Mr. Dooley Remembers

Mr. Dooley Remembers

The Informal Memoirs of

FINLEY PETER DUNNE

~~~~~~

Edited with an Introduction and Commentary by

PHILIP DUNNE

An Atlantic Monthly Press Book

LITTLE, BROWN AND COMPANY · BOSTON · TORONTO

The essay on Warren G. Harding originally
appeared in a slightly modified form in the
Saturday Evening Post.

ATLANTIC–LITTLE, BROWN BOOKS
ARE PUBLISHED BY
LITTLE, BROWN AND COMPANY
IN ASSOCIATION WITH
THE ATLANTIC MONTHLY PRESS

*Published simultaneously in Canada
by Little, Brown & Company (Canada) Limited*

PRINTED IN THE UNITED STATES OF AMERICA

To

CHARLES BRACKETT
WINSLOW CARLTON
AMANDA DUFF DUNNE
ELMER ELLIS
FELIX FRANKFURTER
GEOFFREY GALWEY
MABEL BRADY GARVAN
JOHN F. KENNEDY
EDWARD P. MORGAN
JOHN O'HARA
JAMES RESTON
ARTHUR SCHLESINGER, JR.
PAUL ZIFFREN
MARY ZIMBALIST

*And all the others, known and unknown to me,
who read and appreciate Mr. Dooley.*

Contents

Illustrations

Mr. Dooley Remembers

Introduction

I N PRESENTING Finley Peter Dunne's memoirs to the
reader, I should first make clear what this book is not.

It is not an autobiography in the usual sense. My father
himself disposes of that notion in the first of the essays.

Nor should the material I have interpolated be considered an attempt at biography. "Mr. Dooley" himself took
note of the danger to the deceased inherent in biogra-
phies: "Which wud ye rather be," asked Mr. Hennessy,
"famous or rich?" "I'd like to be famous," said Mr. Dooley,
"an' have money enough to buy off all threatenin' biographers." Besides, a biographer should to some extent
lack bias. I confess that in the matter of Finley Peter
Dunne I am hopelessly biased. I was not only his son; I
was his friend. I am prouder of the latter distinction, because I had to earn it.

In any event, there is no need for a new biography. The
standard work in the field is *Mr. Dooley's America* by Elmer Ellis. It is an accurate, comprehensive and graceful
book. There is nothing I could add to it in the way of
straight biography.

But I feel it would be unwise to publish my father's last

writings without interpolating some background material of my own, based on my own memories.

There are good reasons for this presumption on my part. The first is the inexorable passage of time. It is now more than a quarter of a century since Finley Peter Dunne died. "Mr. Dooley," his unique creation, virtually vanished from the scene another quarter of a century before that. There was an Indian summer in the twenties, when Dooley for a brief period made fun of Mussolini and the Anti-Saloon League and other phenomena peculiar to those times, but Dooley in truth was a creation of the turn of the century; his great days were the days of William McKinley, of "Sinitor Bivridge," Admiral Dewey and Theodore Roosevelt.

So Mr. Dooley and even Finley Peter Dunne have become in a sense Ancient History. They belong to another act in the American drama, an act which began after the Civil War and ended with our emergence as a world power after the First World War. I may be rebuked by historians for setting such arbitrary limits. Perhaps it is purely a subjective judgment. I confess that I see little resemblance between the America in which I spent my childhood and the America in which I have spent my adult life. I draw no invidious comparisons; I merely think that, *mutatis mutandis*, they are different. I am not referring so much to the tangibles of modern life: the supermarkets, the expressways, the jet aircraft and the sundered atom, as to the intangibles: the mores of our society, the judgments men make, the ways in which they look at the world around them. My eyes are not my father's, nor are my children's mine. Whether the differences signify progress or decay, they are nonetheless differences, and they include all the disciplines of human expression, from style to morality.

You will find these differences reflected in the essays themselves. Their charm may appear old-fashioned to the modern reader. They are leisurely and discursive. They were not written with an eye on the clock. Their wit is the gracious wit of another day, and so is their morality. They will evoke for you old worlds which no longer exist: a Washington surprisingly small and informal, even in the time of Harding; a Chicago where by manorial right all policemen were Irishmen; a New York where a white-clad Mark Twain could hold court on a busy street corner, where Madison Avenue was merely that street between Park and Fifth, a New York which was still in my father's time the city of Richard Harding Davis and O. Henry, of brownstone fronts, Delmonico's and "sparrow cops."

The bare facts of Finley Peter Dunne's life are as follows: He was born in Chicago in 1867. After graduating from high school, he went to work as a newspaper copyboy, became a reporter, a city editor (at twenty-two) and eventually an editor. During this period he began writing the Mr. Dooley sketches. At first confined to local Chicago politics, they soon moved on to national and international affairs, as well as general humanistic philosophy. They were widely syndicated here and in England and eventually published in a series of books. At the turn of the century, he moved to New York, where he married and raised his family. He continued to work sporadically as an essayist and editor until 1928. He died in New York in 1936.

A surprisingly large number of people can still quote Mr. Dooley and a smaller number remember my father in person. But to most of my contemporaries and practically all young people Finley Peter Dunne is merely a vaguely familiar name, someone who, as Franklin P. Adams put it, "did something in a literary way, back along about the Battle of Shiloh." I have met people, not poorly informed in other matters, who thought Mr. Dooley was variously an Irish comedian, a comic strip, a vaudeville turn, and the title of a popular song. And a great many want to know when our family changed its name from Dooley to Dunne.

I suppose I shouldn't be disturbed by such confusion. Fame, even garbled, is still fame. If we are remembered at all, it is often for the wrong reasons. John D. Rockefeller is celebrated today for his philanthropies, Benjamin Franklin for some platitudes about thrift, and the least worthy of Walt Whitman's poems is the one most quoted. The veil of time distorts as it conceals.

My father himself put fame in its proper perspective when he had Mr. Dooley say: "What's fame, after all, me la-ad? 'Tis as apt to be what some wan writes on ye'er tombstone as anything ye did f'r ye'ersilf."

Nevertheless, I hope that this book can bridge the decades and create a better understanding of Finley Peter Dunne.

My second reason for presuming to interpolate is that the reminiscences are sadly incomplete. My father always had trouble meeting deadlines, and in the case of these essays, his deadline was death itself.

Late in 1935, I received a call in California from his

close friend John P. Grier in New York informing me that my father was suffering from cancer of the throat. My mother, my two brothers and my sister were also in California at the time. Characteristically, my father had decided not to let us know. Mr. Grier called me on his own responsibility.

I decided to keep my father's secret, but to fly back to him at once. In 1935, commercial airplanes did not cross the country with today's swift ease. The twenty-odd hours of my flight to New York seemed like twenty days. I was prey to the blackest forebodings. I imagined a lonely, dying man in an atmosphere of tragedy and despair.

What I found was something quite different, and much more typical of Peter Dunne. When I arrived at the Delmonico Hotel, where he kept a small suite, a gay and vociferous party was in progress. His friends had dropped in, not so much to entertain the stricken man as to be entertained themselves. It was a scene I had witnessed many times before: my father holding court, dispensing whiskey and wit with a prodigal and practiced hand. Those who remember him will know what I mean. He was always the center of any group into which he might wander, and his chosen group of close friends was made up of some of the most interesting men of his time. He was a private as well as a public wit and nothing ever dammed the stream of his humor. He was the same in a group of intimate friends, among the movie people to whom I introduced him, in a collection of youngsters from college. To quote Frank Adams again, any gathering in which he found himself was always "full of respect for his erudition and bowled over by his charm." And he was the same on this day, forty-eight hours after the cancer specialist had given him his death sentence.

When the guests finally went home, we settled down to a discussion of the situation. He was ready to forgive John Grier for disclosing his grim secret, but he insisted that he wanted no fuss made over him. "It's not all that tragic," he told me. "I'm sixty-eight and I'm already tired of being an old man. Let me tell you something about old age. When you're sixty, all sorts of pleasant things happen to you. Pretty girls fight for the privilege of sitting at your feet, of filling your glass and lighting your cigarette. Callow youth can't compete with you. But when you get closer to seventy, they begin to avoid you. You can see them thinking: is that old bastard still around? Old age is a disease like other infirmities and people are afraid they'll catch it from you. Besides, my notion of hell is having to outlive my friends, and mine are going fast. And that's why," he concluded, "I have no desire to reach seventy."

It was gallantly said, so gallantly that I believed he meant it. But I also believed that the time had come to revive a project we had discussed before: the writing of his memoirs. I thought the effort would prove valuable as an anodyne, and so it did. Much more to the point, I had always felt, and so had his friends and contemporaries, that his recollections of his own times would be of enormous literary and historical value.

I began with great circumspection to drop hints. He saw through me, as he always did. "You want me to work to take my mind off my troubles," he said. "With me, it's always been the other way around. I've invented troubles to take my mind off my work. Very well, I'll work. But on one condition — that you stay here a while and help me get started."

I arranged to stay for three weeks before returning to California. I wasn't much help to him, as it turned out. As he knew well, writing is not something you do with help. I was most valuable as a sounding board. We spent the three weeks blocking out the broad outline of what he was to write: chapters on the Irish in America, on Mark Twain, on Theodore Roosevelt, Robert Collier, Ethel Barrymore, Charles W. Eliot, the American Magazine and the muckrakers, his newspaper days in Chicago, and so on.

He decided to write the memoirs in the form of letters to me, which I could edit and publish or not as I chose.

It was a cheerful and sociable time. He had a trained nurse, a lovely Irish girl with the improbable name of Dorothy Thompson. She was Irish-Irish, having been born in the metropolis of Horse Leap in Westmeath. She was a good nurse and excellent company into the bargain. She delighted my father.

Dorothy had the Irish love of funerals. Since his suite overlooked the corner of 59th Street and Park Avenue, the important funerals from the Fifth Avenue churches used to pass directly under his windows on their way to Queensboro Bridge. She would run to the window exclaiming, "Ah, isn't it lovely!" My father would nod and say. "How can you square it with your conscience, Dorothy, working day and night to save me from just such a delightful journey?" Another time, she mixed him a forbidden whiskey and soda, forbidden by his doctors but not by her great heart. He took one sip and glared at her suspiciously.

"Dorothy Thompson," he said, "what in hell did you put in my drink?"

"Whiskey and soda, like the doctor said you shouldn't," she answered calmly.

"Taste it," he said, giving her the glass.

She tasted it and turned white. "Oh, God save us!" she gasped. "I used the Pluto Water! And me a trained nurse!"

Some thirty years earlier, Mr. Dooley had resolved an argument over the relative merits of doctors and Christian Scientists by saying that it really made no difference which you called in — if you had a good nurse. Dorothy Thompson proved the point. Her gaiety and tenderness helped nerve my father to the task of writing the essays in this book.

After several months, the cancer was arrested to the point where the doctors felt that radiation treatments could and should be discontinued for a while. My father flew out to California to visit the family and come to grips with the work. He had not been able to accomplish much in New York. He wrote me: "I am not blessed with friendship. I am cursed. These are the best fellows in the world, but they will not leave me alone. They are kindness itself, and when they inquire as to the progress of the memoirs, I cannot tell them that they themselves are the reason there *is* no progress. Have you room in your cell at the studio for another aspiring young writer?"

Dorothy Thompson came to California with him, and I engaged a secretary to do his typing.

For two months he taught me a lesson in courage. Writing had never been easy for him. He thought easily, spoke

easily, but wrote in blood. He scorned dictation and called
the typewriter "the assassin of style." Every word was
written out in painstaking longhand. He was sixty-eight
years old when he undertook the articles. He had not written professionally for years. He was ill and troubled with
aggravated insomnia. But it was during this period that the
greater part of the work was completed.

Then I began to notice that he seemed to be wilting.
He became distant and irritable with me. One day, he
suddenly announced that he was going back to New York.
I suspected a recurrence of his malady, but this was not
the problem at all. He finally broke down and explained it
to me. "It's these damn women," he said. "All day long
I'm surrounded by women. And they're all trying to take
care of me!" he shouted in despair.

I should have thought of it myself. I went off to work
every morning at nine and returned at six or later. And
he was left at home with his wife, his daughter, his secretary and his nurse, each vying with the others in solicitude
for his comfort and welfare. All his life he had spent his
daytimes in the masculine atmosphere of newspaper offices
and clubs. And now, forced to sit through lunch with four
benevolent women every day, he was like a fish gasping on
the desert. As a zoologist might say, I had dropped him
in the wrong ecology.

I talked him out of going back to New York and we
drove down to La Quinta, a quiet resort in the desert a few
miles from Palm Springs. It was theoretically a working
expedition for both of us. We were heavily armed with
foolscap, pencils — and a case of whiskey. But we did lit-

tle work. We idled in the desert sun, and talked. In the evenings we idled over a fire of aromatic mesquite logs, and talked some more.

"Bring that bottle over here," my father would say, "and we will discuss life and letters." Then he would talk and I would listen. I can no more reproduce what he said than I can paint a rainbow on the air. If I could, I would go down in literary history along with Plato and Boswell, who both owe much of their fame to the absence of tape recorders in their day. Perhaps the essays in this book will give the reader some notion of how this master conversationalist could sound.

After a few days, we ran short of supplies. The foolscap and the pencils were still intact, but the whiskey had evaporated in the desert sun. We drove into Palm Springs to stock up.

At a service station, we ran into two girls I knew. One was a lovely young actress; the other an aspiring poetess. I had never read any of her poems. She was a mute but far from inglorious Milton, nor was her sweetness wasted on the desert air, as my father was quick to perceive.

"Ask them over to lunch," he said.

Driving back to La Quinta, I did my best to keep a straight face. My father remained unperturbed. "The trouble with youth," he observed, "is that it worships consistency. As you grow older, you will learn that consistency is a vice, like taking regular exercise and eating raw carrots. By these standards, rabbits are the most consistent animals in nature."

During our stay at La Quinta, the girls came to lunch three times. For me they had neither eyes nor ears. My father turned on them the entire battery of his wit and charm. I had never seen him in better form.

When we saw them off for the last time, I said to him: "You know you've spoiled those girls. You've got them both in love with you. They're going to make life hell for the young fellows they usually run around with."

He smiled and shook his head. "They've just been admiring a desert plant," he said. "It's like Dr. Johnson's dog who walked on its hind legs. The miracle was not that it was done well, but that it was done at all. The miracle of the desert plant is not that it's beautiful, but that it grows at all. Now these children are going back to the garden, where growth is no miracle, but the rule of nature. And that's as it should be. Now bring that bottle over here and we will discuss life and letters."

I didn't know it then, but we had few bottles left to us. Soon after he returned to New York, he suffered a hemorrhage at the site of the old growth and died within a few hours, before any of the family could reach him.

It is perhaps fitting that a career founded to a great extent on the subtle use of irony should have ended on an ironic note. If my father had a clearly expressed last wish, it was that no fuss should be made over his death and that above all there should be no elaborate funeral. But he suspected his old friend, the late Francis P. Garvan, of plotting otherwise.

Frank Garvan was a devout Catholic, deservedly honored by a Church for which he had done much during his long and useful life.

My father was at best a nominal Catholic, though I have often heard him leap to the defense of the Church if any atheist or Protestant were foolish enough to attack it in his hearing. His attitude towards the clergy was equally ambivalent. He respected the little man of the cloth, the parish priest who unselfishly served his flock, but he was suspicious of the mighty, as he was in any field of human endeavor. This ambivalence is best illustrated by what he said to me once in a letter. "I have never known an unworthy priest," he wrote. "But the less you have to do with them the better."

He never told me in so many words that he was an agnostic, but it is significant that he spoke with tacit approval of Mark Twain's "unbending atheism" and raised no objection to my own youthfully ardent professions of agnosticism. I would say that he had faith, but not religion.

He certainly did not believe in an afterlife. His several references to such a phenomenon in these essays are purely formal and literary. In conversation, he always scoffed at the idea.

He detested funerals. He considered them not only barbaric and indecent, but an unforgivable invasion of privacy. "The only place where a man can't hide," he told me, "is at his own funeral. Every scoundrel and bore he's spent his life in avoiding is privileged to step up, view the carcass and tell the world what a dear friend he has lost in good old What's-his-name. If that ever happens to me, I'll find the strength to jump up and punch them in the nose."

He was sure that Frank Garvan had plans to bury him with undue ostentation. "Frank is the grandest fellow that ever lived," he said with affection, "but he's by nature a body-snatcher, as dangerous in his way as Burke and Hare. It's a matter of religious principle with him. He's saved his own soul and now he feels a call to save mine as well. Or perhaps he's not quite certain he's saved his own and thinks by saving mine he'll score enough extra points to make sure of Paradise. It's up to you to stop him. He promised me he'd respect my wishes and then I'm positive he went straight to the archbishop who hears his confessions and received absolution for a barefaced lie. So it's up to you."

But I failed. When my mother and I arrived in New York, Mr. Garvan had already arranged for the funeral, a Solemn High Mass of Requiem in St. Patrick's Cathedral. Half of New York was there, including most of the "scoundrels and bores" my father had always detested. But his friends were also there, a host of them, and I think now that both they and I should be grateful to Frank Garvan for giving us all a chance to pay our last respects to a man we loved.

But it was a very long service, made longer by my ignorance of the ritual. Not knowing when to sit, stand or kneel, I stood at attention throughout the service, this seeming to me the most respectful attitude. The rest of the mourners, taking their cue from the family pew, perforce had to do the same. As we finally trooped out of the cathedral, I happened to be walking close behind the late Judge Morgan J. O'Brien, a beloved friend of my father's later days. The Judge was in his eighties and his ancient sinews had obviously felt the strain of so much standing at attention. "Well," he sighed, "Peter spent more time in church today than he did in all the years of his life." I think my father would have appreciated this epitaph. He might only have been jealous that he hadn't thought of it himself.

I have dwelt on his last illness because it was one of the conditions of the writing of these essays. But even now, after a quarter of a century, I never think of him as anything but alive. He may not have believed in an afterlife, but he forgot that artists, the few good ones, are immune to mortality.

I once saw Charlie Chaplin give an imitation of John Barrymore rehearsing in his dressing room for a performance of *Hamlet*. He began: "Now you know Jack has a bad habit of picking his teeth in public." Chaplin used the present tense. Barrymore had been dead at least five years, but to Chaplin he was still alive, and his foibles to be affectionately relished by his friends.

The immunity does not extend to soldiers and politicians. Alexander and Caesar and Napoleon are dead. We think of them in terms of their deaths. We learn the dates of these events in school. But the writer, the artist and the philosopher live on, fixed forever by their own works in the present tense.

And it is so with Finley Peter Dunne. It is becoming the fashion among modern political pundits and academes to quote Mr. Dooley again. They are discovering that his observations are as readily applicable to our times as to his. I am grateful to them for this modest renaissance, though I deplore the efforts of some imprudent individuals to attempt Dooley articles of their own on current affairs. They all make the mistake of trying to guess what position he would have taken on this issue or that. Perhaps they guess right, but I doubt it. I knew him as well as any man can know another, which is not very well, and I cannot tell you what he would have thought of any one of the problems and personalities of our era. I cannot conjure up ideas for him. I can only conjure up a man as I see him through the flawed glass of my memory.

Perhaps he exists only in my memory, but exist he does. He is still the faithful critic of my work and speech. He still restrains me from the literary solecisms and vulgarities he disliked. I will not use certain words and phrases which he despised as the corruption of our language: the transitive verbs "to contact" and "to intrigue"; "shibboleth," "meticulous," "galore," and those near twins so often misused, "flaunt" and "flout"; all gobbledygook, journalese and the pidgin English of Madison Avenue. How he would have detested such gems as "to finalize," "to structure" and "togetherness"!

I still try to meet his social and moral standards. If he didn't always meet them himself, they were nevertheless strict. I don't always meet them either, but he keeps me informed of my transgressions. He remains my stern and benevolent censor, my warm and caustic friend.

And now it is time to let him speak for himself.

On Biography and Related Subjects

Philip Dunne
Hollywood, California

Dear Phil:

WHEN YOU SUGGESTED the other night that I write my autobiography I was flattered. It was a great thing to know that such confidence in my abilities was entertained by a sound judge of letters, a son, and a friend. You did it without condescension — a rare thing in these degenerate days when old age is treated with no more deference than it ever was. So I have given the matter consideration. What you say about my having observed at close range many of the scenes, and known intimately many of the actors in the comedy of my day, is true. My memory seems pretty good to those who have no books of reference at hand. And I need the money.

Besides, I suppose no man who has ever earned a living by writing — if he lasts long enough — escapes the temptation to write an autobiography. Sometimes he surrenders to it and makes a show of himself. But why shouldn't he? You mustn't believe what you hear about the pleasures of old age. Nature is a cynical comedian and paints for dreary age a cheerful picture of slippered ease, omitting the fact that the slipper often encases a gouty foot. Aside from the inestimable luxury that comes from the affection of family and friends, the older people grow the narrower becomes their range of gaieties. Avarice has been recommended as a parlor and bedroom sport, but the practice of that pastime requires early training and few of us can indulge — even in thought — in the "final old gentlemanly vice." Montaigne pretended there was plenty of compensation in loss of appetite for loss of pleasure, but he might just as well tell us a man is better for blindness because he can no longer see the misery about him, or deafness because he doesn't have to hear Herbert Hoover on the radio. He may affect a feeling of youth. He may say he is just as young as he used to be. No one will believe him, but if he has a little skill as an actor and if he has managed to preserve a disposition easily cheered by pleasant sights, scenes, sounds and smiles around him, his buoyancy will at least float him out of those fatal floods of commiseration that always threaten his pride and his peace of mind. It takes a great deal of skill and art in balance to walk perpendicular when you have lumbago. I advise my contemporaries to restrict the appearance of youth to words. Let them talk, not act. If a man thinks that just because he got his numeral for stoop tag at the kindergarten he can compete with his youngest granddaughter at skipping rope, let alone playing tennis or polo or kicking a football, let him have a cane. Above all, let him beware the perils of the dance. In shame and ridicule has many a noble reputation been obscured when its bearer dragged some female dependent to the floor of the night club to dance the conga on her instep. Perhaps I am giving away the secrets of the lodge, but I did have to laugh at a recent statement attributed to the Chief Justice of the United States Supreme Court. Charley — for it is only by a diminutive that I would think of talking about this Boy Jurist — Charley declares that owing to the advancement of medical science, dietetics and so forth, the whole skeletal, vascular and membraneous structure of the human race has been improved to a point where a man is not old at seventy-five! I wonder if Kid Hughes really fancies he is young, looks young, thinks young or decides young. He is perhaps unaware that his opinions are overlaid with a considerable coating of dust. But I am wandering from my subject, which is autobiography and its companion in mendacity, biography.

Years ago I tried to get William James to write a "Life" of President Eliot of Harvard. He wrote back: "I can't. To tell the truth I'm skeered of him." The founder of the school of philosophy called Pragmatism had known Mr. Eliot for fifty years. The great educator was much changed from the blandly domineering young chemist who, when a member of the faculty of the Medical School had asked querulously, "How is it that we have been going on so well in the same orderly path for eighty years and now *within three or four months* it is proposed to change all our modes of carrying on the school?" had replied, "I can answer Dr. ——'s question very easily. There is a new president." The Eliot I knew during the last fifteen years of his life was much gentler, much more tolerant than the soft-spoken young tyrant of the 1860s. Yet even at this stage James dared not write about him.

Now, I am no William James, nor is he a Charles Eliot, but I am skeered of this man Dunne whose "Life" you ask me to write. How can I sit down solemnly and describe the antics of my *animula blandula vagula, hospes comesque corporis*? How can I — whatever *I* means in this instance — how can I write about a spirit that is so elusive and fleeting, or say with certainty that it is today the same guest and companion of the body that lodged there yesterday, or another quite different in its view of life? Besides, this disrobing in public is not to my taste. There are intellectual and spiritual pudenda as well as physical. Even a Hottentot will wear a breech clout before the camera. The more clothes I put on the better I look. A mask, I am told, might further improve me. I was never designed for membership in a nudist colony. I haven't the courage of shamelessness. And I was always awkward at lying. Somerset Maugham said the other day in *Don Fernando* (repeating what has been said a thousand times before): "I do not believe there is any man, who if the whole truth were known of him would not seem a monster of depravity." Let everyone speak for himself. I can't go that far. But I subscribe without hesitation to "W. Tickler's" firm statement in John Wilson's *Noctes Ambrosianae* that all autobiographers are liars.

Of course, you will throw up in my face one of the gods of my idolatry, Montaigne. It is not so long ago that a beautiful young lady reproached me for this love, applying to it that silliest of phrases, "the mauve decade," when

I spoke of my enjoyment of an open fire, a bottle of port and Montaigne. Well, I plead guilty to preferring port and Montaigne to gin and Joyce or crème de cacao and André Gide. Besides, Montaigne was far from indiscreet. That demure little Jew — for he was a Jew by the Nazi standards — made few disclosures of the facts of his life. He affects perfect frankness. He speaks with familiar contempt of his wife and daughter after the best manner of a modern autobiographer. He alludes to his love affairs and often mentions his gallstones (and Cicero's) with pride. But in general his confessions are confessions of opinions, not of acts. He seems to say, "I conceal nothing. I present myself shirtless to the world." But he is really hardly more outspoken than Gibbon or Franklin. His confession is a broad one: I am a man. He admits his concupiscence but the time, the place, and the lady are not identified.

Not, mind you, that I dislike autobiography as such. On the contrary, it is among the pleasantest forms of reading and I sometimes envy these brave or conscienceless fellows who take it up. I revel in Cellini. I suppose there is little truth in his tale. But what a noble lie it is! Was there ever such a self-made bully, thief, adulterer, pederast — and goldsmith? With all his faults, he is better reading than Gibbon. An artist can do wonders with the truth or with a lie; but he can't do much with half-truths. Still, it wouldn't be at all surprising if some good-tempered gossip of the future should dig up facts to prove that, far from being the great ruffian he professed to be, Benevenuto was really a sober and industrious smith who, of a Saturday night when his furnaces were cooling, joined mildly in the fashionable diversions of the hour. To kill your man was as much in the mode of his Europe as it was later of our own cow towns and mining camps. The Grecian vice, with the example of such men of genius as Michael Angelo and Leonardo da Vinci, was as vaunted a fashionable practice in Italy as it ever was in Athens, Sing Sing, or the Paris of Marcel Proust. He was perhaps like our own worthy citizens who put on their uncomfortable silk hats and morning coats and march up and down Fifth Avenue in the Easter parade. During the rest of the week they discard this tiresome harness for more virtuous alpaca jerkins and sleeve protectors. There is no trace of the androgynous man of fashion, the curled and perfumed Clodius, in the work-a-day Cellini. It was no Oscar Wilde who cast the statue of Perseus that you may see today in Florence, if Mussolini has not knocked it down as the challenge of a glorious Italy to his own regimented Italy of macadam roads and castor oil. I'm glad to say, in this connection, that a modern writer has tried to rescue Michael Angelo's good name from this infamous companionship, to prove that he never was a member of the retinue of the ugliest of vice. I say I am glad because I see amazing signs in American newspapers and magazines, and on the stage particularly, of a humorous toleration of this disease.

But I didn't mean to preach. I was gassing about autobiographies and the difficulty of writing one that will hold the interest of the reader and, at the same time, preserve his respect for the author. A writer who attempts a truthful narrative of his life is damned at once. If he tries the other kind and paints himself as a faithful husband, tender son and model father, the day may come when a biographer will summarily dispose of these pretensions. No slyer apology was ever written than Franklin's *Autobiography*. You could not guess from this great plea in avoidance that Franklin was anything but a prudent, temperate citizen with only one illegitimate son. But not long ago a young American got out a book (or so I am told) to show that he was a toss-pot and a libertine, a sort of Quaker Falstaff with a passion for Dame Quicklies. If Franklin is now enjoying the life beyond the grave that he didn't in the least believe in, he will take this accusation as lightly as we do. The vices of which he is accused are not unknown even in the printing trade. And whatever may be said about him at the court of Gertrude Stein he will remain the Father of the Chapel for all type-stickers and scribblers as long as the world lasts.

But that is biography. It is perhaps less justifiable than autobiography. A man has a better right to lie about himself than he has to lie about another man. I like a tender and appreciative biography like Lockhart's *Scott*, Trevelyan's *Macaulay* or Miss Tarbell's *Lincoln*. I like especially Nicolay and Hay's *Lincoln*, which is really a history of the Civil War. John Hay wrote most of the part that treats of Lincoln, and in this we have the benefit of his intimate knowledge of his subject, expressed in the best manner of one of the most graceful writers of our time. But I hate with all my soul such a pretended life of Lincoln as the man who wrote it sent me a copy of a few years ago in which the author, after a laborious search of court records for years, tried to prove the depravity of the woman whom Lincoln called "my dear, dear mother." I'm not going to mention this man's name. He has a son alive who has done no harm that I know of.

Your own moving picture business has gone in for a kind of biography in a big way. We have had portraits or caricatures of Rasputin, Washington, Diamond Jim Brady, Lincoln, Lee, Disraeli, Wellington, Rothschild and other worthies. In a few years you will put on Theodore and Franklin Roosevelt. W. R. Hearst like all of us is growing old. In all human probability he has but a few years of life left and undoubtedly the playwrights will make a story of one of the most curious and interesting figures of our modern world. I hope you young men and your actors will do better with these characters than your predecessors have done with others. I have seen some of these biographical picture plays and I can't say they seemed very convincing. I stood George Arliss's representation of Disraeli until the actor had the languid statesman, who would not run if his house were on fire, scamper down a corridor at a speed that Nurmi never equaled. That was too much. I haven't seen his *Richelieu*, but I can imagine what he will do to it. I am told that instead of drawing the magic circle around the heroine he draws it around himself. Besides, I once saw a great actor play the part in Lord Lytton's *Richelieu*, which the critics of my day told me was the finest *acting* play ever written. I saw him draw the circle of his holy church around Madame Modjeska and heard him tell the king that if he put his foot in that ring he'd launch the curse of Rome on his head, yea, e'en though it wore a crown. And fifty years afterward I can see the noble face and carriage and hear the sonorous, the majestic, the unforgettable voice of Edwin Booth. But Booth was an actor who, like Garrick, sank his own personality absolutely in the character he was playing. I once sat in the flies of a theater and watched his performance of Hamlet. When the curtain went down Laertes, the guilty king, the queen, and all the courtiers began chatting, making appointments for supper that night, or lunch the next day, or talked about baseball or the races. But Booth, his arms folded across his breast and his head bowed, stalked off the stage without a word. He was still Hamlet.

I had always thought H. G. Wells would write an ideal autobiography. He is one of the most engaging of modern writers and he has all the necessary self-confidence, not to say assurance, for such a job. I was not wrong in my surmise. His *Experiment in Biography*, which I have just read, is a pretty work of this class. He gives us much important information about his youth. As, "I did not so much begin masturbation as have it happen to me as a natural outcome of my drowsy clasping of my goddesses — (Tenniel's pictures of Columbia, Erin and Brittania, in Punch!) I had so to speak a one-sided affair with my bed clothes." Having thus delicately introduced the reader to the mysteries of his sex life and assuring the world that he was only lightly touched by homosexuality, he goes on to describe the more substantial erotic adventures of his mature years. And, to prove the truly scientific nature of his mind, he actually gives the name of a young woman who made a successful assault on his continence in his office with their clothes on.

It is also as a scientific recorder that he discusses his family and makes it clear that he can give them no credit for his prodigious success in life. There is, of course, no such thing as physical spontaneous generation. Pasteur ended that superstition for all time. But there is unquestionably an intellectual phenomenon of that nature. "Look," he seems to say, "at the mire from which my greatness sprang! What seed was there in that dungheap to account for my rise to glory?" He deals sharply with his mother. She seems to have been a considerable failure as the mother of such a genius. It is true that when her husband went broke she returned to her old job as a domestic servant and supported the family for eleven years. She earned the money that carried her magnificent son through school. When he was ill she nursed him. And in the end he forgave her for not nourishing his youth with vitamins, and when she was dismissed from her employer's service, he provided for her "suitably." So it can be truly said of him, as it was said of "Scotty Briggs," that he "never shook his mother." But as a man crammed full of science at a Kensington school he refuses to draw a veil over her painful delinquencies. "She was," he says, "the worst housekeeper that was ever thought of." "She was the sort of woman who is an incorrigibly bad cook." "She learnt nothing and forgot nothing." "Every night and morning and sometimes during the day she prayed to our Savior for a little money, for a little leisure to make Joe (the father) better and less negligent, for now he was getting more neglectful." And so forth. We share the great author's contempt for this pathetic but ludicrous figure. But I couldn't write this kind of thing. I'm not large-minded enough! I couldn't write it on the biggest kind of a bet.

Perhaps my inhibitions in this respect are racial. The practice of jumping on one's mother seems to be more British than Irish or American. Every nation has its peculiar amusements. Once Rudyard Kipling, who doesn't

like America but who does like Americans (he married
an American girl) and is most hospitable when he sees
them in England — Kipling, I say, once held forth to his
friend Roosevelt, the great Theodore, on the iniquitous
frequency of homicides in the country. "Yes," said Roosevelt, "it's terrible. But every nation has its peculiar vice.
We Americans kill men; you Britons beat women. We
don't. What we do is perhaps worse. We write mother
songs about them."

In this matter Wells has a distinguished model in Dickens. Her son's criticisms of Sarah Wells will be soon forgotten. They are not very savage at their worst. But as
long as people read *David Copperfield*, they will not forget
the portrait of Dickens's parents drawn by the cruel hand
of that superlative genius, their son. That long will they
scornfully laugh at Mr. and Mrs. Wilkins Micawber.

Wells is, as you know, a Socialist. He and Shaw are the
best known Socialist leaders among people who write English. But they are different from the Socialists I knew in the
hot days of my youth, when Arthur Brisbane, Jack London
and I organized committees to run guns into Russia to help
the Nihilists. (We were promised reduced rates by a son-
in-law of William Rockefeller who was head of the Rem-
ington Arms Company, but we never could raise even the
reduced rate.) They belong to what might be called the
Take-it-Aisy School of Socialism. They are opposed to
Capitalism but not to Capital, when it adopts the form of
a tidy balance in their own name at Barclay's Bank. No one
could imagine them giving up the pleasures of life to wage
endless, unsuccessful war on the British throne. All they can
do is to fan softly the flames of discontent and when they

glow too much quell them with a word about the hopeless-
ness of mass effort against intelligent selfishness. I don't
blame them. But I can't help thinking of the earlier Socialist
leaders. Of John Swinton in New York, in his skullcap, living
in poverty but getting out his little weekly paper regularly.
Of Tschaikovsky, the gaunt figure, with his high cheekbones
touched with pink, his tousled scanty white beard, his glow-
ing old eyes, who had been hunted like a rat from one cover
to another all over the world, who had spent two-thirds of his
life in prison, and who kept uncooled so ardent a faith in the
cause, that we old-young men of his day thought him childish. He went back to Russia when the Soviet was established.
In one or another of Trotsky's whining books I saw an allusion to him as a sort of old moss-back who is tolerated and
pitied. But Tschaikovsky was not the man to hold his tongue
when he saw things going on that he didn't like. I was
afraid that my friend, the old Soldier of Freedom, had
been liquidated in the manner so much approved by Mr.
Shaw, i.e. by a pistol shot in the back of his head from the
gun of one of the Ogpu. It turns out that not even Lenin
and Trotsky dared take this man's life. But they drove him
out of Russia, just as the Procurator of the Holy Synod
had driven him out before, and he died in the peaceful
suburb of Harrow in England in 1927.

I think of Kuropatkin, who spent the money he made
by writing science papers — and he was a real scientist,
Mr. Wells — in pamphleteering in the cause of Com-
munism. Of Steinmetz, who would take from the General
Electric Company only enough money to live on while
contributing something to his Socialist committees. (He
did demand, however, the privilege of smoking in the com-

pany's compound at Schenectady, and he was the only officer or employee who had the privilege.) And back of them all the somber figure of Karl Marx, poverty-stricken, his mind so tortured by what he saw in the slums of London and what he read about the back-breaking child slavery of Cornwall and Lancashire, that he created a new political gospel, which has destroyed one ancient civilization already and bids fair to end many another. It is the proper thing among the socialistic intelligentsia to represent the Marxian theories as cold, carefully thought out, and apart from everything resembling humane feelings. They were, in truth, gestated in a heart embittered by the cruelty, the meanness and the suffering that seemed then to be inevitable partners of our modern social system.

I think too, of Lenin. I wonder if Wells ever knew him or even heard of him when his fellow Socialist was living in dirty lodgings in London and ceaselessly contriving his plots against Tsardom. No more, I guess, than the somewhat lower order of Socialist intelligentsia in this country — Lincoln Steffens, et al. — knew of the existence of Trotsky in New York when that firebrand was lighting to melt the consciousness of the Russian proletarian and fit it for Lenin's annealing hand. The interview of Lenin by Wells a few years before the Russian died must have been high comedy to Trotsky, who was present. You can see the taciturn, cynical Lenin, with his yellow skin drawn like parchment over his high cheekbones, his little restless eyes, his filmy beard, his full pale lips, his great bald head looking as if it might have been hewn out of yellow pine with an adze. There was no more blood in his veins while he lived than there is in his pickled and stuffed carcass in the mausoleum at Moscow. By far the greatest man of his day, he was also the cruelest monster that Tartary has visited on western civilization since Ghenghis Khan. But his work, his accomplishment, had been prodigious. He had first undermined and then, as if with the hammer of Thor, smashed to flinders the greatest, richest and most powerful of modern autocracies. And here was little Wells, earnest, honest, conceited, describing in his falsetto voice the British conception of a Socialist Utopia of semi-detached villas with a pot of geraniums in each window. When the interview ended, which it did when Wells stopped, and our hero had strutted out, Lenin gave one of his arid chuckles and said to Trotsky, "Ah, the little bourgeois; ah, the little bourgeois." That was all.

It is some satisfaction to me to think that I was still a very poorly paid wage earner when I turned my back on Socialism, although I long continued to sympathize with revolution. Certainly my change of mind was not venal. My default went unnoticed, for I never had much to do with the boys who make their living by writing books on Socialism or preaching to ladies' clubs. I never had believed that value was created solely by labor, whether abstract or concrete, and I came to feel that no more good could arise from a dictatorship of the proletariat than from any other dictatorship. A man might be as free and more comfortable physically and fully as comfortable spiritually under Mussolini as under Stalin. The dense stupidity of the labor unions in politics has always been appalling. They follow some labor leader — labor skate we used to call him — like Ramsay MacDonald until he is ready to sell them out to the political gang that will pay him most for them. Then another schemer takes his place and the game goes on as before. What good would come from giving absolute power to a greasy mechanic any more than to a greasy millionaire? But I can still sympathize with the Socialist whose theories honestly spring from a passion for justice and mercy for the helpless and not from his desire to cash in on the thrills he can impart to the bosoms of Englewood, New Jersey. My gorge still rises against a complacent Supreme Court that values property above life and refuses to interfere with that murderous thing child labor. I hate the "rugged individualist" who is utterly incompetent to earn a livelihood in business except by sweating his labor. I abhor cruelty in any form whether it is practiced by a court, a steel boss or a newspaper publisher. Above all I hate humbug, high or low.

I wonder if it isn't a constitutional hostility to authority with me. It is much the same with my feeling about Ireland. My father was only six years old when he was brought to New Brunswick by his parents, and remembered absolutely nothing about the old country. In all my life I have spent only a fortnight there. True it was a delightful fortnight, but it wasn't long enough to root me to the soil. I don't believe all Irishmen are honest, loyal, capable, kind, humorous, brave and musical. But let no Englishman tell me they're not. My languid pulses respond at once to a tale of the suffering of Ireland under British rule. I'm moved, too, but not so much, by the suffering of Ireland under Irish rule. It was no Englishman who murdered Michael Collins. But our emotions control us far more than our calculations and it is well that they should. I remember at a Land League Convention in this country hearing a speech by Willie Redmond, the brother of the Parliamentary leader. While he was talking about the bills that were to be introduced in the House of Commons for the betterment of Ireland no one paid the slightest attention to him. But when he turned to the ancient wrongs of his country there was a sudden silence; and when, to prove that England's attitude had not changed in all these years, he cried: "And now they have sent us a lord left'nant bearing the hated name of Castlereagh," a roar of passionate indignation went up from the convention. Lord Castlereagh had been dead for nearly a century. After a career of cruelty and rapacity, he cut his throat with a penknife. The crowd hooted at his funeral in the Abbey. But as the embodiment of savage misrule in Dublin he could, though dead a hundred years, arouse the passions of practical Irish Americans of this day.

It is well that these ancient grievances should be kept alive. If Irish hatred of England had not been fanned by angry hands, Ireland would not have the measure of freedom she enjoys today. It may not be much, but this can be said of it: that if the Irish people are under another form of tyranny, it is self-imposed and not imported from London or Belfast. It was not John Redmond and the parliamentarians with their love for the amenities of English life that finally tore Ireland from the murderous embrace of England, but Micky Collins and his like with their grim hatred of all Britiannia ware — and their machine guns.

No, it is because I find no sign of sorrow for the sufferings of the poor, and no hatred for the economic system to which they attribute it, among the educated Socialists in England and America, or the professional labor rats in

Stanley Baldwin's Cabinet or the House of Lords, that I see
no hope for leadership of the world's discontent in this
quarter. They look down on the poor, they deride them,
they trade their votes for money, a peerage or a job. In a
quiet way, they make a little cash by writing or lecturing
on the golden future to be achieved not by violence, of
course, but by a patient, intelligent revolution led by some
such radical as Tom Lamont of Morgan and Company,
who in his sale of securities to the public has learned to
appeal to the heart as well as to the head. I don't think
Tom would appreciate the honor, but it is his for the asking. And if he could read the minds of these gentry he
would be fearless of any harm that could come to our present social order from their activities; for no one he has met
in his long experience in Wall Street could feel or show a
profounder contempt for the sad-faced and bedraggled
slum dwellers whom he encounters in London, than the
hermit of Eyot St. Davids, on his way to Henrietta Street
to collect belated royalties on "Widowers' Houses."

But here I go again. I started in, a few hours since, to tell
you I'd be damned if I'd write my autobiography and to
give you my candid opinion of autobiographies and bi-
ographies. And here I suddenly find myself shouting the
views on Socialism that I have fished out of memory forty
years old. I'll not do this again. At whatever cost I'll stick
to my text. Again I say I hate autobiographies and I loathe
the modern biography. I do like the old and gentle school.
I can still read Lockhart's *Scott* with its tender account of
that good man's life. I am told "people don't read Scott
nowadays." Not long ago in a gay little publication I read
a statement by a book reviewer that he much preferred to

Scott — I forgot who it was he much preferred. It may have been Harold Bell Wright, or it may have been H. L. Mencken — he much preferred so-and-so to Scott. Now I maintain that if a man is suffering from this sort of malady, if he really does prefer so-and-so to the Wizard of the North, he shouldn't talk about it. It is a disease. To mention it is like describing your hemorrhoids in public. Scott is still read, you can bet on it, and loved by thousands; and Lockhart's *Life* will be in reverent hands when no one will know which one of the Ludwig School wrote *The House of Rothschild.*

Did you know, by the way, that Ludwig's real name is Cohen? I didn't myself, until the greatest bibliophilist in the world, a publisher who knows more about authors old and new than any other of my acquaintance, told me Cohen is this distinguished author's real name. Why he should change it I don't know. Perhaps he didn't. Perhaps my friend was misinformed. To tell you the truth, he does entertain the most depressing thoughts about the prevalence of the Jews in every department of life. He doesn't find books in the running brooks, but he does find Jews in everything. Most of the Jews are named Cohen.

"There's Frank Harris," he cries.

"But," I say, "surely Frank was Irish."

"Don't you believe it. He was an Omaha Jew and his name was — Cohen. And James Joyce! What was the name of the woman in *Ulysses* — you know — the woman who doesn't punctuate her reveries? What is her name? Isn't it Cohen?" "No, it's Bloom; her husband was named Bloom." "Well, he must have changed it. They do. But Bloom is Cohen, and Cohen clearly is Joyce."

He is almost as bad as Codlingsby, in Thackeray's burlesque of Disraeli, who hints that the Pope is a member of this ancient society. I don't know whether my bookseller would go quite as far as that.

The extent of this Jew-searching and Jew-baiting in New York is amazing. I know scores of otherwise sane men who attribute all that is perverse in public or private morals to them. One friend of mine, a man of great intellectual distinction, last year gave a large sum of money — for what do you suppose? Nothing less than that ancient, that thousand times exposed forgery the Mannheim Protocol. The last previous sucker in a large way had been Henry Ford for his *Dearborn Independent*.

The feeling is more general than it was and infinitely more intense. The late J. P. Morgan would have no dealings whatever with a Jew. Only the other day the president of one of the banks that are called "Morgan banks" boasted that not one Jew was employed in his institution. Henry Cannon, who in other respects was one of the most fair-minded of men, would not even take the account of a Jew in his old bank, the Chase. "If you let one of them in," he said, "he'll bring others and the first thing you know your cashier and your loan clerks are corrupted." "Did it ever happen to you?" he was asked. "No," he said, "but it might." "Did you ever know it to happen in any other bank?" "No, but it might. Anyhow, that's the way I feel about it."

Few Jews have been able to get into a good New York club. I have seen E. H. Harriman, during the Northern Pacific panic, leave Jacob Schiff at the door of the Metropolitan Club because even he did not dare to take a Jew into this not-too-exclusive club. There was no rule against taking him in. In fact, there was a by-law permitting a member to introduce a resident of New York. And at the time Schiff's firm, Kuhn, Loeb and Company, was lending millions of dollars to Harriman in his fight with Morgan. Yet even the audacious Harriman did not dare face the hostility of his fellow members by taking a great Jewish financier in for a cocktail.

Now getting into a club seems a matter of very little moment to me. You join a club because some of your friends ask you to, or because it includes in its membership men who you think will be companionable and because you get good food and drink and tobacco at reasonable cost. Some even join clubs for business reasons, hoping to sell stocks or bonds to the other members. But these enterprising souls soon learn that the older and more opulent members have a plenitude of these same securities which they can be induced to part with at a slight sacrifice, and the adventurer finds at the end of a year or two that he possesses more worthless stocks and bonds than he had when he became a member. But as a general thing men join clubs for the reasons I have given and not for the honor of having a list of their clubs printed in their obituary notices. Yet prosperous Jews appear to be inordinately anxious to gain this doubtful honor, which is nearly always refused them here and in London. There might be some reason for a man wanting to get into a New York club, which often has a pleasant house to meet in, but a London club! Of all mausoleums the gloomiest! I quote from memory something George Moore, a well-known English writer and tout for picture buyers, said: "A London club! A great room with dusty red curtains on the windows and a dusty red carpet on the floor. Here and there worn red leather chairs in which sit members dozing over their evening papers. In the center of the room a long table on which lie the current reviews — *The Nineteenth Century, The Contemporary Review, The Fortnightly,* with an incomparably dull article by the Right Honorable William Ewart Gladstone on 'The Decay of the Pimp in Modern Times.' "

You say it is a trifling matter, but is it? Is it a matter for unconcern that this social ostracism is practiced in the largest Jewish city in the world, a city where the most prosperous newspaper is owned by Jews, where Jews are financial leaders, where they control the great shops, predominate among the judges, where one of their number is governor and another mayor, in a country where they control the moving picture business, direct the most successful and intelligent of the radio companies, own the theaters, have two members of the Supreme Court, and are also represented at Washington by the most influential of all the President's advisers — my accomplished friend Felix Frankfurter — is it a thing to be dismissed lightly that a great scientist like Simon Flexner, a scholar like Walter Lippmann, or a cultivated man of affairs like Bernie Baruch should be denied social privileges that would be freely accorded to any Nordic customer's man in a Jewish brokerage firm? I think not. I think it is highly significant of a feeling of hatred of Jews or jealousy of Jewish influence that grows in intensity instead of decreasing as I hoped it would after Hitler's ruthless persecutions. I abhor it. Coming, as I do, from a race and religion that were cruelly persecuted for centuries, I hate religious persecution wherever directed.

But it is foolish to blind oneself to facts and so to doubt that the time may be near at hand when all who believe in freedom of religious worship will have to fight for the Jews.

Well, bless my soul, I hadn't the slightest notion when I commenced this letter that I'd even discuss anti-Semitism. But old men are notorious preachers. They can't stop issuing warnings to the gay young world. It is the infallible sign of senility. But before I return to my subject, I must tell you of one of the funny consequences of Jew-searching. When I commenced to write Dooley articles about Theodore Roosevelt I made Mr. Dooley call him "Rosenfelt," which I thought was about the way a Mr. Dooley would pronounce the name. *The London Spectator*, which had been most generous in appreciation of these pieces, severely took me to task for "alluding to the President's Jewish ancestry." I showed the article to the President and he laughed and said he'd write Strachey, the editor, about it. "No," he said, "so far as I know I haven't a trace of Jewish blood in me. I wish I had a little. But I'm straight Dutch and Irish." And he sang his favorite song: "The Irish, the Irish, they don't amount to much, but they're a damned sight better than the Goddamned Dutch." Some time afterward I told this to Augustus St. Gaudens, the sculptor. I knew St. Gaudens from the World's Fair in Chicago, but we became great friends through a paragraph I had written in *Collier's Weekly*, quoting a German paper which asserted that a census of all the old men over ninety-five in the city of Dresden showed that most of them were confirmed drunkards. St. Gaudens wrote in eagerly for further information and I got hold of a copy of

the Dresden paper and sent it to him. I found he had two
prejudices. Although he drank little he hated the Borahs,
Bryans, and all the brood of political prohibitionists and
humbugs of our time with a furious hatred. And strange to
say, although he was the gentlest of men, and the kindest
fellow that ever lived, he was distinctly an anti-Semite.
This may have been due to the fact that St. Gaudens's father was a Frenchman and that the great sculptor was at
a malleable age during the Franco-German war, when the
Jews were madly pro-German. When he heard my tale of
the *Spectator* and Roosevelt he said, "Don't you believe a
word of what Roosevelt tells you. He's a Jew. I swear it.
Why I've modeled hundreds of heads of Jews and I've
modeled Roosevelt's and he has the distinctive round head
of a Jew." "But he's blue-eyed and fair-haired." "That
proves nothing. So is Morty Schiff. His skull gives him
away." I told this to T.R. and he laughed again. "Perhaps
he's right," he said. "Anyhow who cares?" And that's perhaps the right answer. Who cares? Who the hell cares?

Now I can return to the subject of my autobiography
and tell you the real reason why I won't write it. I will give
you the truth. It is because I don't trust my memory. I was
blessed once with a most tenacious and exact memory, for
names, places, dates and occurrences, although strange to
say I could recall only in their essence passages out of the
thousands of books I have read. I was famous for winning
"memory bets." I thought this gift would never fail me.
But of late I find that I'm not, at sixty-eight, as secure in
my recollection of things as I was at fifty. I have slipped
and I ask myself, in terror, when this senescence began. For
example, I have often told this story: When I was a lad Gen-

eral Phil Sheridan was appointed to the command of the Department of the Missouri with headquarters at Chicago. I saw him often. His legs were short and his trunk long, so that when he walked he looked undersized, but on horseback he was a giant. He liked the pleasures of the table; he was red of face, with a white mustache, white hair cut *en brosse* and the merriest of blue eyes. There were no airs about him. Those who met him found it hard to believe he was the same man whom von Moltke called the greatest cavalry leader of modern times. He joined freely in the social gaieties of the town and was as simple and unaffected as could be. My friend Robert Hamill's father-in-law, John Lyon, used to tell how the modest warrior wept when a little girl recited Buchanan Reid's "Sheridan's Ride." There was a racing association in Chicago called the Washington Park Association and General Sheridan was elected president of this organization. The merchants and bankers who comprised this association thought it was a high honor — perhaps almost as high an honor as being Lieutenant General. On several occasions General Sheridan acted as presiding judge at the races. On one of these occasions the judges "hung out the wrong number." Two horses in a race were "Red Light," which was number three, and "Baggage," which was number seven. Red Light won going away. Baggage was nowhere. Yet the judges, in a confusion occasioned by frequent trips to the clubhouse, put out Baggage's number as the winner. Instantly a mob gathered around the judge's stand. It was such a mob as only Chicago can afford at times of great popular excitement. There were cries of "Lynch 'em." Pistols were drawn. Two of the judges became panic-stricken and urged General Sheridan to call for the police. But the General (or so my story went) lighted an enormous black cigar and said, "Oh, no. It will evaporate. It will evaporate." And so it did.

Now I could have taken my oath that I saw all this, although Sheridan's supposed remark was repeated to me later. I was all the more confirmed in my belief by the fact that Clint Riley, who was racing editor of my paper, the *Times*, and I went down to the betting ring after the race and I heard the bookmaker ask him if they should pay off and he replied: "Certainly, you must go by the judges' decision." I thought this a remarkably just finding, seeing that both he and I had tickets on Baggage at 8 to 1. Now I believed every word of that story and I told it so often that my family knew it by heart and could chant it when I began on it again. But the other day, while I was following up a reference to General Sheridan, I ran across the fact that the General died in 1888. Of course. Why I saw his funeral in Washington. I recall it as if it were yesterday: the wonderful summer morning, the solemn cortege, the gun carriage with the draped coffin, the black horse, the empty boots, the massed bands playing Chopin's "Funeral March," the Negro women weeping. But if Phil Sheridan died in 1888 how could he have misjudged a horse race that took place in 1889, for that was the year of the Baggage-Red Light race? The truth is that he didn't. My memory had cheated me. General Sheridan was not in the judge's stand on that fatal day; he had not overconsumed that noble tonic compounded of champagne and brandy; he had not hung out the wrong number. It was all a dream. There was no Marjorie Daw!

Twenty years ago I was warned of the fallibility of an

old man's memory by a wise friend, Joseph H. Choate. I had joined a group of writers under the leadership of that best of editors and friendliest of colleagues, John Phillips, in buying the *American Magazine* and attempting to run it on the old line of *McClure's*, that is, the exposure of corruption in politics, business, religion, fashionable society and everything else except publishing. We were called "muckrakers" after the poor men at whom Bunyan's little religious snob Christian turned up his nose. But after we had gone a while we discovered that public interest in these disclosures had all but disappeared. The great jurist Kenesaw Mountain Landis (who now judges the disputes between Gabby Hartnett and Umpire Moriarity) had fined the Standard Oil Company thirty-five million dollars, which sum the Standard Oil Company blithely charged off to petty cash and went on as before. (Or even more so, because the fragments of the Octopus waxed prosperous beyond all reason until parts of the dismembered cephalopod became as great as the Ol' Devil Fish itself and the equivalent of a share in the original Standard of New Jersey which was worth five hundred dollars is now valued at seven thousand dollars or eight thousand dollars.) Nor was it any longer possible for good old Lincoln Steffens to arouse the slumbering virtue of our citizens with his thrilling tale of the rescue of the fire department of Coo Coo, Ioway by Andrew Gump from the hands of wicked Barney Google. In fact the public was tired of muckraking. They had had an overdose of it in the articles of the scamp Tom Lawson, published in a magazine called *Everybody's*, now defunct. Once more in the long history of Reform Politics, the Mammon of Unrighteousness was triumphant and Vir-

tue was taking the count, booed by the sporting American
public, which dearly hates a loser. John Phillips, who was
first of all a professional magazine editor with a great reputation to lose if the *American* failed, thought it was time
we turned our energies towards getting out a readable magazine. This was a harder task than reforming the world, but
it also might be more profitable. In this Ida Tarbell, Ray
Baker and Bert Boyden and I agreed with Phillips. We
also agreed that the memoirs of some American of distinction would be a good thing to get hold of. Memoirs had
often brought gain to the magazines that published them.
Some of them, like General Grant's, were great books of
history. Others could be classed as works of fiction. So I
was asked to see Joseph Choate, our former ambassador to
London, and try to get him to write his Recollections.

Mr. Choate was one of the amplest men mentally of our
day. He had long been the most brilliant member of the
New York bar, he had served with great distinction in
diplomacy, he was a wit, whose drollery was not unmixed
with that slight touch of the malice that Lamb attributed to
the mustard in the salad. He had been a tall figure in the
world. His memories must make fine reading. I thought I
surely could induce him to sign, for our relations had been
friendly. In the first place he was one of that dwindling
band of heroes who read and found consolations in the
talks of one Martin Dooley. Again, he was a fond admirer
of your maternal great-grandfather Stephen Ives, who was a
leader of the Massachusetts bar when Mr. Choate was a
youth in Salem. He was at first enthusiastic about the project but later he weakened and refused to go on; and this

was the reason he gave: "I want to write this book. I think I would enjoy doing it. Perhaps it might be useful to those who come after me to have at first hand my impressions of the world of my day. But I'm afraid to tackle it. Maybe you know that President Eliot and Senator Hoar and I were at Harvard at the same time. We were not in the same year, but we were close friends and have remained friends ever since. Late in his lifetime Senator Hoar was persuaded to publish his Recollections in *Scribner's Magazine*. They had just come out in book form when Eliot dropped in on me. 'Joe,' he said, 'you still like George Hoar.' 'Of course I do, Charles. Why do you ask?' I said. 'Have you been reading his Recollections?' 'Yes.' 'Well,' said he, 'I have too. I think you will agree with me that in spite of his deplorable political connections (which, Joseph, I am sorry to say are similar to yours) he is as honest, as fearless, as straightforward a man as ever lived. Then how do you account for the fact that at nearly every point where he touches on some matter that he and I are both familiar with, my memory doesn't agree with his?' 'I can only account for it, Charles, on the theory that the memory of the President of Harvard College is not as good as it used to be.' 'That may be so. But what has been your experience?' 'My experience has been exactly like yours,' I was forced to admit.

"Now," Mr. Choate went on, "if Eliot and I found so many discrepancies in the Recollections of one of the best of men, how can I trust my aged memory? The Memoirs of Joseph H. Choate must remain unwritten."

He did write a few pages about his boyhood in Salem and his young manhood at Harvard and in New York, but

that was all. He remembered distinctly things that happened seventy years before. He was not so certain of occurrences forty, thirty or ten years before.

So I shall not write my Recollections. But I may send
you from time to time a few notes on the things I have
seen and heard and if you think you would like to gather
these fragments together and make a book of them, they
are yours.

Commentary

Jimmy Malloy, the Irish-American writer in John O'Hara's *Butterfield 8*, claims in a bitter paragraph that the Irish in America are nonassimilable. Malloy explains that he is qualified by ancestry to be a member of the Sons of the American Revolution. "I only mention it to show," he says, "that I'm pretty God damn American and therefore my brothers and sisters are, and yet we're not American. We're Micks, we're nonassimilable, we're Micks."

John O'Hara is one of the most perceptive and sensitive writers of our times. I am assuming that in this case he is using the character of Malloy to express his own views. I have heard him express similar views in conversation. They are views held by many Americans of Irish descent. (This was the locution imposed on us in the Office of War Information during the last war. There were no Irish-Americans, Italian-Americans, German-Americans, etc. We frowned on the qualifying hyphen. There were merely Americans of the appropriate descent.)

O'Hara may be right. Certainly the melting pot is still cluttered with stubborn chunks that have failed to fuse into the mass, or rather that the mass has refused to assimilate. National or racial origin is still an important consideration in our social, political and often in our economic life. We give lip service to our own ideal of total equality, but that is all. Negroes continue to be hampered and restricted in almost every conceivable way, in the North as well as in the South. Jews suffer certain social and even economic handicaps. In many quarters it is more advantageous to be a Protestant than to be a Catholic. The socalled Anglo-Saxon has an edge over the Italian or the Pole when it comes to clawing his or her way on to the society pages. To some extent, we still suspect the "foreigner." The Know-nothing of a hundred years ago has left many of his genes in our chromosomes.

To be sure, some of this classifying of origins is benevolent in effect. It is probably an advantage to be a Jew if you wish to be Governor of New York, a Catholic if your goal is to be Chairman of the Democratic National Committee. In some congressional districts, a white candidate would stand no chance against a Negro. But in general it can be said that the tendency to classify is basically derogatory, if in most cases only faintly so. We still assume a degree of "difference" in the citizens of "foreign" origin. The "typical American" of television and the slick magazines, not that any such animal really exists, is by common acceptance white, Protestant and bears a name originating in John Bull's home island, usually Joe Smith. A television show might star a character named Luigi Marconi, or Stanislaus Kowalski or Manny Cohen, but you would know that the hero was meant to be an Italian, a Pole or a Jew, not a real honest-to-goodness apple-pie Joe Smith American. If his name is "foreign," he is a good American in spite of his ancestry, not because of it. And if your hero is named Pat O'Shea, you are asked to love him for certain traits which are considered peculiar to the Irish, not to "typical Americans."

Political commentators in general seem to agree that John F. Kennedy was elected to the presidency despite his national origin and religion, that these were factors which lost him more votes than they won. His election broke a rule of American politics. That it was broken cannot change the fact that it was a rule.

It is silly that such things should go on in this of all nations, but go on they do, to the extent that an important writer like John O'Hara feels called upon to make the extreme statement that the Irish are nonassimilable.

For myself, I don't know. I am only half Irish or, according to the O'Hara theory, semi-nonassimilable. I do know that when I entered Harvard in 1925, I found that being the son of an Irishman (and a writer into the bargain) made me vaguely suspect in a social sense. In introducing me around, one of my Boston friends, a spotless Brahmin himself, always managed to drag my Yankee maternal lineage into the conversation. He was courteously giving me half of an acceptable pedigree and he never realized that he was also being offensive. In self-defense I took to emphasizing my Irishness, even to cultivating a slight brogue to which I could make no legitimate claim whatsoever. As my father, who spoke pure Chicagoese, pointed out, I might as appropriately have relapsed into Choctaw.

I think I can safely say that my father, who was Irish on both sides, never shared the O'Hara theory at all. Certainly he was a most assimilable individual. He was proud of his

Irish blood, but he never thought of himself as one of a minority, and emphatically not of a minority in any sense inferior. As an Irish-American he was different from those who claimed some other national origin, just as his friend Bernard Baruch was different from him because he was a Jew, and his friend Theodore Roosevelt because his ancestors were Dutch, but only differing from each other as individuals, in just one of the myriad ways in which all individuals differ from each other.

Most of us, even the most liberal, are prey to some prejudices. We may intellectually accept the thesis that only as individuals are men superior or inferior to each other, but emotionally we can still be seduced by those ephemera of race, title and ancestry which have posed as realities since man invented society.

Finley Peter Dunne was one of those fortunate beings who could see them for the shams they are. Not that he was averse to accepting the social amenities which were offered him. He belonged to some of the "best" clubs in New York, London and Washington, because he liked the company he found in them. He was listed in the New York *Social Register* because it pleased my mother. But he was no more proud of such social adornments than he was ashamed of his origin in Chicago's Irish lower middle class (to use a phrase which wouldn't have occurred to him).

He was proud of his Irish blood, but he disliked being described as an Irishman. In his own view, he was simply an American whose ancestors happened to have been Irish. And his view was entirely correct. His Dooley articles, though written in the brogue, are humor in an essentially

American tradition. They are concerned with American politics and America's position in the world. He saw the world through his American eyes and set down what he saw with his American pen. Remove the brogue, rewrite the articles in plain English, and there is little of Ireland left in them.

He was American, but in no sense a chauvinist. His animosity against the British which sometimes appears in these essays was political, not racial. He was as much at home in London as he was in New York and many of his closest friends were British. He disliked British imperialism (including the British treatment of Ireland) as he disliked American imperialism, the "expansionism" which flourished briefly at the turn of the century. Some of his most savage satire was aimed at our shameful experiment with colonialism in the Philippines.

He was a patriot, though he would have derided the appellation, for he despised the flag-wavers. I do not have to guess what he would have thought of those specimens of the breed which infest the country in our time, because they were there in his time too, and ranked among his favorite targets. We sometimes forget that our generation has no monopoly on patrioteers and witch-hunters. Waving the flag was just as profitable a venture in my father's time as it is now, and just as satisfactory a substitute for thought.

He was proud of being an American simply because he was an American, not because he thought Americans were better than anyone else. But both as a writer and as a man, he was a peculiarly American phenomenon. (And so, for that matter, is John O'Hara.)

I often run across people who think that he must have

talked with a brogue. As a matter of fact, the very few
times I heard him make a verbal assault on the dialect, he
couldn't master it for the life of him. It rang completely
out of tune with his native Chicago wood-notes. Others are
surprised when they see his photograph for the first time.
They seem to expect a stage Irishman, with top hat and dudeen, something in the nature of the cartoon representa-
tions of Mr. Dooley done over a period of years by Opper,
Flagg, Kemble and Dana Gibson. Instead, they see him as
he really was: a prosperous American of indeterminate national origin, living in New York during the first half of the
century.

He was conservative in dress and manner. He was far
from being a dandy, but he patronized only the most expensive tailors, who made him beautiful suits which he
promptly ruined by stuffing the pockets with boxes of
wooden Swedish matches. When it came to matches, he
was an outright kleptomaniac. He was forever asking me
to return for him little silver matchboxes he had inad-
vertently picked up at dinner parties. (He smoked no
dudeen, but only flat Turkish cigarettes.) His hats were
expensive if somewhat shapeless, and his shoes handmade
in England. In none of this did he differ from the well-
dressed, affluent men of affairs in New York and Washington who were his friends. He didn't copy them; he was one
of them.

In only two ways did he declare sartorial independence.
In the twenties, the flat straw hat called a "skimmer" was
de rigueur in the summers. Men who were entitled to a
somewhat doubtful privilege used to ameliorate this harsh
and unlovely headgear with colorful club hatbands. On
Friday evenings when the Cannonball had rolled in from

New York, the Southampton station of the Long Island Railroad bloomed like a garden with the colors of the Links, the Knickerbocker, the Racquet and other famous New York clubs. I could always pick out my father even at a distance by his Spartan black hatband, the only one in sight. Nor would he wear knickers or plus-fours on the golf course. "I put away such childish things," he informed me, "when I was six."

No, in Peter Dunne as a personality there was no trace of Martin Dooley. And why should anyone expect it? Nobody expected Ring Lardner to talk like one of his gloriously semi-literate ball players. Lardner was a writer, a great writer, who created characters. And so was my father. One of the secrets of Dooley's success, as Elmer Ellis has shrewdly pointed out, is that Mr. Dooley was something much more than a puppet expressing his creator's views. He was a complete and rounded fictional character. He was the creation of Finley Peter Dunne, not his alter ego.

So when Peter Dunne speaks of the Irish in the following essay, he speaks not as the Irishman Dooley but as the American Dunne, two generations removed from the "soft fair" days, the peat-smoked twilights and the appalling poverty of the land where his grandfather was born.

He was tolerant but scornful of professional Irishmen, (but no more than he was of professional Jews, professional Christians or professional Americans). You will find both the tolerance and the scorn reflected in the article itself.

Personally, I feel that the essay is mistitled. I only use the title "On the Irish" because it was his own choice. It is one of the incomplete essays. He intended to write a great deal more on a subject which was very close to his heart, and on which he was more than adequately informed. As he left it, it is less an essay on the Irish than a collection of reminiscences vaguely touching Ireland: a discussion of police methods, the fascinating story of a journalistic scoop, character sketches of his friends Jack Shea, Lady Gregory, Lord Birkenhead and John Devoy.

He makes one reference to the position taken by Irish-Americans during the First World War, including a brief mention of his own stand, which was not a popular one among some Irish-Americans at the time. In the text, the paragraph is ambiguous and I feel that it could stand some clarification.

Many Irish-Americans in the First War adopted what we learned to call later an isolationist position. They were not so much pro-German as fanatically anti-British. They saw the war, and even a possible British defeat, as a golden opportunity for Ireland to achieve her freedom. In 1916, a large majority of them voted for Wilson, the "peace" candidate, as against Hughes, the "war" candidate.

My father was one of the exceptions, not the only one, but perhaps the most prominent and influential among Americans of Irish descent. At the risk of seeming to labor the point, I repeat that he looked on the world through purely American eyes. And in this he differed from many of his Irish-American friends, who could not see the American forest for the Irish trees. It was possible for a patriotic Irish-American to work and speak against an alliance with the hated British, but not for one who was also an avid student of history like my father. He was well aware of the fact that the United States had been allowed to grow to rich maturity in splendid isolation mainly because throughout the period of our growth the British Navy dominated the seas of the world. (Ironically, I know Britishers today who are intellectually neutralist or anti-American but who don't hesitate to admit that they can survive as a free nation only under the shield of American power.)

My father didn't like the British as a nation. He didn't like to appear as an ally of the Anglophile snobs of New York and Washington who banned Beethoven from the concert repertoires and swooned over the British officers who were sent here to fan the war fever in American breasts, while collecting any loose cash which might be lying around. He disliked the snubs he received from some of his Irish friends who were such bellicose partisans of peace at any price. He simply considered it his duty as an American to stand for our entry into the war as a matter of self-defense.

And he did more than merely state his opinion. He worked hard at it along with Theodore Roosevelt, Robert Collier, Mark Sullivan and others who led the crusade for what was called Preparedness but meant intervention. It was one of the few times that he ever entered actively into national politics as leading spokesman for a cause.

From this time and condition dates his otherwise inexplicable antipathy to Woodrow Wilson. As he would often admit in later years, Mr. Wilson was one of the greatest of Presidents. Wilson's enemies were also the enemies of Mr. Dooley: the hypocrites, the social frauds and the greedy pirates of politics and finance. There was nothing in his liberal intellectual political philosophy to which the liberal intellectual Peter Dunne could take major exception. Yet he never really liked him.

I believe that this lack of enthusiasm sprang from their difference of opinion over Preparedness. It was no doubt fanned by my father's close association with Theodore Roosevelt, the leading apostle of Preparedness and Wilson's bitterest critic. Even our entry into the war did nothing to effect a reconciliation between these two strong characters. The Roosevelt faction was furious when Wilson by-passed General Leonard Wood, a Roosevelt man, and appointed General Pershing to command the American Expeditionary Force in France. The Colonel's own romantic offer to raise and lead a division of volunteers to France was also rejected by the President, a predictable action with predictable results. Hell hath, then and now, no fury like a Roosevelt scorned.

And some of the Rooseveltian fury lingered on in the Dunne household. I was too young at the time to understand what it was all about, but I remained loyally anti-Wilson until I took my first American history course in college. It seems clear to me now that Peter Dunne, the aloof and disinterested commentator, had involved himself in a political quarrel he normally might have ridiculed. But then he always ranked friendship above consistency.

All this is far afield from the subject of the Irish, but it had its origin in Irish-American affairs. The non-Irish who led the fight for Preparedness, or intervention, pushed my father to the fore precisely because he was Irish.

I think my mother must have done some pushing too, once the direction of his sympathies was clear. She had suffered snubs from people who assumed that because her husband was Irish he must be pro-German. As I remember her telling it, she was pointedly not invited to a dinner for an exalted Englishman given by an acquaintance of hers. This lady, who held an American patent of nobility in the meat-packing business, spread the word round New

York that the Dunnes had not been invited because the Dunnes, being pro-German, wouldn't accept in any case. It is true that my father wouldn't have accepted, but only because both the lady and her husband bored him. So, as a matter of fact, did the Englishman. But my mother felt the snub keenly. In her circles, it was the equivalent of being accused of Communist sympathies today. And it was grossly untrue.

My mother had always had a difficult time with her own personal Irish problem. She had been brought up in a Boston still deeply prejudiced against the sons and daughters of the Ould Sod. When she was a little girl, Honey Fitz had not yet been elected Boston's first Irish mayor, nor had Brickley and Mahan, Daly and Kiernan done heroic deeds on the gridiron for Harvard. No one could have guessed then that in two generations the Boston Irish would produce a President of the United States.

The Irish were the coachmen, cooks, cops and comedians of my mother's Proper Bostonian world. And she had broken all the rules of her caste and married one. On her frequent returns to Boston, she ran into the same kind of inverted snobbery that I experienced at Harvard. A friend gave a dinner for her and took pains to announce to the guests that she and my mother had "been out to Mount Auburn to visit Mrs. Dunne's ancestors." Mount Auburn, for the uninitiated, is a cemetery favored by the Brahmins. In Boston it is as important to end well as to begin well. If you are buried in Mount Auburn, you are in, in more senses than one. My mother's hostess was setting her guests straight on this apparently upstart wife of an Irish humorist. One of them, with ill-concealed surprise, asked my mother: "Do you mean you bury in Mount Auburn?"

My mother, maintaining a poker face, assured her that she did, constantly, and the party was a great success.

My mother gallantly conquered her native prejudice against the Irish. But until she died she adhered firmly to the belief that Boston — Puritan, Yankee Boston — was in truth the Hub of the Universe. An Irishman might rise to eminence and social respectability, like her husband, but a Boston Yankee was born to both. The pious Bostonian is as unshakably orthodox as the pious Jew, and as convinced of the essential virtue of his institutions and beliefs.

And so my mother set out with dedication to turn her half-Irish New York children into Proper Bostonians. It went without saying that her sons would go to Harvard. My father had no objection to that, but he did put his foot down when she, warmly abetted by Old Grotonian Theodore Roosevelt, entered us for Groton. As a matter of fact, although my father had once had Mr. Dooley describe Groton as a "siminary for young Englishmen bor-rn in America," he acted only when another Old Grotonian friend of his maliciously pointed out that Groton was officially a church school and that the nominally Catholic young Dunnes would be educated as Episcopalians. My father had taken no pains whatsoever to give his children a Catholic education, but this was too much for him. So my brothers and I were sent to Middlesex, which was recommended to my father by President Eliot of Harvard and which was officially nonsectarian, meaning that the compulsory chapels on Sunday were vaguely Unitarian. If you are sufficiently confused by this, you will have some understanding of the religious confusion that reigned in the Dunne household.

The root of it was that my father didn't really care. Religion never weighed heavily on him. Once when he was asked if he was a Roman Catholic, he answered, "No, I'm a Chicago Catholic." His veto of Groton was purely a reflex action to the needling of his friend. A man who never went to mass himself was in no position to provide his children with sound Catholic leadership. When he was a boy, there had been some talk of educating him for the priesthood. His father, my grandfather, had turned the idea down flat, saying that there would be no "made priests" in his family. Himself a pious man, he may have guessed that his son was basically irreligious.

In his lack of religious attachment my father revealed once more his nonconformity with the usual pattern of Irish-American life.

But for all his aberrations, for all his fundamental Americanism, his love for Ireland and the Irish lasted as long as he lived. He reveled in the legendary deeds of Finn Mac-Cool and Cuchulainn. He wept over the martyrs Robert Emmett and Michael Collins. He loved the Irish songs — not the imitations with which modern "Irish" tenors pollute the airways — but the genuine folk music used by generations of Irishmen to salute their beloved and misruled land. One of my last memories of him is the sound of him, in company with the actor Joe Kerrigan and Colonel Geoffrey Galwey, U.S.A., friends of mine who became friends of his, sending down a dying California moon with renditions of "The Blarney Roses" and "Ballyjamesduff." It was my father's humble boast that he knew sixty-eight verses of "The Blarney Roses."

He was, after all, an Irishman.

FINLEY PETER DUNNE

On the Irish

B OB PINKERTON and I used to differ as to who was the
best policeman in America. I don't mean the best
detective. He knew that. It was Bob's brother Bill. Like all
good detectives, Bill Pinkerton was without romantic notions about his profession. He would not do for a hero
for Doyle or Wallace or Mason. His theory was this:
"Most criminals are professionals. I care nothing about
amateurs. If they are stupid, as nearly all criminals are,
they give themselves away the minute they are suspected.
If they are clever, the only persons who can turn them
up are their own associates in business and they can be
relied upon not to talk. I know of a fellow who stole a million dollars from a bank that he was president of. He was
accused of the crime by the chairman of his finance committee. He smilingly admitted that he was guilty. 'But,' he
said, 'I'm not the only fellow around this bank who has
done queer things with its funds. And then,' he went on,
lighting a cigarette, 'besides the million I stole, I grabbed
three million dollars more when you began snooping
around instead of coming to me, as a friend and an honorable man would have done. Do you think there wouldn't be

a run on the bank if it got out that we'd lost four million dollars? And do you think you could realize on the old hats and rubber boots your friends have up as collateral? I'll tell you what I'll do. I don't want to be harsh, but it is clear that the board and I have lost confidence in each other. If you promise not to prosecute I will return all of the four million except two hundred and fifty thousand to start going again in some other place.'

"And they did it," Bill went on. "I would have no chance with that kind of crook. But I know all the professional criminals in the country or know about them. And I know that when a safe is blown in a bank the safe blower is sure to turn up in a hock-shop, or a barroom or a race track and show off his new money to a girl, or the bartender or the gambler. And that's where we get 'em."

So the star Pinkerton detectives and Bill himself would stroll casually about all sorts of resorts, and one day one of the experts of the brace and bit, or the acetylene torch, would be betting a sure thing on the nose with his friend Costigan or Big Eddie or Honest John, when a firm hand would be laid on his shoulder and two others on his wrists and in no time he would be on his way to Sing Sing or Joliet. The sign "American Bankers Association" on the door of a bank was a warning that only the tyros neglected. The seasoned robber knew that "the eye" was on him. The eye that never slept.

But it was not about detectives that Bob and I talked. It was about policemen qua policemen, that is, officers of the peace. He thought Bill Devery of New York was the best, I thought Jack Shea of Chicago. It was an honest difference of opinion, for both Bill and Jack belonged to the

same school of thought and both looked with a good deal
of contempt on officers like the celebrated Inspector
Byrnes, whose fortune was made by scaring millionaires
into the belief that there was about to be an uprising of
anarchists and assembling an army of cops to surround a
few hundred garment workers in Union Square who had
gathered to hear a squeaky little tailor rant in Yiddish
against the tyranny of Capital.

Devery and Shea had the same antipathies. Both hated
a thief as they hated a snake, and both grew savage when
crimes of violence were committed in districts under their
control. Prostitution and gambling they tolerated. They
looked with contempt on officers who took money from
streetwalkers, as is the London practice. But, like the London police, they regarded gambling as a necessary evil —
necessary to the principal officers of a well-regulated police
force who have families to bring up. It was not until Prohibition was put in force and crime became big business
that the police in New York and Chicago began to grow
rich by harboring and protecting murderers and kidnapers.
You may be sure that under these two peace officers the
Als, the "Dutches," the Rothsteins and the "Luckys" who
have made fortunes by robbery and murder and kidnaping
would not last twenty-four hours. "Take the night stick to
them, men," were Devery's orders. "These rats are only
frightened by a beating. Give 'em the night stick. They're
not afraid of a revolver. Ninety-nine times out of a hundred an excited man will miss his mark with a gun. But
you can't miss with a night stick." If Devery were chief
in New York now, Mr. Lucky Something-or-other with a
hue-and-cry out against him, wouldn't be drinking cham-

pagne in a New York hotel. He'd be lying on his stomach
in some out-of-town hide-away with his lady-love applying
poultices to his bruised rump.

Scores of times I have rambled with Jack Shea through
the night streets of Chicago, talking ancient Irish poetry,
about which he knew a great deal and I was sort of dab.
Often have I heard him say, "Excuse me, please," and stalk
across Polk Street, grab a big ruffian by the neck, knock him
down (for my poetic policeman was a terrible fighter) pull
him to his feet and boot him to the corner into the inhos-
pitable arms of a patrolman who knocked him down
again for luck, disarmed him of his pistol and sent him off
in a patrol wagon to be booked for carrying a concealed
weapon and vagrancy. Then John would rejoin me and say,
"You'll not see that duck in this neighborhood again with
his gun. I'll have no killings in my district. The Red will
get off light. The judge is a friend of Joe Martin's and
Red is one of Joe's fellows. But he'll steer clear of this part
of the South Side. Now what was it you were saying about
Finn MacCool being a fabulous and not a historic character?"

Jack Shea and Devery hated crimes of violence, and if
you told them that organized bands of assassins existed in
New York and Chicago without the purchased connivance
of the police, and possibly the district attorney, they would
laugh in your face. They knew different. No money could
buy them off from pursuit of these murdering thieves,
blackmailers and kidnapers. But political killings were different. And killings in the unending conflict between Ireland and the British government were acts of war.

My older brother was a friend of Shea, and one day in

1882, while I was still a schoolboy, we dropped in on the great policeman just as a tall, redheaded young man without a hat ran out of his office. He was a loose-jointed fellow with high cheekbones and small, mad eyes and he was apparently in a state of great emotional excitement.

"Who is that?" my brother asked.

"I can't talk now," said Shea, who knew how sound was my brother's belief in dynamite as a political agency. "But some day I'll tell you."

About a month later we picked up a paper and read that Carey, the informer in the Phoenix Park murder case, was traveling under an assumed name on a P & O boat and had gone into the lounge for a drink when a fellow passenger, an Irish-American named O'Donnell, stepped up to him and shot him dead. O'Donnell had been taken off the boat at Port Said and was now on his way back to Liverpool to be hanged.

When my brother saw Shea that afternoon, the policeman had a copy of the paper on his desk.

"Did you see this?" my brother asked.

"Yes."

"Do you know anything about it?"

"A little. Do you remember the loon you saw coming out of my office last month?"

"I remember him well."

"That," said Shea, "was O'Donnell."

He would say no more at the time. But years later he told me. We were sitting over a toddy in the back room of Tom Moran's friendly barroom in Randolph Street, talking about politics and crime, how the Sullivan–Kilrain fight at Mississippi City would come out, did Curt Welch compare with Jimmy Ryan as a fielder, and this and that and the other, and the disgraceful betrayal of Parnell by the Bantry band and their sympathizers, when Shea said, "Do you remember that lad O'Donnell that you once saw in my office?"

"I do indeed."

"Well," said Shea, "I'll tell you how I came to get mixed up with him. You remember the murder of Cavendish and Burke in Phoenix Park. Well, nobody wanted to kill Lord Frederick Cavendish. He was a kind, simple-minded sort of a fellow, a little soft, who wished to be friendly and thought he might do some good as Lord Lieutenant when the British gave him the job. But Burke, his secretary, was hated. He was an Irishman and a Catholic, but everything wicked and hurtful to his people that came from the Castle was charged to him. He was always in danger. But he was a brave man and I'm told he would go to mass with a shot-gun tucked under his arm. The boys of Pat Egan's Invincibles made up their minds to kill him in the Park the first morning they got the chance. Unfortunately, they found him walking with Cavendish. Both men resisted. Cavendish was carrying a folded umbrella and he lunged at the jackeens as if it were a sword, crying, 'Ha! Dastards!' So the boys cut them both down with their knives. They were soon caught. The police had been watching them. They first took Carey, who kept a pub and was a leader of the group that the laborers and car men belonged to, and he gave way to threats and bribery and turned queen's evidence. So the poor men were hanged.

"Our fellows over here felt bad to think that an informer — and such a rotten one — should be traveling around the world at ease with all his expenses paid by the British government. So they raised a fund to get him killed. You wouldn't think it, but there were many who volunteered for the job. The men who raised the money picked out O'Donnell, who lived in St. Paul. He was far from being the fool he looked. He was really quite an intelligent fellow and a brave one, but he was a thorough fanatic, from Mayo, God help us. So they gave O'Donnell the money — ten thousand dollars it was — and they figured this would be enough to take him over and seek out Carey and leave considerable for a good lawyer. It was a million to one against O'Donnell knocking Carey off and getting away with it, but he took the chance.

"Coming down from St. Paul, he fell in with a gang of three-card monte men. By this time he had maybe a drink taken. Anyhow, they got him into the game and cheated him out of the whole ten thousand! They didn't leave the unfortunate man a sou. He was in despair when he got here and hurried over to see Cusack. Cusack sent him to me and he told me his story. Of course I knew, as any copper does, that if a gang of cardsharpers works on a railroad train, they can only do it under the protection of the conductor, the brakeman and the railroad's chief of police. It's the same on an ocean liner. The professional card players on the boats hardly make a living after they've split with the head steward, who reports to the purser, who reports to the captain. I knew this railroad dick and I sent Grab-All Murnane to bring him in. The dick was a German man. I told him as much as I wanted to tell him. I had enough on him to hang him, anyhow, but when I hinted something about the Invincibles and their long knives, he caved in completely. 'I'll have it all here by five o'clock,' he said. And sure enough he made good. I took the money, gave it to O'Donnell and sent Grab-All down to the train to wish him Godspeed and see that he didn't buy a gold brick on his way. The next I knew I saw by the papers that he'd blown Carey's head off on that boat.

"It was a tough spot to put an honest American police-man in, but feeling the way I felt, I couldn't do anything else but what I did."

"Haven't you ever regretted it? Hasn't your conscience ever reproached you?"

"Divvle the bit," said Jack Shea cordially. "The beast Carey had to be killed. There was no way out of it. If that was the greatest sin I had on my soul I wouldn't be bothered about my salvation. Look at the way I swear when I'm mad."

It is impossible to understand this attitude of Shea, unless you appreciate the intense hatred of the British Government that the Irishman in every part of the world cherished in his heart. "What! Condone political assassina-tion?" you cry. By no means. In our own country the assas-sins have ended the lives of three presidents. In all of these cases the offense was unjustified and horrible. In none was it condoned except on the ground that the murderer was insane. That was true of the slayers of both Garfield and McKinley. Whether it was true of Wilkes Booth is a mat-ter for conjecture. But who can regard the murder of the lewd, petty tyrant Huey Long as a public disaster? And who will deny to an oppressed people the privilege of tyran-nicide? When all is said and done, war itself is nothing but massed assassination. The reply of the unorganized

Irish to the rifles of the British soldiers and the bludgeons of the British police was the dagger and the dynamite bomb. When this assassination was closely organized and firmly directed, it became a form of warfare far more humane than the air raids on defenseless cities which are to be the great feature of the "next war." Brave men risked their lives to march into public places and shoot down officers who had been sent across the Irish Sea to shoot them down. The ferocious Black and Tans and Auxiliaries slew and spared not; the still more ferocious Irish Republican Army slew the Black and Tans and the Auxiliaries by the hundreds with bombs and machine guns manufactured by ex-soldiers in Dublin cellars and the caves of Wexford hills. And in the end, Great Britain made peace with as much formality as she would have shown in dealing with a continental power.

After the failure of the Fenian invasion of Canada, the anti-British sentiment in this country organized a Society known as the Clan na Gael. An old friend of mine, John Devoy, was one of the leaders of this movement. He and I had worked on the same papers, where he was an admirable foreign editor, and he taught me the little French I know, which I speak with a slight brogue. Inflamed with patriotism, Devoy as a boy made up his mind that an organized military movement against Great Britain was possible, and with this in mind he bent his soul toward acquiring an accurate knowledge of the art of war. He imagined, as a boy might, that he could best acquire this knowledge by enlisting in the French Foreign Legion under Napoleon III. He spent the usual term of service in Africa, and when he came out he was assigned by the

Fenian leaders to the business of proselytizing Irish soldiers in the British army. His failure was foredoomed. With a sentence of death hanging over him, he escaped to America. But he had made one distinguished convert. John Boyle O'Reilly was a sergeant in a British regiment quartered in Dublin. He joined the movement but was soon suspected, for he knew no such thing as concealment of his thoughts, was arrested and sentenced to death. This sentence was commuted to transportation to Australia for life. Later he was taken off by an expedition organized by Devoy. The ship employed sailed from New Bedford. Her captain was a Yankee who had no great love for the Irish but made up for that by an inherited hatred of the British. O'Reilly was brought back to Boston, where he became editor of the Boston *Pilot*, a Catholic weekly that grew into one of the most distinguished literary magazines of that time. He wrote much charming verse, was champion middle-weight amateur boxer of New England, and a man much admired and loved.

While the Clan na Gael was under Devoy's leadership, it was purely an Irish organization and was of great help to Charles Stewart Parnell. Parnell knew the value of suggesting force as a possible alternative to an unsuccessful parliamentary campaign. He could say to the ministers of the Crown in effect: "Oh, very well, if you won't concede anything, we'll step aside and let the dynamiters take our place." He was in constant touch with Stephens, the old Fenian leader who lived in Paris, and with Devoy, who was in New York. When Parnell came over to this country, the only man who met him at Quarantine was John Devoy. They understood each other.

But as time went on, Irish-American politicians saw the possible usefulness of the Clan in promoting their own interests, and gradually the camps were filled with politicians, under the leadership of one Alexander Sullivan, a Chicago lawyer, whose wife was one of the ablest and most influential journalists of her day. Sullivan had distinguished himself by shooting down in cold blood an unarmed man who had said something derogatory about Mrs. Sullivan's political activities. But as leader of the Clan he became a great political force. He was a Republican in politics and by his adroitness and his wife's remarkable political ability, he succeeded in building up a large Irish Republican faction which worked for the election of James G. Blaine as president. So large was this body that Blaine came within a few hundred votes of election. The Irish Blaine vote more than offset the so-called Mugwump vote of disaffected Republicans. But on the Saturday before election day, a silly, bigoted Protestant clergyman, one Dr. Burchard, turned up at headquarters with an address from some hundreds of his fellow bigots which he read to the candidate. Blaine had received hundreds of these addresses. He thought they were all alike. His mind was elsewhere as the minister droned on. He did not hear the phrase in which the smart-aleck dominie summoned apt alliteration's artful aid and congratulated Blaine on his coming victory over the party of "Rum, Romanism and Rebellion." But the newspaper reporters didn't miss it. The next morning pamphlets hastily printed by the Democratic Committee were distributed at the door of every Catholic church in New York and Brooklyn. And poor Blaine was beaten out of the New York electoral vote by — I think — about a thousand votes. Was ever a wise man, a great man, so undone by a perfect fool? And is there, in all the history of human folly, a greater fool than a clergyman in politics?

Sullivan was greatly disappointed at Blaine's defeat. The candidate had promised him the Attorney-Generalship in his cabinet. But he was a resourceful and a persistent character and he continued in power. It was through his influence that Pat Egan, the chief of the Invincibles, to which the murderers of Cavendish and Burke belonged, was appointed Minister to Chile by Benjamin Harrison, in whose cabinet Blaine was Secretary of State. Egan made a mess of things in Chile by harboring the deposed dictator Balmaceda in the American legation. Balmaceda afterwards slipped over to the Argentine legation. There, I imagine, his reception was not altogether ardent, for he soon decided to commit suicide and thus escape his enemies, who would have strangled him with all the good will in the world.

Sullivan's control of the Clan na Gael led eventually to its subsidence as a political factor through the murder of Dr. Cronin. This was one of the great "news features" of my career as a newspaperman, into which I threw all the eagerness of my youth and my professional ambition. I was city editor of the Chicago *Times* when the doctor was killed. And I was twenty-two! I had known Dr. Cronin as a harmless sort of character, who possessed an agreeable tenor voice and could wring the impressionable hearts at an Irish picnic with "The Harp That Once" or "The Vale of Avoca" or "Let Erin Remember." He was the last man in the world I should think anyone would want to murder. But I was wrong.

Alexander Sullivan, after gaining political control of the

Clan na Gael, began to take a deeper interest in its financial affairs. Although Devoy always said he was a British
spy, my old friend had not the slightest proof of that except that Sullivan was born in Canada which, I submit, is
not entirely convincing evidence even for an Irishman
against a political enemy. But there is no question that the
large sums of money that passed into Sullivan's hands were
not used for the purpose for which they were intended —
namely to arm agents of the Clan with weapons to destroy
Windsor Castle, Buckingham Palace, the Houses of Parliament, the Bank of England and other monuments to England's power. These points of interest to tourists are still
standing. Eventually it leaked out that Sullivan had been
speculating on the Chicago Board of Trade and his enemies surmised that he was gambling with money from the
war chest of the Clan. This turned out to be true. He made
the usual excuse — that he had only borrowed temporarily,
that he intended to pay it back to the last cent, etc. This
excuse was good enough for Sullivan's political heelers but
not satisfactory to such firebrands as Devoy and Cronin.
Urged on by his leader and friend, Cronin began a sys-
tematic campaign against Sullivan in the camps of the
Clan. He could talk as well as sing and his eloquence was
informed with hatred of Sullivan and a thorough belief
that he was an enemy, not a friend, of the "cause." Which
was not true. The worst that could be said about this man
was that he looked upon the Irish agitation chiefly as a
means to his own financial and political advancement.
Apparently Cronin's tirades did not diminish Sullivan's
power in the least, nor deprive him of the support of his
followers. He was as strong a factor in politics in Washing-

ton and Chicago as he had ever been. He must have possessed qualities imperceptible to my eyes, for his friends stood by him through good and evil report with unwavering constancy.

Strange to say, no word of this mutiny in the Clan reached the newspapers. But there can be no doubt that Sullivan felt the attacks keenly and was exasperated to a point where he denounced Cronin as a spy and hinted that a spy's death was his due.

Then, one night — the night of May 4, 1889 — Dr. John Patrick Cronin disappeared.

A few weeks before this, he had made a contract with a man named O'Sullivan to attend employees who might be injured at O'Sullivan's icehouse on the outskirts of the city. On this May night a buggy, drawn by a white horse, was driven up to Cronin's residence and word was sent up that the doctor was wanted at O'Sullivan's icehouse. He packed his instruments in a bag and drove off with the stranger. And he never came back.

The next day, his landlord reported his disappearance to the police. No one paid much attention to it at first. The case was turned over to Daniel Coughlin, a detective of experience and excellent standing. Coughlin treated the affair lightly. He knew Cronin. Probably the doctor was off on a spree somewhere. He was a bachelor and bachelors are notoriously erratic in their movements. Cronin's landlord, one Cochran, insisted that there had been foul play, but no newspaperman believed it until suddenly John Devoy appeared in Chicago. He had resigned from his position on the New York *Herald* and had come west without a penny in his pocket, but with vengeance in his heart. I was one of the first newspapermen whom he saw. He flatly declared that Cronin had been murdered and proceeded to give me an account of Cronin's campaign against Sullivan.

Devoy was well known to many Chicago newspapermen, who respected him for his rugged honesty, and they began to take the disappearance seriously. Then commenced one of the strangest conspiracies to baffle investigators of a great crime that I have ever heard of. Day after day men, not all of them Irishmen either, whom I knew and respected, dropped in at my office to chat about nothing in particular but always ending with something more than a hint that they knew Cronin was a British spy who had been uncovered by Sullivan and was now on his way to London; that he had been killed by his landlord, who had discovered him lying with the landlord's wife; that he had fled to escape the wrath of the brother of a patient whom he had seduced. But the most concrete evidence that he had furtively escaped came from Canada. The Associated Press reported from St. Catherine's, from Kingston, from London, from Toronto that he had been seen in each of these towns. It was puzzling beyond words, so I turned to my constant friend William Pinkerton for help. In those days the agency, and particularly Billy himself, maintained close relations with all the police chiefs in the United States and Canada, as well as with Scotland Yard and the Paris Sureté.

"I'll wire the Chief Constable of the Dominion," (I think that is what he was called), Pinkerton said. "Come around tomorrow afternoon and I'll let you know."

When I called the next day he had decoded a message from the Canadian police chief. It stated bluntly that no

trace of Cronin had been found, but that the statement
that he had been seen in various Canadian towns had all
been given to the newspapers by one Sharkey, whom Pinkerton and I identified at once as an employee of the claim
department of the Chicago City Railway Company — for
which Alexander Sullivan was counsel.

Pinkerton, after reading the message, calmly remarked,
"Cronin was murdered." But when I tried to pump him
further he exclaimed, "No, this ends my connection with
the case. You newspaper fellows all think you are better
detectives than we are. Go find the murderer. I'll not help
you. I don't care what you Irishmen do to each other. I'm
Scotch."

I published the facts without mentioning Pinkerton and
instantly the messages from Canada ceased. I sent a reporter to see Sullivan. Sullivan angrily refused to talk.
O'Sullivan, the ice man, stoutly maintained that he had
not sent for Cronin. The detective in charge of the case,
Coughlin, put off his appearance of indifference and apparently began to apply his keen mind to a solution of the
mystery.

The newspapers had the greatest confidence in Coughlin. He was a tall, powerfully built fellow, with a white
face and small quick eyes of the lightest blue. He was a
slow, patient man whose manner created confidence in his
ability and honesty. When the facts came out about Sharkey, he spent all his days and most of his nights in examin-
ing persons who might know something about the case. He
had Cronin's landlord at his office twenty times. He sent
for O'Sullivan, the ice man, again and again and put
him secretly through an inquisition that, as he said, "would

have broken down a man of iron." But he made no headway.

One morning he called the reporters in. He looked utterly tired out. "Boys," he said, "I give up. Unless Cronin is a British spy who is now in hiding in London, I can't even guess what has happened to him. I've searched high and low until I'm exhausted and I can get nowhere. *But this you may be sure of, there isn't a shred of evidence that Cronin was murdered!*"

The next day a gang of city workmen, who had been looking for the cause of the stoppage of a sewer in a remote part of the North Side, found the evidence. It was a dead body that had been stuffed into the sewer. They hauled it out and sent it to the morgue, where it was unmistakably identified as the body of Dr. Cronin. It had been mauled by clubs and heavy boots as well.

Dan Coughlin, for the first time in his career, showed excitement over this discovery. "I'll find the men who did this job if I have to spend the rest of my life looking for them. Poor, poor Cronin," he said, and he went to work with the air of a man who is determined to do his duty at any hazard to his fortune or his life.

By this time, I could think of nothing but the Cronin case. I slept with it. I ate with it. I drew on the cashier of our struggling newspaper for what he considered enormous sums to pay the expenses of reporters lodging in the same houses with a score of persons under suspicion.

One day at noon, I went to Billy Boyle's celebrated chophouse "in the alley" for lunch, and there encountered an ex-detective named Patrick Ryan. I should like to write a good deal about Ryan if I had time and room. He was a good man, a staunch friend and one of the wisest beings I have ever known. He had the most amazing knowledge of what was going on everywhere and a fine memory to retain his knowledge. He was Pinkerton's closest friend. He jeered at me.

"A fine lot of detectives you newspaper fellows are," he said. "Why don't you find out who killed Cronin?"

"We're doing the best we can," I explained. "We're relying a good deal on Dan Coughlin and we turn over to him anything we get."

"Do you ever see Dan?"

"Once in a while."

"Well, when you see him why don't you ask him who it was who tried to get Paddy Guerin and Jack Harvey to beat up Dr. Cronin at a Hibernian picnic last August."

"You mean — ?"

"On second thought, you needn't ask. I'll tell you. It was Dan Coughlin."

I don't think I was ever more astonished by anything in my life. I ran back to my office and from that moment every act of Mr. Daniel Coughlin's daily life was watched. Slowly we wound about him an unbreakable chain of evidence. Finally, the last link was forged. We had on the paper one of those creatures of the underworld who somehow manage to maintain a position in journalism. His name was Joe Dunlop. He was a night bird, a collector of evil gossip for purpose of blackmail, but he had been partly instrumental in inducing the widow of Wilbur F. Storey to sell the *Times* to its present owner, J. J. West, and the lady had made the transfer conditional upon the hiring of Dunlop at a large salary. He had an office on my floor, but what he did except look disgusting I never knew. I never spoke to him. But one night, when our progress on the case had halted because we couldn't locate the livery stable where the white horse had been hired, Joe Dunlop came in and told our proprietor that he had found the place and the man.

The man who hired the horse and buggy was Dan Coughlin.

West called me in, had Dunlop repeat his story, and ordered me to hold the city edition while he and Dunlop went to the Mayor and the Chief of Police. Then the Chief took two policemen with him to Coughlin's house.

When I got word that the murderer was taken, we rushed the story to the composing room, where it was set up in an incredibly short time, and about six o'clock in the morning the newsboys were running through the streets yelling "Huxtry." Their cries were hardly more shrill than my headlines announcing to the awakening citizens that the Cronin mystery had been solved and that the chief detective officer in the investigation of the crime was in a cell charged with the murder of Patrick Cronin.

It was the biggest "scoop" I ever took part in in my whole newspaper experience. Come to think of it, it was the only one. Oh yes, there was one other, which I will describe later in these notes.

Eventually the murderers were put on trial and convicted. Eleven of the jurymen voted to hang them but one man held out for life imprisonment, and after many hours of argument the eleven gave in and the verdict was "Guilty" and the penalty imprisonment for life. The finding was afterward reversed by the State Supreme Court, but meanwhile, two of the other prisoners, O'Sullivan the ice man and a deluded fellow named Martin Burke, died at Joliet and Coughlin alone was retried. By this time public interest in the case had waned, witnesses had died or disappeared, the public prosecutor was a friend of Alexander Sullivan, and after a farcical hearing, a farcical verdict of "Not Guilty" was returned. Coughlin, freed, went to work for Sullivan in the streetcar company's law department. There he was guilty of one malfeasance after another, and was obliged to flee the city. We heard of him later in bad repute in the Northwest, then in the Argentine. Finally he was caught up by the maelstrom of life in the Far East and disappeared — I hope — forever.

In after years, out of curiosity, I pieced together the true story of this remarkable crime, from the lips of men who knew and were no longer afraid to talk. In the first place I assured myself that Alex Sullivan had no guilty knowledge of the murder of Cronin until after it had been committed. He was not accessory before the fact, although by force of inevitable circumstances he became accessory after the fact. On the morning after the murder, Sullivan called up Dr. Leonard St. John, a well-known physician, and asked him to take him for a drive. The doctor found the Clan leader, who usually presented a front of ice to any great emergency, in a state bordering on hysteria.

"I'm in a terrible position," he cried. "A group of my men, headed by Dan Coughlin, have killed a man called Cronin. Cronin was a nuisance. I may have said he was a spy and ought to be killed. I never thought the fools would do it. But they've murdered him and now I must stand by them and get them off."

The doctor gave him a sedative powder and took him to his office. After this, Sullivan presented to the public the same demeanor of cool self-confidence that had carried him the great distance he had gone. He did take care of his men. He got a new trial for Coughlin, saw that he was adequately defended and inadequately prosecuted, found a place for him after his acquittal and took care of him financially up to the time of his death.

The story of the actual crime was briefly this: Coughlin was under great obligation to Sullivan whom he, like many other followers of this strange man, fairly worshipped. When he found that his "leader" was disturbed by Cronin's savage attacks, he made up his mind to silence the doctor. His first thought was to have him roughed, perhaps maimed for life. But he didn't find it easy to get even the criminals under his protection to do this kind of job. Cronin was growing more and more savage in his attacks. Finally Coughlin determined to make away with him altogether and in looking for accomplices he hit upon O'Sullivan, the ice man. This O'Sullivan was what old country Irish people would call a "dacint man." He had a nice little business of his own. There was no stain on his character. He was at heart no more of a murderer than any man you know. But his people had been treated with all the savagery that the landlord classes in Ireland called the "Iron Hand" and he was a monomaniac on the subject of Irish Freedom. He thought Alex Sullivan was the greatest Irish leader since Robert Emmett. He would believe no wrong of him. When he was told Cronin was a spy, he blazed with anger and readily joined Coughlin in the plot to make away with the doctor. It was in his cottage that the victim was destroyed. Confronted by the murderers, Cronin, who was a powerful man, made a strong resistance. But he was struck down with clubs and kicked with heavy boots until he was dead. Then a strange thing happened. As the doctor fell, his shirt front, which had been torn in the fight, came open and disclosed his scapulars. Coughlin was about to kick him again when O'Sullivan saw the scapulars and called on him to desist. "D'you want to defend a bloody spy?" Coughlin demanded. "Let him be," O'Sullivan cried, pointing his revolver at the detective. "If you kick him again I'll shoot you."

Did the thought flash on O'Sullivan's brain at that moment that he had been deceived? No one will ever know, for the little fellow went to his grave without opening his lips to any layman. I have always felt a deep pity for O'Sullivan. What a fate it was that made his love of country lead him into this dark and dreadful plot to murder, not an enemy of Ireland, but one of her most faithful sons!

The Cronin case did much to cool the patriotic ardor of Irish-Americans who had felt the political passions of their fathers revived in their hearts by the brilliant and uncompromising leadership of Charles Stewart Parnell. They were further alienated when a majority of the Irish parliamentary leaders and a great part of the Catholic clergy, hitherto the staunchest friends of the cause, turned on Parnell and destroyed him, after the Kitty O'Shea scandal. And for what? To satisfy the "Non-conformist conscience" which had looked with the greatest complacency on the spectacle of the Marquess of Hartington (later Duke of Devonshire) and his mistress dining with Queen Victoria, while Gladstone, in the sanctity of his spotless, home, received John Morley and *his* mistress. Is there any hypocrisy in the world equal to British hypocrisy? Only one — the American brand derived from that good old Anglo-Saxon stock, upon whose hypocrisy the sun never sets without a blush.

In the years that followed, most of us lost interest in Irish affairs, although Devoy reorganized the Clan na Gael and, coming to New York, started the *Gaelic American,* in which I was glad to take a small stock interest which I later presented to my friend. Devoy grew older very slowly, but he was much softened as his days drew in. It was as though to the wild eyes of this man whom people thought a mere visionary there had appeared the figure of Ireland with the manacles stricken from her wrists and the color swarming back to her cheeks. Only occasionally, and that over some matter too trifling for the attention of men of sense, was his passion for Ireland aroused beyond reason, as in his quarrel with Lady Gregory and the Abbey Players over the presentation of Synge's farce, *The Playboy of the Western World* in New York. *The Playboy* was nothing much worth troubling about. It is not a particularly valuable piece of literature. It is not even a good play. It had been presented in Dublin with indifferent success and a minimum amount of rioting — for a Dublin first night. But Devoy got it into his head that it was "an insult to the Irish race" and determined to stop the New York opening. I wonder what he would think, if he had lived to see them, of the books and plays of Mr. O'Flaherty and Mr. O'Casey? And what would he say to the motion picture of *The Informer?*

Now this Lady Gregory whom he challenged was as gentle and lovable and kind a person as I ever met. She was a delightful old lady with the most graceful mind, the pleasantest turn of wit. She wrote little, but what she wrote was good to read. Her conversation was a delight to listen to. Her diction was — how shall I put it? — yes, perfumed is the word — perfumed with a delicious brogue. But as my friend Devoy soon discovered, she was Irish. Isabella Persse of Roxborough in the County Galway was every bit as Irish as any Devoy that ever came out of Kildare. And as eager for a fight, she didn't care how rough. John had no sooner announced his intention of stopping the performance of *The Playboy* than Isabella proclaimed her intention to produce Synge's farce as soon as it could be properly rehearsed. The battle was joined and, as usual, I found myself between two friends just as they decided to throw the chinaware at each other. I decided to do what I could to prevent the duel. I thought I could bring the two combatants together, but after I had seen the militant Devoy I put this thought aside as foolish. I went to one of the early performances of the Abbey Players. I saw no disturbance, but I was told that at the end of an act a big bosthoon of a fellow who had misunderstood instructions from headquarters got up and started to denounce the author. Whereupon one of the brilliant and charming Emmett girls, descendants of the great Robert, marched down the aisle and, taking him by the arm, declared him under arrest. "And what for, ma'am?" demanded the astonished fellow. "For disorderly conduct," said the determined Rosina. "Come with me." The great gawk actually followed the pretty girl to the station house where she first charged him and then withdrew the charge. I never knew whether this had actually happened, although I met Miss Emmett in the street the next day. She didn't give me a chance to ask. After reducing me to a pulp with a look of cold contempt from her lovely blue eyes, she proceeded to tell me in language as forcible as the rules of polite society and good breeding will permit (and a little beyond) precisely what she thought of me and her brother-in-law, Justice Martin Keough, who wouldn't "stand up for the right because you are, both of you, afraid of John Devoy." I have never yet fully recovered my self-assurance.

But, as I have said, I didn't see this occurrence. I was talking with Devoy. I slipped out in the middle of a dull curtain raiser to smoke a cigarette and saw John standing in the rain, wrapped in a frieze coat with a high collar up over his ears and his slouch hat pulled down. But there was no mistaking the cleft nose and the quick glance of the gray eyes and we were soon whispering together as if in a conspiracy to blow up the Nelson monument. "Is anything going to happen tonight?" I asked. "Not tonight," he answered in a hoarse whisper and, dropping into the vernacular, "Next Choosday," he said. I took him to the rathskeller on the corner and pleaded with him over a half liter of Pilsner not to bother about the players and their *Playboy*. But he wouldn't listen. He was reasonable and good-humored about other things; on *The Playboy* he was inexorable. "If you're around Tuesday," he said, "you'll see a noble ruction." And he smiled a smile of great content.

I made up my mind there and then that I wouldn't be around and so I told Lady Gregory when I went to tea with her the next day. We talked of one thing or another, of the Irish language movement, of the budding Sinn Fein society, of her nephew Hugh Lane's pictures, and then as if by chance, of her reason for asking me to tea. "Oh," she said, "I've saved a box for *The Playboy* and you must come. Just Colonel Roosevelt and Colonel Robert Emmett and you and I." I gave her a hundred reasons for not going to the play; she blandly ignored them. "Why do you want me particularly?" I asked. "Because you are a representative Irishman," she said. "But I'm not. There are two hundred thousand Irishmen born or of Irish parents in New York alone who know they are more representative, each of them." She blandly ignored my protest. "Never you mind," she said. "Have a cup of tea." When I left, protesting, she laid her hand gently on my arm and said, "Tomorrow night. You won't fail me." The next morning who should call me up but Colonel Roosevelt, for whom I would do almost anything. "I want you to come to dinner with me at the Algonquin. Nobody but you and I and Lady Gregory and Colonel Emmett." I was now about at the end of my defenses. But I fortified myself with a contrived invitation to another dinner and went to the Algonquin. There I blurted out my real excuse. It was a frank confession of cowardice. I told them there would be a riot, that the rioters knew me as a friend and ally of Devoy, that they would suspect I had turned traitor and that the bad eggs, potatoes and onions intended for the players would bounce off my devoted nose. Indeed, I feared that my friend Devoy would himself become so filled with the spirit of the occasion that he would go out and provide himself with something more substantial as a missile in the form of a brick or an empty bottle to fling at his old associate. Colonel Emmett listened with the air of approval slightly tinged with envy of a patriot who is in the

tumbrel himself and sees a confederate freeing himself
from the guards and legging it up an alley. Lady Gregory
grew hilarious over my predicament. "You needin come,"
she said soothingly. "They might miss you and I don't
want to have me new frock spoiled." But Theodore Roosevelt was made of sterner stuff. When I got up to go, he
went with me, clutching my arm. He was determined
that I should appear in the box, and by this time I was so
spent that I was about to make a sulky surrender, when my
luck returned. It came in the form of a tall man wearing an
enormous Stetson hat, a black frock coat and black trou-
sers that covered, but did not conceal, a pair of old-
fashioned high boots. He ran up to the Colonel with two
great hairy paws extended and cried, "Well, by the great
horn spoon, Colonel Roosevelt!"

Now the Colonel had few weaknesses, but one of them
was that he couldn't resist an invitation to shake hands
with a man in a Stetson hat. "Dee-lighted," he cried, and
he let go of my arm to seize the rancher's hands in one of
his notorious clasps. I was off like a flash and I did the hundred to the corner in a good deal less than Duffy's time.
And my record was made from a standing start.

The riot at the theater came off according to schedule
and was highly satisfactory to all concerned. A few potatoes and onions were thrown at the male members of the
company and one reckless patriot nearly obscured the gaiety of nations by hitting one of the best of modern Irish
comedians, Joe Kerrigan, on the ear with an Ingersoll
watch fired at close range. But most of the rioting was
declamatory or musical in its nature. There were cries of
"Down with the Sassenach," meaning Bella Persse of the

County Galway. Part of the audience sang "The Wearing of the Green" and "God Save Ireland," but others, who looked on the demonstration with greater levity, rendered such ditties as "Down by the Tan Yard Side" or "They'll kiss you and they'll caress you, they'll spend your money free and of all the towns in Ireland, Kilkenny for me." The police were called in to eject the rioters, whereupon the ladies of the company forgot about the potatoes and onions lying at their feet and urged their compatriots to "desthroy the peelers" and made faces at the constabulary, who were all Irishmen in complete sympathy with the demonstration they were suppressing. And in the midst of the tumult Lady Gregory was standing up in the box crying to the city and the world, "Reserve your strength. Reserve your strength. We'll play it all over when this is ended."

And so they did. This very moderate comedy has the distinction of having been played twice in one night, or at least once and a half. After that it was done a good many times until it passed permanently into the repertory of the company.

Both these two great and true characters are now dead and gone. If they are in the Elysium for which all good Irish men and women are destined, they have met and made it up by this time. They will be talking Gaelic, at which difficult tongue Lady Gregory was far more proficient than John Devoy. They will like each other. Perhaps John can be persuaded to do, for the assembled saints, the same handspring that he did in my office when he was over seventy.

People of our time have no conception of the power once exercised by the Irish patriotic societies on American

politics. Mr. Blaine, a great statesman, was an outspoken
enemy of England, not, I guess, because he was of Irish
blood, although the name Gillespie implies such a strain,
but because during the Civil War and afterward he had
become convinced of the deadly hostility of the ruling
classes of British to this country and of the utter crooked-
ness and chicanery of the permanent staff of the British
Foreign Office. Both Grover Cleveland and Theodore Roosevelt reluctantly came to this same attitude of suspicion in
their time. The latter once told me that he had in his pos-
session "absolute proof" in both the Venezuela and Alaska
boundary cases that the Foreign Office had substituted
fake maps for the genuine surveys and had hastily with-
drawn them when the fraud was discovered.

Of course the patriotic Irishmen as well as the professional Irishmen took full advantage of this feeling. Much
of the time of Congress was spent — I won't say wasted
— in long, one-sided discussions of the Irish question.
They used to tell a story of Richelieu Robinson, a Brooklyn Congressman, meeting on the steps of the Capitol
John F. Finerty, a Chicago representative. "Anything going on inside, Jawn?" Congressman Robinson asked. "No,"
replied the Chicago Congressman in a tone of contempt,
"nothing but some damned American business."

But the occupation of a friend of Ireland in those days
was by no means free from peril. In fact, it might well be
ranked as an extra hazardous risk, for there were many factions in the party, and many factions in each faction. Between these factions and between the factionettes there
were decided differences of opinion, if the word decided is

not tautological in describing any Irish difference of opinion.

Judge Morgan O'Brien tells a story about the early days of the agitation in New York. The Judge was on the conservative side, that is he was for peaceful and parliamentary measures. But the time came when he and others decided that it would be well if the peace men and the armed force men were brought together. So they had a meeting in a hall in Lafayette Street. But let the Judge tell the story. "We had a great meeting. The hall was packed. Miles O'Brien, who had strong friends in both factions, was chosen chairman. On the platform were a number of the most highly respected and richest Irishmen in New York — ex-Mayor Grace, Eugene Kelley, Joseph O'Donoughue and others. With the election of Miles O'Brien, we settled down for a quiet discussion. But Mr. O'Brien had hardly finished his speech when a tall young man rose in the hall and said, without being recognized by the chairman, 'Misturr Chairman, I have listened to your speech with great interest. Ye spoke well and I suppose it is a good thing to get these gintlemen up on the stage who believe in conciliation to meet those of us that haven't the least faith in the world in British friendship. But I only wish to say this — that we'll have to come to force finally, and I tell ye now that under this very platform where these friends of peace are setting so comfortable, there is enough dynamite stored to blow both Houses of Parliament and the Bank of England to smithereens.'

"He sat down and looked up at the stage and my old friend William R. Grace had a violent fit of coughing and walked off and didn't come back. Joe O'Donoughue looked at his watch, whispered a few words to the chairman and left, followed by Mr. Kelley who called 'Wait for me, Joe.' That's the last we saw of them. Well, we had the meeting and appointed a number of conciliation committees and adjourned. As I was walking out I saw Miles O'Brien ahead of me. As he got to the head of the stairs, a big man stepped out of the crowd and hit him over the back of the head with a piece of lead pipe. He pitched forward down the whole flight of stairs and I heard the voice of a man near me say angrily, 'What the hell did you hit that man for, ye omadhaun?' 'Well, you told me to hit O'Brien, didn't you?' 'Yes, but that wasn't the O'Brien. We wanted you to get *Morgan* O'Brien.' 'Well,' said the other fellow sulkily, 'I done the best I could. How was I to know which O'Brien you wanted me to soak?' I didn't listen to any more, but I never stopped running until I got up to the Manhattan Club. The leaders of the force movement were apologetic about the faux pas, but the apologies didn't help Miles much. He stayed in the hospital for a month and since then I have gone to a good many meetings of my fellow Irishmen but I have always specified that they shan't be conciliation meetings. An Irish conciliation is too rough for me."

But in spite of all these factional fights, cross currents, savage differences of opinion, corrupt ward politics, betrayals, murders and the other natural disfigurements of every revolutionary movement, the Irish in America did the greatest imaginable service to the Irish in Ireland. They never wavered in their constancy but, poor men and women as they were, poured millions of dollars into the treasury of the Land League or its auxiliary armed force societies. They thought their sacrifices were amply rewarded by the progress of their people towards freedom. I know my father contributed far beyond his means to Parnell's fund, although he hadn't set foot in Ireland since he was a child; and the rest of our family did the same, after the traditions of our tribe.

But as the attitude of the British Government became more tolerant the feeling of the Irish in America softened too. Ireland was well off. Her land troubles were settling. A bill for home rule was in train for passage in Parliament. Then, to the amazement of nearly every sane person in the world, the British Government surrendered to a small group of mutineers and rebels who were prepared for bloodshed rather than give way to an Act of Parliament that did not suit the ravenous Irish landlords and their wives around the court. Among Sir Edward Carson's associates in this enterprise against the Crown by paid servants of the Crown were two soldiers, Sir John, later Lord French, who, notwithstanding Lloyd George's attempt to place Lord Haig on that eminence, was afterward considered by all recognized military authorities to be the most incompetent general who ever took the field, and Sir Hubert Gough who led his Fifth Army in the most hasty retreat in the history of modern warfare. The old feud rose again in this country. Were the three million Catholic Irishmen in the South of Ireland to be denied Home Rule because these mutinous mercenaries were ready to order out their troops to shoot down the farmers of Galway and the mechanics of Dublin and Cork? If the Sinn Fein were rebels and traitors what were Gough and his gang?

Then the Great War broke out and the young men of Ireland were asked to volunteer service under their most hated enemies, Carson, the Galway lawyer who was loyal only to his present client and Hubert Gough, the soldier who was loyal only to the Orange Grand Lodge. As a piece of political impudence it has few parallels. Of course the Irish resisted, and their resistance was echoed in this country by a powerful opposition to those of us who thought we ought to go into the war in sheer self-defense. For nearly three years, President Wilson's determination to "keep us out of war" was backed up by formidable groups of Irish-Americans. But England is the luckiest country in the world. The dunderheads in London by their foolish treatment of Ireland did their best to prevent the United States from joining forces with the Allies, but the chumps at Berlin outdid them in thickness and gave new point to the old joke, "What is stupider than a stupid Englishman? Answer: a bright German." The inconceivable senselessness of the sub-normal Kaiser in following the advice of the blockhead von Tirpitz made it impossible for us to stay on the side lines. We declared war on Germany, sent three million men to support the worn out and faltering lines of the French and English and, what was almost as valuable, poured billions of dollars into their depleted treasuries, thus imposing on their honor a debt too heavy for their honor to bear. We saved the British Empire, not to speak of France and Belgium. And into this war none stepped with more cheerful alacrity than the young Irish-Americans.

But the Irish in Ireland were not to be coaxed into enlisting or forced into the army. They carried on incessant warfare against the government. The government retorted in kind. Assassination was met with assassination, until the will of the British broke.

I don't intend to write a history of the last Irish Revolution, but I wish someone would, a real record of that terrible conflict, not the romantic mush that passes for Irish history. I would especially like to know more about Michael Collins, who appears to my imagination as a man out of the ancient world. He had all the soldierly qualities — craft, energy, courage — animated by a fierce patriotism that was like religious fanaticism. I am glad to think that this opinion of Collins was shared by a man who hated him up to the time when they met in London to sign the protocol of the treaty that created the Irish Free State.

This was F. E. Smith, better known as Lord Birkenhead. He himself was a man of no small stature. He and Sir John Simon were the two great leaders of the English bar twenty years ago. But they were as different in type as in politics. Simon is a pleasant-spoken man, full of humor as becomes an Englishman who has had the great good luck to marry a charming Irish wife; Birkenhead had rough and ragged edges to his bearing. He could be fierce, even uncouth at times. Although he was an Oxford scholar, there was little suggestion of good breeding or education in his manner of speech. He was a mirthful man, but his cheer was large and boisterous, better suited to the tavern than the drawing room. And he was one of the most heroic drinkers in history, unless you accept the Reverend François Rabelais as a veracious chronicler. I doubt if our own Daniel Webster surpassed him in accomplishment at either kind of bar. Yet, like the great Daniel, his mental proc-

esses were little affected by his conviviality. I remember
that he turned up late when he was the guest at a dinner
of the American Bar Association. The arid Charles Evans
Hughes, who presided, was plainly nervous about him and
when Birkenhead lurched up to speak, Hughes's apprehen-
sions seemed warranted. But only for a moment. The British Lord Chancellor steadied himself with one hand stiffly
on the table, while with the other he produced from his
pocket a small bundle of notes. He stared at the first of
these pages for an instant, then his eyes came into focus,
his face became animated and he flung the notes on the
table and delivered a speech of the most dazzling eloquence. Men who were there still talk about it. It was one
of the best after-dinner speeches I have ever heard. But
English public men are much better at this form of enter-
tainment than our own countrymen about whose bril-
liancy we boast so much. To tell the truth, we have had
very few really good after-dinner speakers. Chauncey Depew was a great treat; Patrick Francis Murphy was marvelous and it was a pleasure to listen to the musical ca-
dences and the delicate humor of Joseph Choate. But most
of our speakers have no ease or grace or distinction. Having
pronounced that part of the ritual imposed by American
taste on post-prandial speakers, and told that funny story
about Pat and Mike, they launch out into an oration as
pompous as Webster's at the Dedication of the Bunker Hill
monument. I think their victims should not be denied the
privilege of hissing them. Fortunately these commensals
are usually so stunned by wine and food that they don't
know what the Demosthenes is talking about.

Birkenhead was much liked over here by those who met him. He was a spare, bony, bright-eyed man with one of those durable constitutions that defies doctors and dietary rules. He seemed always in the best of physical condition. He had been a great football player and boxer at Oxford and he told me he still boxed or punched the bag every day, although by this time he was nearing sixty. He was a friend of Georges Carpentier and one of his diversions after a long week on the wool sack was to take a boat for Calais and go up to Paris and box with the French prizefighter. "I like to box with Georges," he said. "Of course he pulls his punches. If he didn't, he might knock my head off my shoulders. But he doesn't just tap me. He hits me hard enough to get me angry. *He makes me fight. That's what I like about him.*"

Birkenhead dearly loved a row. He should have been Irish. When Gough and his crowd mutinied and Lord Carson beat his briefcase into a sword, Freddy Smith became his galloper, an act which Irishmen of both parties resented, rightly thinking that this was purely a family affair and none of an Englishman's business. He was full of audacity. He was more than that. He was what an Irishman would call "saucy." Although he spoke like an angel he wrote like Poor Poll. This did not prevent him from writing a good deal. Most of it I never heard of but I did read a book that he called *Celebrated Cases* or *Famous Trials* or something of the kind in which he told about some of the great legal trials of history. I forget now exactly what trials he included, but it ran something like this: "Trial of Joan of Arc," "Trial of Sir Thomas More," "Trial of Anne Bo-

leyn," "Trial of Charles I," "Trial of Warren Hastings"
and "Trial of the Case of Goldberg *vs.* Gluckstein, F. E.
Smith Counsel for Defendant." But it could not be by audacity alone that he won his position. He must have been
an amazingly fine lawyer and a forceful and adroit politician to gain the lord chancellorship at the comparatively
early age of forty-six. Both British and Americans like their
judges ripe. A man must be close to his dotage to be eligi-
ble for Lord Chancellor or Justice of the Supreme Court.
But notwithstanding Birkenhead's infantile weakness, he
managed to do a good job as Lord Chancellor, although he
regretted ever accepting the position. He was elevated to
the peerage, first as viscount and afterward as earl, but as
he explained to me, he had apparently forgotten that once
a man has been chancellor he can no longer practice law.
True, the Lord Chancellor receives five thousand pounds
for life, but what was that to a man who could easily earn
ten times as much at the bar? And Birkenhead was like
my old acquaintance John Moore who, when reproached
for exacting too large a commission for forming one of the
earliest industrial trusts, replied, "But, gentlemen, I am a
man of large necessities." However, the English have a way
of getting around an immemorial custom, when said immemorial custom is in the way of a practical career.
Lord Birkenhead "retired from the bar and entered business," i.e., he became a director of companies to whom he
could properly give legal advice and receive adequate pay.
When I saw him last he was far from destitute. He was a
great loss to English public life, and while his death did
not exactly eclipse the gaiety of nations, it left the British

political world without any antiseptic to the stodgy ineffi-
ciency of Stanley Baldwin.

Naturally I was eager to get from this keen, outspoken
Englishman his opinion of the Irish leaders. He thought
little of any of them except Michael Collins, but he spoke
of Collins with the enthusiasm of one good fighting man
for another.

"Collins was a great fellow," said Birkenhead. "For the
first time in my life when I talked with him I realized how
impossible was the task of coercing Ireland. With such in-
domitable men leading them, no nation can be broken
down. When he came over to London to discuss the treaty
that was to make the Irish Free State, I found him clear-
headed, honest, courageous and extremely able. He seemed
always full of fun, and that I liked especially. In Winston
Churchill's dining room there hung framed a proclamation
of the Boer government offering a reward of one hundred
pounds for the capture of Winston Churchill, an escaped
prisoner from Pretoria. Poor, dear Winston was strutting
before this broadcast. Michael Collins said quizzically,
'Well, Mister Churchill, I don't blame you for being proud
of that thing. But, if we're to judge by rewards I'm a hundred times more valuable than you, for there's ten thousand pounds offered by your government for my capture.'

"As you know, the protocol was a compromise. Both
sides had to give in. I felt dejected and humiliated. I knew
how my old friends and colleagues would hate me for making vital concessions to the rebels whom I had fought for
years. But there was no way out of it. I was finished with
public life, or so I thought. I signed, threw down the pen

and said, 'I have signed my political death warrant.' Collins turned to me with a smile and said quietly, 'I've signed my actual death warrant.' "

And so it was. Within a very few weeks this dauntless man was murdered from ambush near his birthplace in the county of Cork. His murderer is known and still lives.

God save Ireland!

Commentary

Finley Peter Dunne was not a politician, but his entire professional career was based on politics. He won international renown principally as a political writer. His Muse was no Grecian demi-goddess from the springs of Parnassus, but a hard-boiled lady who knew her way around Capitol Hill, the White House and the steaming wards of Chicago. Nor was she any stranger to the chancelleries of Europe.

She inspired him well. He knew politics and politicians intimately and sympathetically. He understood that the men who practice this most curious and most important of the professions are neither saints nor devils, but only fallible human beings. He had his likes and dislikes, but personal tastes seldom colored his judgments. A good newspaperman needs a trace of the judicial in his temperament and my father, even in retirement, was always a good newspaperman.

He loved to talk politics and politicians. Whenever we settled down to discuss "life and letters," to use his pet phrase, we soon found ourselves straying into political fields.

Once we were talking about Winston Churchill's *Life of Marlborough*, which my father considered the best historical biography in the English language. He had known Churchill in London when the great Englishman was Home Secretary in Asquith's cabinet before the First World War. "One thing is certain," he said, "Churchill may have failed as a politician, but this book will secure his place in history as a writer. This, *The Aftermath*, and *The World Crisis*. He is the greatest historian of our time — perhaps the greatest since Thucydides."

"Do you think he's completely through as a politician?" I asked.

"Oh, yes," he answered. "He's offended the party managers once too often — in fact about a hundred times too often. Both sides hate him now. He's finished." And then he thought a moment and made a remarkable prophecy: "*Unless*," he said, "this obscenity Hitler manages to push the Germans into another war. Then the English will remember Winston. He has a talent for crisis. The English resent talent. It embarrasses them, so in peacetime they stifle it and crush it. But let there be a crisis and they know where to look for it. And even if they didn't, Winston would tell them. Modesty is not one of his vices."

He also credited Churchill, often accused of being a tactless man, with the greatest single display of tact in his experience. Ethel Barrymore had just opened in a West End play which, in spite of her usual brilliant performance, was quite obviously destined for the ash-heap. My father and other friends of hers went backstage to try to dispel the gloom with the customary cheery lies and false display of optimism. Miss Barrymore, thoroughgoing professional that she was, refused to be cheered. She knew better. Then Winston Churchill came in, walked straight to the crestfallen star, threw his arms round her and said only, "My poor darling!" Miss Barrymore started to laugh, the others joined in, and the wake became a celebration that lasted until dawn.

Perhaps this is far afield from politics, but it reveals another and charming side of one of the most successful politicians of our time.

The essay which follows concerns one of the most unsuccessful, President Warren G. Harding.

To those who knew him, my father's involvement with Harding's quest for the Republican nomination has always seemed out of character. As a matter of fact, he thought so himself, as the essay makes clear. He had always held himself scrupulously above the political battle. Indeed, Mr. Dooley's phenomenal success was based on this quality of aloofness. Not that Mr. Dooley didn't take sides. When the situation called for a blow, he hit and hit hard. But the blows fell impartially. You were not immune because you happened to be a Democrat or a Republican or a businessman or a labor leader. Too many political writers today are utterly predictable. They are committed to a party, or a personality, or a cause. They are not commentators, though that is their style, but merely pamphleteers.

Mr. Dooley's modern admirers often express the wish that he were with us today, to expose the foibles and prick the bubbles of our era. For instance, when Mr. Nixon made his famous "Checkers" speech on television, at least a dozen people called me to lament the absence of Mr. Dooley from the scene. One or two of them even asked me to try a Dooley of my own on the subject, a temptation which I wisely resisted.

Now obviously my father could not have refrained from shooting at so fat and luscious a target for ridicule as the Nixon speech. It was right down Mr. Dooley's alley.

So were some of the pompous and pious pronouncements that used to emanate from President Eisenhower's White House. President McKinley's regime was also marked by self-righteousness and Mr. Dooley called attention to this relatively harmless foible in one memorable sentence describing the opening of the Republican Convention of 1900: "Th' proceedins was opened with a prayer that Providence might r-remain undher th' protection iv th' administration." This could have been written of the convention which renominated President Eisenhower in San Francisco fifty-six years later.

Now my father liked McKinley and respected him. He might as easily have liked and respected Mr. Eisenhower. He might even have liked and respected Mr. Nixon. But that wouldn't have spared them. He would have taken a shot at them when he felt they deserved it.

But never as a partisan. Based on what I know of his tastes in strong characters, I believe that he would have shared my own admiration for President Kennedy, but I don't think he could have resisted the target presented, to give the obvious example, by quite so many Kennedys in public office. Even when he and Theodore Roosevelt had become close friends, that great President was not thereby armored against Mr. Dooley's shafts.

Roosevelt, being Roosevelt, sometimes hit back. In one letter, he said: "Now, oh laughing philosopher (because you are not only one who laughs, but also a genuine philosopher and because your philosophy has a real effect upon this country) I want to enter a strong protest against your very amusing and very wrong-headed article. . . ."

This rigorous nonpartisanship had its drawbacks. My father once felt compelled to write in turn to Roosevelt, when the then President was heavily engaged on the trust-busting front: "You have always been so good-natured about Dooley that it never occurred to me that he might carry a joke too far until recently when I was congratulated by some people who are as objectionable to me as they are to you. Now, I am very strongly of the opinion that the character of a man's work is accurately reflected by the character of his admirers, and I am disturbed by the congratulations of Wall Street. . . . If I thought my feeble fun was in any way harmful to the present undertakings of your administration I would sacrifice my necessities."

His prime necessity, as the quotation suggests, was to maintain at least the appearance of nonpartisanship. Mr. Dooley could then become not only a comment but a positive political force. And this is precisely what he was. The articles were read aloud at the cabinet meetings of three Presidents. The public figures of his day thought twice before they embarked on any undertaking or uttered any important statement. They asked themselves first what Mr. Dooley would have to say about it and therefore prudently tempered their actions and their words. To borrow his own phrase, "The Eye was on them." He was truly, in Elmer Ellis's apt phrase, the wit and censor of the nation. Perhaps I may be permitted to believe that if Mr. Dooley had been lurking in ambush, piece loaded and cocked, Mr.

Nixon wouldn't have made his "Checkers" speech at all.

When we were discussing my father's part in helping procure the nomination for Harding, he said to me: "Put it down to the inexperience of age. When I was a young man I knew better. You know I was a sports writer for a few months. I used to travel with the old Chicago White Stockings. I never hesitated to tell Cap Anson how to swing a bat or Billy Sunday how to catch a fly, but I did it from the grandstand. I never stepped on the field. Therefore I have a perfect average. I have never struck out nor made an error. But politics is a more seductive game. You see all those fellows swinging at the air or throwing to the wrong base and you start thinking you can do better and before you know it you've picked up a bat to show them how. But the only thing you show is yourself — up."

I am often asked if my father was a Democrat or Republican. The obvious answer is that he was neither, but perhaps it isn't quite that simple. Though he wrote as a nonpartisan, Peter Dunne was personally a man of decided and often partisan views, which he didn't mind expressing. He only refused to wear a label. His fundamental sympathies were with the Democratic Party. Given his background in Irish Chicago and his basic liberalism this was inevitable. Mr. Dooley, true to his character, was always identified as a Democrat, even when making fun of Democrats.

But in middle life many of my father's associations were Republican. His friends in New York, the bankers, manufacturers and corporation lawyers who belonged to his clubs, were almost as inevitably Republican, with a few striking exceptions, in his day as in ours. They took a proprietary interest in the GOP, which was then quite openly under their control. My father could disapprove of the power and greed of Wall Street, but he felt at home in the company of Wall Streeters.

He never let politics interfere with friendship, but it is possible that to some extent his friendships colored his politics. The most powerful influence drawing him towards the Republican Party was that most atypical Republican Theodore Roosevelt. I say "drawing him towards" because that was about the extent of the process. But I know that he voted for Hughes, Harding and Coolidge, as well as for T.R. himself.

After 1925, and particularly after the economic collapse of 1929, he moved back to the faith of his Democratic fathers. He liked and supported both Al Smith and Franklin Roosevelt.

Both were personal friends. Smith was something of a boon companion of his in Southampton and New York. Politically, he approved of the second Roosevelt's efforts to reform the economy, and he admired him for his enemies. In a letter to me, he described the opposition to F.D.R. as coming from "those greedy pirates who for years have been selling the public illuminated bumwad in the form of first mortgage bonds." The slight vulgarity here is not characteristic, but he felt strongly on the issue.

Smith was champion of a cause even dearer to his heart: the repeal of the Eighteenth Amendment. On the subject of Prohibition, my father was somewhat less temperate than William Lloyd Garrison on the subject of slavery. In the uncompromisingly Wet Al Smith he found a perfect soulmate.

My father's hatred of Prohibition was both personal and political. He resented its invasion of privacy and personal liberty. He was galled by the effectiveness of the Dry lobbies which had pushed the Volstead Act through Congress, notably the Anti-Saloon League and the Women's Christian Temperance Union. They had set up a virtual reign of terror in Washington, and both southern legislators who liked their juleps and northerners who liked their drams consistently voted to deny the cheering cup to their constituents. In 1898, Mr. Dooley's crystal ball had been clouded indeed when he had said: "Polytics ain't bean bag. 'Tis a man's game; an' women, childher an' pro-hybitionists do well to keep out iv it."

He disliked having been so wrong, but above all it was the hypocrisy of the Drys that he scorned. He was a heavy drinker himself, but he never forced conviviality on those of his friends who happened to be teetotallers. Prohibition was not an issue between himself and his abstemious friend Gifford Pinchot, for instance. Three years after his death, my wife and I were given a small dinner by the Pinchots in Washington. Governor Pinchot, in proposing a toast to my father's memory, raised his glass of unsullied soda water and said, "I'm sure Peter wouldn't mind my toasting him in this innocuous beverage. He knew and forgave my weakness for the stuff."

My father reserved his scorn for those who voted Dry and drank Wet. This included the patricians at the Links Club who would smugly announce that Prohibition was "good for the working classes," while putting themselves outside three double martinis before dinner.

But not all of the financial aristocracy was so hypocritical. One of the most valiant fighters for Repeal was Pauline Morton Sabin, wife of Charles M. Sabin of the Guaranty Trust Company. An attractive and forceful woman who was also a power in the officially Dry Republican Party, she had organized the wit and fashion of New York into a virtually solid phalanx for Repeal. My father used to call her "my little Joan of Arc."

Then John D. Rockefeller, Jr. came out publicly for Repeal. His statement was a tremendous blow to the Drys. Not only were the Rockefellers Republicans, but there was a definite odor of sanctity about them. They were so very rich that the public had learned, with the help of Ivy Lee, to forget how the money had been obtained in the first place. (Mr. Dooley had summed this up in an imperishable description of the original John D.: "His heart was pure seein' that he had niver done wrong save in th' way iv business.")

Shortly after the junior Rockefeller's statement, my father met Mrs. Sabin at a party. He walked past her without speaking. Never one to suffer a snub in silence, the redoubtable lady went right after him. "Peter Dunne," she said, "aren't you going to speak to me?" He turned to her with an affable smile. "It's just that I don't need you any more, my dear," he said. "You made Repeal fashionable, but now John D. Rockefeller, Jr. has made it righteous."

Perhaps it was Prohibition that finally put an end to my father's rather languid flirtation with the Republican Party. It is sometimes forgotten that, in spite of the depression, Repeal was an important issue in the 1932 campaign, especially in the eastern, or drinking half of the nation, with

Hoover running as a Dry and Franklin Roosevelt as a Damp. (The genuine Wet, Al Smith, had been eliminated at the Democratic Convention.)

During the campaign, there was very little difference between the two candidates on the straight economic issues. Both took an essentially conservative stand. F.D.R., of course, was playing it safe. He had the election won if he could avoid alienating any sizable bloc of voters apart from the professional Drys who were not going to vote for him in any case.

But my father pointed out that Roosevelt would be forced to move to the left after his election. "He'll have no real choice," he said. "It's a case of preventing a revolution by organizing one. The country will have to be vaccinated, as you vaccinate with cowpox to prevent smallpox. Hoover doesn't understand this. He keeps on saying that prosperity is just around the corner. He still believes in fairies. He thinks someone will wave a wand and cure the depression with a shower of fairy gold. But the good fairies in Wall Street have all hocked their wands and buried their gold fifty feet underground.

"Mr. Hoover's statements," he continued, "remind me of the time when President Garfield was dying after being shot by an assassin. I was only a boy then, but I used to follow the bulletins in the Chicago papers. The White House doctors would announce daily that the President was improving and that there had been a 'healthy flow of laudable pus.' It's the same today. Much laudable pus flows from the White House, but the patient gets no better rapidly."

As between Roosevelt and Al Smith, my father definitely favored Smith, who was a close friend, impeccable on Repeal and an Irish Catholic into the bargain. But he laughed at his pro-Smith friends who charged that Roosevelt had double-crossed Smith when he took the Democratic nomination away from him in Chicago. "Do you think for one moment Smith wouldn't have done the same thing to Roosevelt if the positions had been reversed?" he asked an important Democratic politician who had made the charge. "Don't be ridiculous. You'd act the same yourself if anyone were lunk-headed enough to propose *you* for President. Fortunately, no one will and to that extent the Republic is safe."

He was dismayed by the subsequent rift between Roosevelt and Smith which finally, and to both of us incredibly, drove the once liberal Smith into the arms of the extreme right-wing opponents of the President, the virulent Roosevelt-haters whose rage ran beyond the cosmic into the comic. My father had no choice but to side against his old friend, but the whole affair distressed him deeply. "Of all poisons," he said, "political ambition is the most deadly. It's not that Al has gone back on a whole lifetime of principles. Many have done that before — and been remembered as patriots if they happened to pick the right side — but to allow himself to be bracketed with such fools! It's a shame. A damnable, damnable shame. I thought he had more sense." This was in California, only a few months before his death. I don't believe that he ever saw Al Smith again.

He had known Franklin Roosevelt well around New York and had seen a great deal of him in Washington during the campaign for Preparedness, when the second Roosevelt, then Assistant Secretary of the Navy, was a leading spokesman for that cause within the Wilson Administration itself. Roosevelt's chief in the Navy Department at the time was the virtuous and courtly Josephus Daniels. "The only trouble with Daniels," my father told me later, "was that he assumed all human beings were as saintly as himself. One of his first acts as Secretary was to discontinue the use of prophylactics in the Navy. He felt that our brave jack tars could be trusted not to consort with loose women. As a result, the venereal disease rate shot up to a record high, and this great and good man became known throughout the fleet as 'Syphilis Joe.' Franklin pleaded with him to rescind the order, but he refused to retreat. 'Damn the spirochetes!' he cried. 'Full steam ahead!' Luckily, Franklin is a wily and resourceful man. He went behind the Secretary's back and borrowed medicines from the Army. He saved the Navy, you might say, with bootleg Salvarsan."

As a connoisseur of politics, my father was quick to appreciate the magician's touch F.D.R. brought to the craft. In this respect, he ranked him with Lincoln and Jackson, the other two presidents whose strength lay in their knack of direct communion with the people. He accurately forecast the Roosevelt landslide of 1936. "It's very simple," he said. "He's hand-picked his enemies. He's taken all the characters the public has good reason to dislike and distrust and arranged for them to be against him. The Republicans will carry the Social Register and the Ancient but Dishonorable Order of Bucket Shop Operators and that will be all. It's lucky for Jim Farley that he draws no salary as Democratic National Chairman. In this election, Jim could be arrested for obtaining money under false pretenses."

Mrs. Roosevelt was a great favorite of his. He had known her as a young girl around the house of her uncle, T.R., and recognized in her the qualities which later made her the respected and beloved champion of the oppressed in this and other lands. I think he would have been pleased when years later Clare Boothe Luce adroitly applied a phrase from Mr. Dooley to the First Lady in referring to her as one who had always "comforted the afflicted and afflicted the comfortable." It could have been written for her.

He was somewhat dubious about some of the Roosevelt experiments, particularly the N.R.A. (National Recovery Administration). He saw it as a step toward monopoly and eventual control of the government by business cartels, once Roosevelt was safely out of the way. But he favored the great bulk of Roosevelt's economic and social reforms. "It's about time," he said. "We call ourselves the most progressive nation in the world, but we've been ages behind other countries, even England, which is always Tory no matter what the government calls itself. But the English Tories are housebroken. They had their South Sea bubble in the eighteenth century and we waited until the twentieth to have ours. The difference between our Tories and the English variety is that the English Tory knows he has to be elected, but the American believes he was appointed by God."

He was always amused by the tendency of reaction in this country to cloak itself in piety. In 1902, when a ludicrous industrialist named George F. Baer had declared during a prolonged and bloody strike, "The rights and inter-

ests of the laboring man will be protected and cared for —
not by the labor agitators, but by the Christian men to
whom God in His infinite wisdom has given the control
of the property interests of the country," he had had Mr.
Dooley retort with a two-line snapper which made Baer a
national laughingstock and is still quoted today:

"Mr. Hennessy asked: 'What d'ye think iv the man
down in Pinnsylvanya who says th' Lord an' him is partners in a coal mine?'

" 'Has he divided th' profits?' asked Mr. Dooley."

As a young newspaperman of twenty-seven, my father
had had the rare thrill of being applauded in the composing room of his paper by the typesetters who had just run
off the proof of his famous piece on the Pullman strike.
("But what's it all to Pullman?" Mr. Dooley had said that
day. "Whin Gawd quarried his heart, a happy man was
made. . . . Th' lad that can go his way with his nose in
th' air and pay no attintion to th' sufferin' iv women an'
childher — dear, oh, dear, but his life must be as happy as
th' day is long.") Perhaps he mellowed with age, but he
never changed. His scorn for the cruel, the pompous and
the hypocritical stayed with him all his life.

As a thoroughgoing civilian and democrat, he was highly
suspicious of uniforms and the delusions which sometimes
go with wearing them. He used to quote with glee Clemen-
ceau's famous dictum that "war is far too serious a matter
to be left to the generals." He remembered too well Miles
and Shafter and the other — to use his own phrase — "absurd heroes of the opéra bouffe Spanish-American War."
Speaking of our soldiers in that conflict, he wrote in 1936:
"The Spanish General Incompetence they could beat. But

the relentless General Incompetence of their own army was too much for them."

When in 1931 General Douglas MacArthur, then Army Chief of Staff, was ordered to use federal troops to drive the Bonus Marchers out of their Washington bivouac, he was offended not by the act but by the manner in which the order was complied with. "I suppose the poor devils had to be kicked out," he said, and then added in a sudden burst of fury, "But who in Christ's name ordered the General to wear his medals?"

He laughed at those Americans who followed the British custom of retaining military titles in civilian life. Colonel Robert R. McCormick, the publisher of the Chicago *Tribune*, used to pride himself on his military acumen. The cannon never volleyed and thundered as loudly on the battlefield as from his office in the Tribune Tower. Once, I am told, the Colonel was asked in my father's presence in which war he had earned his brevet. "No war," said my father instantly. "Bertie once won a sword in a raffle." This was perhaps unkind, since McCormick had actually served in France in World War I, and my father knew it, but he had a point to make, which was that the title should have been left off with the uniform.

During my freshman year at Harvard, I joined the R.O.T.C. I did rather well and received an A in the course, which was called Military Science. Unfortunately, I didn't do as well in my other courses and my Military Science A bloomed alone in a dark forest of C's and D's. When my father received my report card, he fired back a succinct telegram: "I didn't raise my boy to be a soldier." It wasn't necessary to say any more.

He hated war itself with all his soul. In 1936 he wrote of "the humbug and sham and cowardice and false pretense that are as inevitable companions of war as lice and pneumococci and taxes." He told me that his decision for intervention in the First World War had cost him many sleepless nights. "But I wanted us to go in," he said, "while we still had allies — the British and the French. If they had gone under, we'd have had to fight the Germans all alone. I'm glad you're a pacifist. Any sensible man is. But the true definition of a pacifist is one who never *starts* a fight. I won't live to see it, but if Hitler isn't stopped soon, you'll have the same decision to make in your own time. I hope you'll temper your noble principles with a little ignoble good sense."

Four years after he said this, his old friend William Allen White, the liberal Republican and beloved sage of Emporia, Kansas, enrolled me as an active participant in an organization he had founded called The Committee to Defend America by Aiding the Allies. We were the direct heirs of Preparedness. It had been the Kaiser then; now it was Hitler. I was proud to be following in my father's footsteps, but not too proud to adapt some of the things he had written during the crisis of 1916 to the crisis of 1940. I am sure he would have forgiven this bit of filial plagiarism. His material made my job as a pamphleteer much easier for me.

Indeed, the parallel between the two crises was striking. In 1940 we were not only faced, as in 1916, with the prospect of a brutal German militarism dominating the world, but we had to overcome powerful domestic opposition, in our case that provided by the Communists and the rightist

America First Committee. As so often happens, the two extremes had joined to make an unholy circle. The Communists, with their slogan, "The Yanks are not coming," had been largely discredited, but the America First movement attracted the support of many wealthy and prominent citizens. These included some articulate political writers with capable research staffs. In support of their cause, they quoted copiously from the writings of prominent Americans of the past. They inevitably came to Mr. Dooley. By quoting him out of context, picking up a phrase here and a phrase there, they managed to make my father sound like a man with isolationist tendencies, and then compounded this felony by claiming that if he had lived he would have been one of them. There were many instances of this sort.

In Los Angeles in 1941, I engaged in a public debate with Theodore Dreiser and others on the subject of American intervention in the war. Mr. Dreiser, ignoring Hitler, denounced the British for their addiction to fox-hunting. He seemed to think this sufficient reason for letting them go under. He drew no moral distinction between the pink coat and the brown shirt. This was before Hitler had attacked Russia and Mr. Dreiser was supported in his isolationist position by two articulate spokesmen of the extreme left. I was speaking on behalf of the William Allen White Committee. After the debate, I had a short meeting with Dreiser. He shook his head at me sadly. "You're no son of your father," he said. "He'd have been ashamed of you." And he went on to give me a summary of my father's beliefs which in every detail was at variance with what my father had not only told me himself, but had published in

Collier's Weekly and other periodicals during the older crisis. I didn't argue. There was no point in it. Dreiser was a great writer who had been sadly misled.

This process of misquoting my father and misprojecting his opinions still goes on today. A few years ago I read an article in an extreme right-wing national magazine which told you exactly what position Mr. Dooley would have taken on every issue of the day, some twenty years after my father's death. By some strange coincidence, the "opinions" expressed coincided exactly with those of the article's author.

This presumptuous scribe apparently had a crystal ball which worked in reverse. He asserted with airy confidence that "Mr. Dooley would have said this" and "Mr. Dooley wouldn't have stood for that." My only answer is: how in hell would he know? I don't know myself.

I wish there could be a law against this kind of literary and political grave-robbing. Even the greatest of Americans have been prey to these ghouls. Lincoln was glibly misquoted by the Communists in the thirties and is being misquoted by the racists in the sixties. Washington, Jefferson, Paine, both Roosevelts, Mark Twain — the list of victims of this deception is endless. I suppose I should be pleased to find my father so often in such company. It is, after all, a form of flattery. But I would advise anyone who is moved to quote an isolated phrase of Mr. Dooley to read all of him first.

A writer is blessed or cursed beyond other men in that he reveals himself through his writings. If no act of Abraham Lincoln had come down through history, we would still have the measure of this great man through what he wrote. The power and resourcefulness of Churchill are carved in the rock of his great histories. The vigor of Robert Browning's personality shines through his verse. Gray's "Elegy" is a perfect portrait of the shy and modest gentleman who sent his friend Walpole this "thing to which I have at last put an end." And so it is with Finley Peter Dunne. His writings reveal the warmth and humor of his character, as well as the entire structure of his political belief.

He was above all a humanist. Perhaps I have done him an injustice earlier in calling him a political writer. Politics provided the skeleton of what he wrote, but he fleshed it out with humanistic philosophy.

He was a pragmatist. As the essays in this book will attest, he was no devotee of the single cause nor propagandist for the single solution. His pluralism, incidentally, is another purely American trait. The doctrine of William James has never flourished on the embattled soil of Ireland. My father equated pluralism with Americanism. He believed that the philosophy of diversity was the foundation-stone of our national virtue.

He was a libertarian. He resented all invasions of personal liberty, whether the invading power was government, business or plain bigotry. His dedication to personal freedom was total, in which he differed from those who remember "liberty" only when their bank balances are put in jeopardy.

Last and most important, he was a democrat in the purest sense. He was one of those rare souls who really believe in the absolute equality and the absolute brotherhood of man. His first and last allegiance was always to humanity.

The following essay on Warren G. Harding (and related matters) was previously published in a bowdlerized form in the *Saturday Evening Post* for September 17, 1936. My father left two slightly different drafts. I have used the one which was eventually the basis for the *Post* article, with some interpolations from the other, which I believe should not be lost. I have also provided a summary of the Teapot Dome scandal based on my memory of his remarks on the subject.

On Warren G. Harding and Others

I SCARCELY KNOW why I should feel called upon to defend, all alone, the posthumous fame of Warren Harding. I knew him well (but others knew him better). I saw him often (but many others saw him more often). I had helped in a small way to nominate him for the presidency (but others had done much more). I am under no obligations to him (and there were hundreds of men, including at least two professional political writers, who were under such obligations, and have since remained silent). Then why should I raise my feeble pipe in defense of his name? Probably it is because, with all lazy, good-natured men, I am an unreasonable partisan of the underdog. This is bad philosophy and bad practice too. The underdog morally is probably no better than the upperdog. Besides it is against common sense. The better, the more profitable rule would seem to be: "Don't jump on a man unless he is down." But that rule is beyond my habit. Against my better nature I find myself inevitably, and unsuccessfully, for the weaker against the stronger, the little fellow against the big, the dead against the slanderous living.

The old maxim *de mortuis nil nisi bonum* has of late

been translated "about the dead say nothing but evil." There is no libel law for the dead. If you slander a living man you can be taken into court in a civil or criminal action. The latter doesn't amount to much, for great freedom is allowed the defense to prove that the complainant's general reputation was so bad he couldn't be libeled.

But a civil action for damages is another thing. As a former publisher of magazines and newspapers, I speak with feeling on this subject and confess that I always settled libel actions out of court. The jury system may be one of the bulwarks of our liberties but no publisher who is not foolhardy wants to take a chance with it.

No, there is no libel for the dead. Once the pennies are placed on their eyelids, the season is open for slander. No matter how distressed may be the widow and the children, who knew the late lamented only as a tender and beloved companion, any author who has access to certain lewd publishers of the baser sort can print his vilifications and falsehoods without fear of reprisal unless public opinion comes to the rescue of the dead. This happened in England a few years ago, where they order matters of good taste, good manners and good feeling better than in our own self-sufficient Republic. Mr. Gladstone used to walk home late every night from the House of Commons, and it was the custom of the spotless old man, when accosted by the streetwalkers who infested London, to stop and talk with them and by kindly questioning learn something about their lives. Once he took one of these unfortunates to his house and introduced her to his wife and gave her supper. But the story whirled around London that he was the willing victim of these drabs. The good Queen Victoria, who would listen to anything bad about the Prime Minister, who always talked to her as if she were a schoolgirl, firmly believed the tale, and you may be sure that neither Gladstone's enemies nor some of his cabinet were at any great pains to shake the simple pious faith of their Sovereign in the wickedness of her constitutional adviser. But, after his death, an adventurer published a book in which he rather more than hinted at this subject. Gladstone's son had no remedy at law. But he did all he could by printing a hot attack on the libeler. The force of public opinion was so great that the scandal-mongering publishers thought it wise to withdraw the book from circulation.

Nothing like this could happen in our free country. Since Harding's death two books have been published about his private life. I venture to say they bear no closer resemblance to the truth than a clever forgery does to a genuine signature. There are dates, letters, incidents which cannot be denied, but they are woven so shrewdly into the mass of falsehood that no man can easily tell where the truth ends and the lie begins. But nobody has attempted to deny them. Harding left no sons to defend his good name. His poor little wife soon followed her adored husband to the grave. And the ghouls were left to do their damage without interference. The consequence is that the general opinion of our late President is that he connived at corruption and was a promiscuous fellow with women — one wife here in Memphis and a hundred back in Pike. Also, that his wife murdered him. A trifling matter, for both are dead.

My own political connection with Warren Harding dated from the spring of 1920. I happened to be in Washington and dropped in on my ancient friend, Davis Elkins, senator from West Virginia. Mr. Elkins was serving his second term in the Senate, one by interim appointment of sixty days to succeed his father; the other by election, which happened while he was serving with the troops in France. Mr. Elkins has many attractive qualities, but the fact that will preserve his name most honorably in history is that during the six years he served in the Senate, he NEVER MADE A SINGLE SPEECH. NOT ONE. He said no more than, "Aye, Aye," and "Nay, Nay." When his bosom friend, Mr. Ad Kelly, told him that this was due to the fact that he never had anything to say, his reply was, "Well, that didn't stop the other senators from hollering." Davis was elected while he was abroad. I have always thought he got a commission in the army and risked his life (for he was in the midst of the fighting) because he was running for senator and was afraid he might be called upon to make a speech. He was like the lion tamer in the story who took refuge in the lion's cage from his angry wife. Coward!

I found him waiting for me alone in the deserted Senate Chamber. Of course, we talked politics. The two leading candidates for the Republican nomination and certain election — for the country was sick of the Democrats — were General Leonard Wood and Governor Frank Lowden of Illinois. Both were good men. General Wood's candidacy was backed by the money of a Cincinnati soap boiler, one Proctor. Mr. Lowden had the use of his wife's fortune. She was Harriet Pullman, the daughter of the inventor of the sleeping car. The disbursers of the money were not Whitneys or Hannas. They over-advertised their benefactions and there was much scandal. "Wood and

Frank will deadlock the convention," said the sage of Morgantown. "It's a great chance for a dark horse."

"Why don't you start your friend Harding?" I suggested.

Harding, I may say here, had been the candidate of a Senate clique for the nomination in 1916. He was a leisurely, good-natured man who, having been brought up in the Ohio school of politics, was disposed to look with indulgent eyes on the sins of his party friends. He was an extremely personable man, the very picture of what a senator should look like, who needed only a toga to complete the illusion that he had come out of the ancient world. He was mild of speech and kind and thoughtful in all his relations in life; he spoke well; in the opinion of those who knew all three, he was a far abler man than either of his successors, Coolidge and Hoover. His one fault, if you can call it such, was that he was too much of a "good fellow." He liked his glass, he liked his game of poker, and — strange as it may seem in this chaste age — he liked women. And women liked him.

It was the theory of the senatorial cabal in 1916 that if Harding could be elected Temporary Chairman at the Republican Convention, he might make a keynote speech which, with his own warm and charming personality, would turn the convention away from the human icicle Hughes, whom nobody wanted but who, the practical politicians thought, might appeal successfully to the public as a puritan in politics, and so help them carry their own states, counties, cities and wards as a tail to his kite. But this was not to be. I ran into Harding the morning he got to the Blackstone Hotel and asked him about his speech.

He looked discouraged. "It's rotten," he said. "I wrote a good one but my friends in the Senate made me put in things they were interested in — the tariff, reciprocity, public lands, pensions and God knows what else, and now it's a rag carpet."

"My friends made me do it." That about sums up the reasons for Harding's failure as President. As it turned out, his speech at the 1916 convention was dismally unsuccessful. It cost him the nomination and he suffered the additional humiliation of having his audience walk out on him, although this was not as humiliating as what happened to Henry Cabot Lodge when that statesman's own Massachusetts delegation forced him to place in nomination a leaden State Street stockbroker, one John Weekes. Lodge himself would have given an eye for the nomination. Or perhaps that is going too far. Let us say he would have sacrificed his dearest friend for the honor. But when I come to think of it, "poor Cabot," as Theodore Roosevelt got to calling him late in life, would do that for a much smaller honor than a presidential nomination. Friendship and gratitude were just two words to Cabot. He understood they were descriptive of emotions existing among the lower classes of South Boston, but knew nothing more about them. He read his speech nominating the stockbroker in a scarcely audible tone, and when he had finished, threw the manuscript contemptuously on the floor and walked off the platform amid a timid cheer from the delegation representing the State of the Adamses, Webster and Sumner.

But to return to the Senate Chamber and Davis Elkins. "Harding could win if he had any money behind him," said the Senator, "but he hasn't. He has no money of his own except his salary and fifteen or twenty thousand dollars income from his two papers in Ohio and he blows that in as fast as it comes. Harry Daugherty, who just about worships him, has spent his last cent in trying to get delegates. His friends here have helped him a little but he can't do much against the weight of metal behind Wood and Lowden."

"It seems to me that some money could be raised for him," I answered. "Who is Daugherty?"

"Oh, he's just a nice fellow down in Columbus. He's a pretty good lawyer and he's a tough old-time politician. He'd cut off his arm for Harding, just as Mark Hanna would for McKinley."

I thought no more about the matter until a few months later when I had a telephone call in New York. Mr. Daugherty of Ohio wanted to talk with me. I joined him at breakfast the next morning at the Waldorf. I rather liked him. He was a pleasant man to talk to. This morning he was dejected by the political situation. His tale was a sad one. He had come up to New York to get help for his idol and everywhere the coldest of cold shoulders had been turned on him. He had felt sure of something from Harry Sinclair, the oil refiner, and another man who was a friend of Harding. But Sinclair wouldn't even see him, and the other man would do nothing. I won't tell this gentleman's name. He's a good friend of mine. He is an honest man, shrewd, able, intelligent, whose opinion on any subject except politics I would attend gladly. But in politics he is the greatest Fall Guy in history. I don't know how much money his fancy for this game cost him, but I do know that he gave over one hundred thousand dollars to the Re-

publican Party in New York and received the high honor of
a nomination for delegate-at-large to the national convention. There were sixteen candidates to be voted on, fifteen
to be elected. He ran sixteenth! He was nosed out by a den-
tist. The professional politicians of his own state should
have been kinder to him. He would have made a much
better governor than the one then in office and an infinitely
better senator than the legal messenger boy for a great millionaire who held down the chair in the Senate. But they
chose to regard him solely as a Christmas tree. After
awhile he rebelled against this role and moved to a Southern state where he was received with outstretched hands
that didn't wait to grasp his, but went straight to his
pocket. He still cherishes the delusion that he can make
the ignorant crackers vote against a Democrat who is not a
Catholic. The net result of his efforts has been that he rests
under the utterly unfounded suspicion among Catholics
that he is an enemy of their religion. It was in his state
that Al Smith encountered a Negro caddy on the golf links
and asked him if he had any religion. "Yes, sir, I sho have."
"Are you a Catholic?" "Good Lawd no, boss!" the caddy
cried in alarm. "It's bad enough to be a nigger down here!"

Daugherty wanted me to see this man and Sinclair. "We
have no money," he said. "We haven't as much as a thin
dime in the treasury. The campaign has cost me fifty
thousand dollars, every penny I had in the world. We have
elected a good many delegates but I've been beaten in my
own district. Now I haven't enough money to open headquarters in Chicago. That is the actual fact. I can't pay the
fares of our men and I haven't enough even to pay rent for

a suite of rooms at the hotel. If I can only get him out there, the nomination will drop in his lap."

Now, I liked Harding — I liked and admired him. And as you know, I'm a good deal of an amateur politician myself. Years ago I asked W. C. Whitney what was the best game in the world. "You've tried them all — law, racing, women, politics, which is the best?" "There's only one," he said, "politics. The management of men. POWER!" I agree with him. It's a great game, but like all great games it's tough. It's no profession for amateurs.

In Daugherty's request I saw possibilities for myself as a Warwick. I would be a president-maker like Whitney and Hanna. So I went to call on the gentleman at the head of the sucker list. He refused to give anything and did so with a speed and abruptness that left no doubt as to his feeling. He added this gratuitous information: "Poor old Warren hasn't a Chinaman's chance." I told this to Daugherty that afternoon. "Then," he said, "can you get an interview with Sinclair for me?" I knew Sinco pretty well, and I had no hesitation in asking for a meeting. We got together in an open room in plain sight and hearing of the clerks. Sinclair was cold and anxious to get away. But by this time I was a furious advocate of Harding. I was determined that he'd get to Chicago and have headquarters there if I had to go out with a gun and stick up a bank. If I do say it, who shouldn't, I made such a speech as would have inflamed the iciest heart. I must have affected Sinclair deeply for, after I had poured out my raptures over the good, the great, the generous and the possibly useful Harding, he turned wearily to Daugherty and said, "Oh, for God's sake, Harry, I'll lend you seventy-five hundred dollars. It's not a contribution. I'm for Wood. It's a loan. Harding hasn't a chance in the world."

The next day Sinclair called me up to say that Harry Whitney would lend Daugherty another seventy-five hundred to oblige Harding, whom he knew well and liked. Harry was partner of Sinclair in Sinclair Oil. So Daugherty had now fifteen thousand dollars and he was grateful. He was so grateful that he asked for more. This convinced me anew that Mr. Daugherty was a qualified Ohio statesman. But it also chilled my ardor. I no longer regarded myself as a Warwick. I was definitely down on the Ohio list as a sucker — no better than the friend of mine I have been talking about. Yet it is with some pride that I read of Warren Harding's departure from Columbus, the opening of headquarters in the Sherman House at Chicago, the favorable personal impression made by my candidate.

Some time during the course of the convention, Harry Daugherty incautiously told the reporters something to the effect that "pretty soon a dozen men will meet in a room full of smoke and name the candidate." There wasn't a political editor in the country who didn't know that this is precisely what happens at every convention when there is a deadlock. Yet when Daugherty got into trouble later through the acts of the crooked and stupid crowd whom he gathered around him, this interview was cited by the papers as proof of his cold cynicism and they slammed him about as if they were country policemen and he had trampled on the flag. And it actually was what happened in the convention of 1920. It was clear that neither Wood nor Lowden could be nominated. So the senators, who had stood in the background waiting for just this situation, got together, agreed on their colleague Harding, convinced their delegates that he was the man and nominated him. His election was a certainty.

This convention marked the entrance of a great millionaire on the political stage and as his adventure was similar to that of a number of rich political amateurs, its course may interest you. The hero was William Boyce Thompson, who had made a vast fortune in mining in the West and in marketing mines in the East. In the wide open spaces he was known as "Boulder Bill," after the Colorado town from which he emanated. I think that even in that neighborhood he was considered a pretty ruthless man in business, who gave and asked no quarter. So he came to New York. All the toughest men in this country come to New York, where they are first tamed and then further toughened. I must hasten to tell you that Mr. Thompson was not a border ruffian, or anything of that sort. He was an educated gentleman — a mining engineer by profession. He was gentle in manner, soft of speech, with a round, benevolent, almost sacerdotal countenance. His bald head, his amiable manner, his benignant eyes behind huge spectacles, all contributed their share to a presence that at once lulled into a feeling of security the object of his attentions in business or poker. At first he yielded to the emollients of New York life. He chipped into the kitty for the Metropolitan Opera House, he bought fresh, hand-painted Old Masters, he gave a great sum of money for a really valuable scientific foundation to investigate the causes of the diseases of plants (like wheat rust and the ergot on rye), and to devise remedies to cure them. But the call of the jungle was too irresistible to let the Boy from Boulder remain idle. Within a year he became known as one of the most skillful operators in that part of the island that for moral as well as geographical reasons is known as "lower New York." In fact, he was so proficient that the senior Morgan took him up and gave him the place formerly held by Jim Keene, whose duty it was to impart couleur de rose to securities which Mr. Morgan desired to pass into the hands of the investing public. This was done by "making a market," a feat at which Mr. Thompson was the very top of proficiency.

But every man has his weak spot. As the gamblers say: "Watch a man long enough and you'll find out what he'll fall for." Bill Thompson was no exception to the rule. The man of iron whom the brave lads on the Denver mining exchange dreaded, whom the Wall Street "jigglers" looked up to with awe, the bold operator who, if Hungry Joe or Dock Owen had met him on the ferry and tried to sell him a line of gold bricks, would have taken the aforesaid Joe or Dock by the arm and led him to the Equitable Building and sold him a package of Electric Bond and Share stock, and pushed him out of the door before he had time to protest — this great man, who could beat any other hazard in the world with his eyes shut, fell for the brace game of party politics. He wasn't asked in; no one capped him; he just pushed the green baize doors open, said, "Gimme a stack," and sat in.

He went to Chicago as one of Bill Ward's delegates from Westchester County, where he lived. Once in the convention hall, he assumed an air of gentle authority with the New York delegation, ninety per cent of whom were devoted followers of Senator James Wadsworth. Mr. Wadsworth sat back and watched with the grin that used to so vex the opposing pitcher in a baseball game that he would peg the ball, not at the plate, but at the innocent smiling face of the Yale first baseman.

At first the new delegate from Yonkers voted for his friend, Bill Ward, who was an adroit suburban politician and an ironmonger in a small way on the Connecticut state line. "But," Jim Wadsworth told me, "Thompson always had another candidate up his sleeve. So when I came back from a little meeting and started to tell our fellows that we had decided on Harding, Thompson took me by the lapel of the coat and protested, 'You can't do that. You can't nominate Harding. If you do, you can't elect him.' 'Well,' I asked, 'who's your candidate?' 'Will H. Hays!' he shouted. 'Will Hays, Will Aitch Hays!!' " And James threw back his comely head and gave one of those whoops of merriment that have often infected his neighborhood with his gaiety and will, I hope, continue so to do as long as I live. He went away gurgling, "Will H. Hays! Will-Aitch-Hays! Good God!"

But William Boyce Thompson, I'll say this for him, was a good loser. He was no quitter at anything he undertook. And presently he appeared as a tremendous contributor to the Harding campaign fund. The national committee promptly selected him to get contributions and oversee disbursements and he did both on a scale unexampled in our political history. Never was there so much money in a campaign. If Mark Hanna had had, in 1896 (when, according to practical politicians of both parties, he bought the election for his friend, McKinley), an equal sum, he

could have made McKinley not President of the United
States, but Emperor of the Cosmos. For one dollar that
Mark Hanna got, Bill Thompson got twenty, thirty, fifty.
Never was there such a distribution of the unearned incre-
ment. In 1896, the scared capitalists gave because they
wanted to save what the panic of 1892 had left them. In
1920 they saw a chance of doubling their already incredi-
ble fortunes and were willing to pay for it. If you knew anybody at headquarters money was as free as beer in a brew-
ery. All you had to do was to turn on the spigot and fill
your can.

Of course Harding was elected. He would have been
anyway, but the fact that their money had been spent in
the cause gave the industrious millionaires a chance to
preen themselves on their generosity. And no one was more
clearly entitled to a good preening than Bill Thompson. It
was taken for granted that some very important office
would be offered him. The only question was which one
would he select. He was at first disposed to have himself
appointed ambassador to the Court of St. James. But his
friend, W. E. Corey, opposed this. Mr. Corey was like Mr.
Thompson in many respects, although somewhat less
tender-hearted in business. "You wouldn't like it, Guts," he
said. (This was "the Chief's" affectionate name for his pal
and referred, of course, to Mr. Thompson's enormous
girth.) "You must go into the cabinet. Harding needs a
sound business man there. I'll take two cards — off the top,
if you please." Bill felt that he was not equipped for the
Secretaryship of State. Either Hughes or Root would get
that post. Harding chose Hughes. He would have been
wiser if he had selected Root. In that case he would have

been sure of having at least one loyal member (besides
Daugherty) in his cabinet, for Mr. Root was steadfast in his
devotion to his political chief even when he differed with
him, as he did with Theodore Roosevelt. The Harding
monument at Marion, Ohio, would not have gone so long
undedicated as it did under the presidency of Harding's
friends, Calvin Coolidge and Herbert Hoover, if Elihu
Root had been in Washington. Mr. Thompson naturally
turned to the Treasury, but when he heard that Andrew
Mellon was under consideration, he withdrew his own
name. Andy's fortune was so much bigger than Bill's that he
felt the same reverence for the Pittsburgh millionaire that
the philosopher from Saturn, in Voltaire's tale, who was only
six thousand feet tall, felt for the philosopher from Sirius
who measured one hundred and twenty thousand feet from
head to foot. Mr. Corey next discussed Mr. Thompson as
Secretary of the Interior. He was well acquainted with the
western country and he had no absurd notions of letting the
conservation cranks interfere with the business of cutting
timber. One of the candidates for this position was Albert
Fall, a senator from New Mexico — a man generally respected for his integrity, admired for his ability as a lawyer
and loved for his endearing social qualities. There was no
more popular figure in the Senate than this rugged plains-
man, who thought nothing of money, but rejoiced to leave
the exhausted atmosphere of Washington, go down to Santa
Fe, put on his chaps and spurs, his ten-gallon sombrero and
his forty-four, leap on his bronco and ride herd over his
vast ranges. Mr. Thompson didn't care particularly about
the job of Secretary of the Interior. He decided to leave it to
Albert Fall and take the place of Secretary of Commerce

himself. Both he and his friends thought that his services and the money he himself put up for the Harding candidacy entitled him to the place. But when he ventured the suggestion that he would like this job, he found it was not his for the asking. In fact, it had been promised to — of all people — Herbert Hoover. I think this was Harding's first mistake. So far as I can find out, Mr. Hoover put in his spare time (and that's what a Secretary of Commerce in those days had most of) in building up a Hoover organization whereby, to the amazement of the politicians, he ran off with the Republican nomination for the presidency in 1928. He was a long time deciding which party he wanted to lead, but he finally chose the Republican as the most promising prospect. At that, he wouldn't have been nominated if Calvin Coolidge had not suffered from an attack of the cold feet from which he had long been a sufferer, which prevented him from clearly telling the country whether or no he was a candidate. As I say, Thompson would have been a better Secretary of Commerce than Hoover. He was much more intelligent and more successful, judged by the yardstick of financial gain in the game in which both gentlemen were engaged, i.e., mining, and mining stock promotion. It was a frightful blow to Bill Thompson, but he never gave up hope until the last minute. I saw him in Florida in the winter of 1920, and he wanted to know where he could get hold of Harry Payne Whitney, whose brother, Payne, was Senator Wadsworth's brother-in-law. "I think he might talk with Wadsworth. It is he who is blocking me." In this surmise Mr. Thompson showed his usual sagacity. Jim Wadsworth is as straight as a string, but as a politician he is perfectly well equipped to draw cards with anybody. The Senator hadn't the slightest intention of letting a very rich man, and a clever one, challenge his leadership in New York. I feel that I'm not injuring my debonair friend when I air the suspicion that he conveyed to the President-elect, who was an intimate friend, some hint of Mr. Thompson's words in the convention.

In any case, Bill Thompson never got to Wadsworth. Harry Whitney was shooting quail and duck at his place near Thomasville. But he had developed to an amazing finesse the art of being "out" to anyone who was seeking a favor. Mr. Thompson came back from the telephone with the impression that Mr. Whitney was not only "out" but that he was in some remote part of Alaska and could only be reached by a five months' "mush" with sledges and dogs.

I saw Bill a few months later in New York. I asked him if he got an office. He looked sheepish, but he had a lot of humor and his face suddenly broke into a broad grin. Yes, he had received an appointment. What was it? Will you believe me when I say that this enormously rich, extremely able man had been named as one of the commissioners representing the United States at the World's Fair in Peru! AND HE HAD ACCEPTED IT. And I think he was rather proud. He had been "recognized" at last. I don't know how many members were on that commission — perhaps one for each state in the Union. The honor was accompanied by the privilege of going down to Peru on a man-of-war and of meeting the famous statesman who was momentarily president of our sister republic but whose name unhappily escapes my memory.

I have gone into this long rigmarole about the Thwarted

Ambition of Boulder Bill because you are a young man, you have Irish blood in you, you might try to get into politics, and I want to warn you of the melancholy effect of being bitten by the political tsetse fly. The other fly causes physical coma; the political insect puts to sleep a man's moral nature, his proper ambitions, his self-respect, his pride. No one can take a chance with it. One attack doesn't give immunity. The oldest and craftiest men in politics suffer as badly as the novices. No one would ever suspect Elihu Root of undue susceptibility. Well, Root went into McKinley's cabinet as Secretary of War and kept on until 1904 under Theodore Roosevelt. He then resigned and went to New York. He told his friends he was sick of public life, would never go back to it, was determined to regain his independence, Mrs. Root was utterly disgusted with the shallow, stupid social life of the capital, and so forth. In New York he stepped into a fabulous law practice. Never before had such fees been asked and collected. He gave a commission to Thomas Hastings, the architect, to build him a house on 71st Street and Park Avenue. Tom was spending a few days with us in the country and he thought he might not go back until Tuesday or Wednesday; but on Sunday night he told me he must return the next morning. "Root has just called me up," he said. "You know he told me he'd never go back to Washington. Well, he's ordered me to stop work on his house. He has accepted a place in the cabinet. He is to be Secretary of State."

So the cool, careful Root gave up New York, gave up his new house, gave up his enormous practice to go back to "that Hell on Earth Washington" and work for a niggardly ten thousand a year, ten times as hard and twice as long as he worked for his clients. He was an admirable Secretary of State, about the best, I think, since Hamilton Fish of the Grant Administration. The speed and accuracy he showed in disposing of important questions were marvelous. He did twice as much business in an hour as one of the loafing old politicians would do in a day. He gave me the privilege once of sitting in his office for a few hours while he disposed of suggestions that were put up to him. One assistant after another came in — Bacon, Adee, I forget who. Root sat behind his bare desk and listened to what they had to say. It was a lively time in the State Department. President Roosevelt had just given the German Emperor one of his frequent dressing downs. There was trouble in Santo Domingo. There were rows elsewhere. Root sat listening, with his finger tips together and his head thrown back. When the assistant had placed the details before him, he appeared to think for a while, then snapped out an order so clear and definitive that there seemed to be nothing left to say. Perhaps he was showing off a little. The ablest of men are not averse to these little displays, and in every good professional man there is something of the actor. Besides, with us in the room was an extremely shrewd political observer in the person of Whitelaw Reid, who had lately come back on his vacation from London where he was ambassador. But histrionic or not, it was a most convincing exhibition of the workings of a vigorous, alert and accurate mind.

Mr. Root went back later to Washington as senator from New York. I think all his friends were surprised at the poor showing he made in the upper house of Congress. Intellectually he was the superior of any man you could name

in the body. But he was in new surroundings, dealing with
men who had acquired knowledge from daily discussion
of the details of legislation that he had never thought
about except as a lawyer for some client who was fighting
the constitutionality of an act of Congress. What chance
had a newcomer in the Senate in debating railway legislation with Bob La Follette, or national finances with Boies
Penrose?

But possibly the thing that acted most destructively
against his success as senator was the fact that Mr. Root is
essentially an advocate, a pleader at the bar, a lawyer in-
tent on turning every point to the advantage of his client.
Lawyers of that type rarely succeed in the Senate. He seldom saw his duty as a public man transcending all private
concerns. So it was when he argued the appeal on the Prohibition law before the Supreme Court. He never could
have won that case. The notion that you can give the legis-
latures the right to amend the Constitution but can take it
away from them because the amendment is contrary to the
intention of the Framers, in other words, that the Supreme
Court can declare a part of the Constitution unconstitu-
tional, was too subtle for any mind but Elihu Root's. He
also insisted on calling the Constitution "a Constitution of
the laws of the United States," which, granting his genius,
is *not* the name of that much prostituted instrument. But
he would have come out of defeat with great good will on
the part of the public if he had taken the case to Washington under different auspices from those offered by his
client. A mild drinker himself, he hated this foul law, and
the kind of people in whose brains it had germinated. He
might have gone to the court as a champion of the people,

a kind of *amicus curiae*. His ingenious mind would have found the way. But, instead, he elected to take a great fee from some distillers' organization — a body as much disliked by moderate men as the Ku Klux Klan or the Anti-Saloon League. Of course, he lost, but what was worse, he lost without glory. No glamor attached to the People of the United States *vs.* the United Dealers in Lush. He was beaten before he finished his argument.

In those days it was his practice after the Library Board meetings to come over, with Payne Whitney and Lewis Cass Ledyard (the elder of that name), to our grubby little lunch club in 45th Street for a cocktail or two. We asked him if he thought he had won his case. "No," he said. "I knew I had lost it before I was halfway through my argument. The court was against me from the start. I knew five of the justices well enough to call them by their first names. I had been instrumental in the appointment of two of them. Yet, when they interrupted my argument with questions, their tone was angry or querulous. They seemed to complain, 'Why do you want to drag your old friends into such a dangerous position!' " That this was the feeling of that courageous body of old gentlemen was further proved by their failure to make public the division of the court on the decision. They were ashamed or afraid to let the country know how they stood on this question. I don't think anyone (outside the court) knows now how they voted. But I do know this, that in his declining years, Chief Justice Edward White would actually weep over his failure to let the world know his real feelings, which were that the amendment could not be disturbed, but that he abhorred this indecent attack on the liberty of the people. But he missed his chance. Fear of public opinion is almost as bad a disease as contempt for it.

But I have strayed far from Harding. A few weeks before his inauguration in 1921, he came down to Palm Beach with Harry Daugherty, Senators Cummins of Iowa, Medill McCormick of Illinois, Fred Hale of Maine, Frelinghuysen of New Jersey and others. We played golf in the afternoon, Harding and Leonard Replogle against Senator Frelinghuysen and me. We beat them two and one. It was the first time in the twenty-five years I had toiled at this loathsome and humiliating game that anyone had considered it important to photograph me in one of my convulsions. But this day there were scores of antique ladies and nasty little boys and girls in attendance with Kodaks and there were at least ten professional criminals with movie cameras. In a few days I saw myself on the screen in a Palm Beach theater, clearly revealed not only as a man who couldn't play golf (a fact which I secretly knew already) but as one who couldn't even act and dress like a golfer.

That night Harry Daugherty gave a dinner for his hero and his party at the Everglades Club, and was kind enough to place me at the right of the President-elect. I found that Harding had changed a good deal from the cheerful companion I had known. He had gained dignity and, although he talked enough, he was much more reserved than I had ever known him to be. He seemed to be grieved because the newspapers were making jokes about his drinking and poker playing and he wasn't at all pleased when I told him that the last time I had seen him was when I went around to the Senate to pay him twenty dollars I owed him from a two-dollar limit poker game the night before, in which we had as a fellow player no less a classical exemplar of our once great American pastime than the Honorable Charles Curtis of Kansas. I tried to soothe him by telling him that every President had been treated in the same way. If the people believed that he was a drunkard or a gambler, they never would have voted for him to the number of sixteen million. I recalled to his mind that every guttersnipe in the world believed that George Washington contracted pneumonia at the age of sixty-seven through paying a visit in his nightshirt to a woman in the slave quarters at his plantation, and that Woodrow Wilson had appointed Louis Brandeis to the Supreme Court because Brandeis had recovered letters Wilson had written to a lady with whom he was having an affair. The guttersnipe writers always prefer a lie to the truth. (I would have spoken less lightly if I could have foreseen what happened to my poor friend after his death — how the lying tales of the convict, Gaston Means, about him and his wife were spread abroad by publishers who should be in the penitentiary themselves.)

But nothing cheered him. He didn't even smile when Senator Cummins sang and danced the familiar dirge "I'm Just as Young as I Used to Be." The dear old fellow played the part of the aged optimist perfectly without the aid of make-up. He was just himself. But Harding didn't smile. The sad austerity of Power had begun to envelop him like a garment. It was not the first time this had happened. Nearly every President is overcome by the awful responsibility of his position and buttons all the buttons of his frock coat the moment he hears a knock at the door. There were three noted exceptions. Lincoln, of course, who used to wander around the White House in his shirtsleeves, Theodore Roosevelt, who, at first dizzied by the suddenness of his elevation, was soon as much at ease in the office as if he had been born to it, and McKinley, who was the same kind, soft-spoken, tolerant, pensive soul he always had been — a fine character much abused and greatly underrated as to ability. Even Coolidge assumed the Louis XIV attitude on a suburban scale. A Republican leader tells me that when a member of the cabinet gave a dinner for President Coolidge, the butler handed the after-dinner coffee to a guest who was chatting with the President. Mr. Coolidge eyed him sternly and said, "Serve the President first." And he didn't smile, either.

Harding talked seriously about his cabinet. Had I heard his selections? What were people saying about them? I told him the nomination of Hughes apparently was well received. People liked the appointment, although nobody liked Hughes — nobody at all. I didn't tell him that one or two of his warmest friends had hoped he would choose Root, who was far abler than Hughes, and resented Harding's uncivil treatment of the senator when he went to Marion. Apparently the grudge was a personal one and not to be discussed. I informed him that Andrew Mellon was agreeable to most of the hundreds of persons in the hotel lobbies, brokerage offices, golf links and horseshoe pitching contests who had been told of the coming appointment as a great secret. He seemed surprised to hear that so many knew of his choice. He thought there must be a leak somewhere. "Well," he said, "if Andy takes as good care of the government's money as he does of his own, we'll be all right. He knows more about finance than any other man in the world." And he then uttered the prediction that afterward became a common saying, "He ought to be the greatest Secretary of the Treasury since Alexander Hamilton." This prediction scarcely came true. But it is a fact that Andrew was — up to 1932 — acknowledged to be the greatest Secretary of the Treasury since William G. McAdoo.

I asked him who was to be Attorney General. He said, I thought somewhat apologetically, "My best friends want me to appoint Harry (Daugherty). There is a lot of opposition to him, but I'm going to appoint him, anyway. He has been very faithful to me." Faithful, indeed. Harding's middle name was Gamaliel. But no Paul ever sat at the feet of another Gamaliel more humbly than Daugherty did at the feet of this one. I believe that if Harding had refused him the appointment he would have gone into a corner and cried. But then he would have wiped away the tears and come back and served as faithfully as ever. I never could understand why his nomination was so ferociously attacked unless it was that "twenty-six Broadway" * was bent on giving its enemy Sinclair a foretaste of what was coming to him later. Daugherty aimed at popularity. He was far too much of a hail-fellow-well-met for my taste. He belonged to the have-a-good-cigar-put-it-in-your-pocket-and-smoke-it-after-dinner school of statesmanship which prevailed at the time. He was not as unctuous in address as Vice President Fairbanks, of whom George Ade said that when he talked with anyone he "gave him a spinal massage." But Daugherty was pretty well liked. And he was as well fitted for the Attorney Generalship as many another

* The Standard Oil Company.

who had filled this office in the past. He was certainly a better lawyer than Moody or Bonaparte and a score of others I could mention. If he was not as great a lawyer as Philander Knox, he was no more of a machine politician than that adroit fellow. *Arcades ambo.* Both belonged to identical political schools. Yet he was blasted out of office by such a sirocco of abuse as never a man in public life had borne, and he was finally put on trial under a criminal charge so baseless that any judge with the conscience and courage of a tadpole would have taken it away from the jury after the government had presented its case. At that, so great was public animosity against this unfortunate man, that the best he could get was a hung jury. But the prosecution was not continued. Public wrath subsided. The prosecuting officers of Mr. Coolidge's administration could no longer depend on lynch law in the courts.

Well, after dinner, we went down to the assembly room of the club, attended by a squad of secret service men, automatic pistols protruding from the pockets of their dinner jackets. There the President-elect met the beauty and the chivalry of Palm Beach in winter. He was introduced to Mr. and Mrs. Aniline Jell, Mr. and Mrs. Imitation Coffee, Mr. and Mrs. Five-and-Ten, Mr. and Mrs. Odd Lotz, Mr. and Mrs. Coal Oil Johnny, Mr. and Mrs. Customer's Man and other social leaders. He seemed as much at home with them as he would have been at an Elks reunion in Marion. Perhaps they had been the same people once — before Fortune not only smiled, but guffawed on them. Being of a more or less unsocial disposition, I decided to go over to Ed Bradley's gambling house and tempt the Goddess of Chance, who was represented by a bored-looking old gentleman who used to deal bank for Curt Gunn and Cy Jaynes in Chicago. Daugherty said he would go, too. I didn't want him to. Bradley's is a pleasant place to lose your money in. The food is the best to be got since Dick Canfield was running wide open at Saratoga and had a ten-thousand-dollar-a-year French chef. The ice water is free. The president of the Beach Club is a genial soul who can tell you the name of all the best horses whose names begin with the letter "B." But, in spite of all that, it is a gambling place and not, or so I thought, the discreet environment on this particular night for the Attorney General designate. I didn't say so. It was none of my business and Daugherty could handle himself. So he came along and all the way down in the roller chair he told me how austerely he intended to run his new office. "I'm going to get the best lawyers I can find. Of course, they'll have to be Republicans, but there are just as good Republican lawyers as Democrats. There'll be no politics or graft in my office." And he really meant it!

At the Beach Club the first man we saw was the Bill Thompson of whose tragedy I have already written. Bill was sitting at a roulette wheel, looking bored. At the manly game of faro he would bet the limit on cases against any dealer and a square box. At the virile game of stud poker, I have seen him set in a stack of seventy thousand dollars on a four, ace, king, queen showing and a four in the hole. But he looked upon roulette as a foolish, effeminate game, and on those who play it habitually as mentally deficient. In gambling he preferred a shade the best of it, or would willingly bet much money on an even chance. But the perpetual and invariable percentage of five-and-fivenineteenths per cent against the punter at roulette, no matter where or how he placed his bet, offended the sense of fairness of this just man. He seldom played, and then only to relieve the tedium that any man of intelligence must feel in Palm Beach. It was his habit to stroll over to Bradley's after dinner, and listlessly play a five-dollar chip on one of the "sections." Any old roulette player will tell you that a man playing this system in very bad luck might lose seventy-five or a hundred dollars in the course of a few hours, or if the luck was with him, he might win thirty-five or fifty dollars. It was to a partnership in this modest venture that Thompson invited Daugherty. "Let's play joint account," he said. Years afterward I read in the New York *Times*, which seldom loses its pride in its own accuracy, a statement to the effect that "Thompson staked Daugherty to $25,000 which the latter lost." I am only recalling this trivial incident to show the extent to which absurd tales were told about officers of the Harding Administration even before Harding was inducted into office. I have never been an intimate friend of Harry Daugherty. For all I know he may have done murder. But I'm bound to say that of all the scandalous stories printed or told about him, none upon which I was in a position to pass judgment was true.

I saw Harding but once after that. In the summer of 1921 I went down to Washington to visit my old friend, Frank Garvan. Daugherty telephoned me that the President wanted me to lunch with him at the White House. Of course I accepted. I joined Daugherty at the Attorney General's office, where he was nervously preparing for his first daily encounter with the Washington newspaper correspondents. I never could understand why he was so uneasy at the

prospect of meeting a lot of amiable young fellows from
the papers. He never had been when he was managing
Harding's campaign. Just as the lads were coming in, a
friend of ours happened along and said, "You don't want
to sit here and listen to this inquisition. Come on down to
Jess Smith's room." On the way he explained who Jess
Smith was. "He's an old friend of Harry's brother, the
banker at Washington Court House, Ohio. He has retired
from business but he thinks he'd like to sort of sit around
and watch over Harry and Harry has given him desk room."
We found Smith behind a large desk smoking a dark cigar.
He was a lank, pale man, with pale, pink-lidded eyes and
a red mustache. I was told he had owned a general store
at Washington Court House. He looked it. But what struck
me as curious was that, sitting opposite this mild purveyor
of calico and ten-penny nails, was one of the most notorious
lawyers in the East, one Tom Felden, who had come up
from Atlanta to practice law in New York and whose activities had attracted even the attention of the New York
Bar Association. But he was safe with this body. So far as
I know, the New York Bar Association has never disci-
plined any lawyer who had more than eleven dollars in the
bank. Felden was not only sitting there but he had his feet
on Smith's desk, his hat was on the back of his head and he
was puffing a great volume of smoke from a cigar in the
corner of his mouth. He seemed entirely at home. I never
knew why till months afterward. The mild, rheumy-eyed
storekeeper from Ohio turned out to be one of the most
flagrant grafters in the history of American politics. He and
his agents shook down every corporation they could reach,
peddled his real or pretended influence with the Attorney

General to anyone who would pay for it and, of course, squandered the proceeds in that great Reformatory for Crooks, the New York Stock Exchange. When a thieving politician, bookmaker, blackmailing editor or lawyer gets out of that institution, he is not only bereft of his ill-gotten gains, but he doesn't even get the ten-dollar bill and the suit of clothes that are given to the released prisoner by other penal institutions. Not only was Jess Smith found out. That was bad enough. What was worse was he was broke. He confessed, I am told, to Daugherty. What passed at the interview I never knew. But Jess Smith went to his room, got a forty-four out of a drawer, put the muzzle to his temple and blew out his brains.

The Attorney General took me over to the White House. As we went to the President's office, I saw a line of men and women reaching almost to the street. The President was receiving them, shaking hands with them and passing them on. I asked George Christian who they were. "They are Hoo Hoos." "They're what?" "Hoo Hoos," he repeated. "The Concatenated Order of Hoo Hoos. The President is a member." Then I remembered. Many years ago, an old newspaper friend of mine, B. Arthur Johnson, started a lumber trade journal in Chicago. In order to divert his friends and advertisers in the timber business he organized the Hoo Hoos. Now and then the eminently respectable and teetotal members of the organization would go to Benton Harbor or St. Joe for a convention or, to put it in business terms, on a bender. But in time the association became rich and powerful. It was no longer used for convivial purposes. When the members went to the conventions they were invariably accompanied by their wives.

And Brother Harding was a member in good standing of this illustrious society. How many similar convivialities he belonged to, I never knew. But he was an inveterate "joiner." It was the Ohio idea.

When the last of his fellow lumberjacks had gone, the President came into his office. His hand was still moist, for he was as yet unpracticed in handshaking on a large scale and had not acquired the art which Coolidge and Hoover mastered of letting the presidential hand drop like a dead fish in the extended palm of the visitor. He was as good-natured as ever. He cried, "What the hell are you doing here?" To which the natural reply seemed to be, "What the hell are *you* doing here?" And indeed he did seem a little out of place, a little too whole-souled, familiar and good-natured for the job. But he soon assumed the pose of a public man and complained of the amount of work he had to do. He pointed to a file of papers on his desk. They were some sort of Indian warrants, which the Great White Father is supposed to sign personally, or the wards of the nation will be hurt in their pride and come whooping down on Washington — the Navajos from the Santa Fe station at Albuquerque with their bows and arrows and the Osages in their Hispano-Suizas from Tulsa — and scalp Jim Ham Lewis. I asked him why he didn't have the act of Congress repealed that compelled a President to waste time on this futile labor. He said it would be too much trouble. I suggested that he buy one of those thingamajigs that the treasurer of a holding company uses when he is in a hurry to get his securities out before the police arrive, whereby he can sign a thousand or maybe ten thousand certificates at a time. "I tried it," he said, "but I couldn't make the durned thing work." I may say in passing that the only statesman I ever knew who didn't complain of the hard work of his office was Theodore Roosevelt. The sole fault the Colonel found with the presidency was that it made him fat.

We had a furtive cocktail in a side room and then went to lunch, where we were joined by Daugherty and Mrs. Harding. The talk was general and pleasant until the President got on the subject of the Washington Treaty. He talked with much bitterness about the failure of the Senate to follow his advice. I mildly suggested that I had heard that Wilson made the same complaint about him and his colleagues. "That was different," he said sharply — that is, sharply for him. I didn't ask him why it was different. I didn't argue. Arguing with the President of the United States in the White House is not my idea of an even match. If he thinks he is losing the argument he may call out the army and navy. When Theodore Roosevelt was President, he used to box with his military aides at the White House. The President had been a good boxer in his day and he was always full of fight, but he was middle-aged, stout and somewhat scant of breath. I asked Senator Root how he managed to spar with young fellows just out of West Point. "I should think," I said, "they'd knock his head off." "They haven't a chance," said Mr. Root. "You see the President is also commander-in-chief of the army. So when one of these young lieutenants begins to force him, the President cries 'Shun,' the boy comes to attention and the President punches him in the nose."

I spent an hour or two pleasantly with the Hardings. The President came to the door to see me out and was

Finley Peter Dunne, in the great days of Mr. Dooley, as caricatured at
the turn of the century in London by Spy.

Mr. Dooley, drawing by E. W. Kemble (from *Mr. Dooley's Philosophy*, R. H. Russell, Publisher, New York, 1900.)

Mr. Dooley, drawing by James Montgomery Flagg (from *The American Magazine*).

Mr. Dooley, drawing by W. A. Rogers (from *Harper's Weekly*).

Mr. Dooley, drawing by Steele (from *The Century Magazine*).

Mr. Dooley, drawing by F. B. Opper (from *Hearst newspapers*).

Finley Peter Dunne, before the Dooley articles brought him fame.
Drawing by Art Young.

Finley Peter Dunne, playing the Dooley harp. Drawing by Oliver
Herford.

Finley Peter Dunne, as editor of The American Magazine, 1912.

At a Preparedness Pageant, 1916. Philip Dunne as John Paul Jones;
T. R. as himself.

The Dunne family minus one — Southampton, 1925. *From left:*
Philip Dunne, F.P.D., Margaret Abbott Dunne, David Leonard
Dunne, Finley Peter Dunne, Jr. *Absent:* daughter Peggy.

Finley Peter Dunne, as he appeared in his later years, at home in Southampton.

once more the same old Harding I had known and liked so much. I never saw him again.

My adventure in backstage politics was at an end. But quite possibly it had been my conversation with Harry Sinclair the year before which enabled Harding to go to Chicago and by his distinguished appearance, his natural tact and good nature, to charm the delegates to a point where they were ripe for the sickle of the senatorial clique. And in that conversation was also the innocent beginning of the Teapot Dome affair, which provided more noise than any scandal that has disturbed the political life of the country since the Credit Mobilier.

Warren Harding probably had never read the remark attributed to Charles James Fox to the effect that friendships are not the least of the possessions of a successful statesman. But this was all too clearly his belief. His tragedy was that he chose unwisely.

He was intensely grateful to the two men, Harry Sinclair and Harry Whitney, who had helped him in his need, although the amount contributed was no more than they would have lightly paid for a yearling colt at a Saratoga sale. So when Sinclair went to Washington with his plan for leasing the "Teapot Dome," an oil field in Wyoming, the stage was set for him. If he could make terms satisfactory to the Navy and Interior Departments, the President naturally would prefer to grant the lease to a friend rather than to a stranger.

How Sinclair managed to induce Secretary Fall to agree I don't know. There is room for a guess. Sinclair has protested in private as well as public that he never paid Fall anything while he was in office. But he had other friends in Washington. The lease was drawn up and carried to the White House by Theodore Roosevelt, Jr., who was then Assistant Secretary of the Navy. He had also been a director of a subsidiary Sinclair company, and his brother Archie was vice president of the parent corporation. There was no need to bribe anyone. There was no thought of wrongdoing. At this time — as well as before and since — Americans of large affairs thought nothing of using their connections in government to promote their private schemes. The government was looked on as merely another link in a chain of interlocking directorates. Wall Street explodes with fury today at the mention of Franklin Roosevelt's name simply because he broke the chain. And poor complaisant Harding was no F.D.R. He signed the fatal document.

Sinclair thought he had a fortune in his grasp. And so he might have had for a time if "oil geologists" were altogether reliable. My personal acquaintance with these experts leads me to believe that I would as lief trust an old-fashioned well-finder with a willow wand as one of them, with their talk of 'domes,' 'faults,' and such. Apparently, although the geological picture was perfect, the wayward oil had been seeping down into an adjoining valley. So that when the Navy Department, at some future time, undertakes to develop this "great reservoir of national wealth bartered away by corrupt government officials," it will be lucky if it finds enough oil to supply its admirals' high-powered motor launches.

But the scenario was good and for a while the oil stocks gyrated on the Exchange.

Sinclair had at Washington a most determined enemy in

Senator Walsh of Montana. Senator Walsh may or may not have been the "greatest constitutional lawyer in the Senate" — a compliment we have all heard about many other senators. But he certainly deserved his reputation as a pious man who would pursue an evildoer with the relentlessness of a Spanish Grand Inquisitor. Moreover his brother John Walsh was Washington representative of a rival oil company and had probably suffered from Sinclair's roughshod methods. He was, too, a friend of E. L. Doheny, the California oil man, also an enemy of Sinclair. At one time Doheny had offered Senator Walsh the position of counsel for his company, an offer which the Senator had sensibly declined. Walsh felt instinctively that there was something wrong with these oil leases. He did not think of the lease to his friend Doheny of the California fields. His mind, after its kind, was centered on his first suspicion. He never once let go of his bulldog grip on the belief that Sinclair had bribed Fall.

Meanwhile a tale had been circulating around the country about Fall. It was first told in the little New Mexico town where Fall borrowed money to keep up his ranch. It was heard from again in Los Angeles, then in Cleveland, again in New York and finally in Washington, which is always the last place to hear the real news from the rest of the country. It was, in a word, that Secretary Fall had received a hundred thousand dollars in currency from an "oil man" to pay for a government lease. I was not privy to Senator Walsh's mind, but one can guess that when he heard this information he said to himself, "Now I have this scoundrel Sinclair where I want him," having no doubt that his enemy, and his brother John's, was the guilty man.

He instituted a senatorial investigation by a special committee, which was followed by others, and these inquiries were conducted in a spirit that amazed the innocent people who imagine there is something in the Constitution that, in substance, protects a citizen against punishment except by "due process of law." The committees, with a fine disregard for the Constitution and all the accepted tenets of fair play, prosecuted the witnesses, judged them and finally punished them. There is no arrogance to match that of a congressional committee which believes that its cause is just. The lofty magnates, themselves steeped in arrogance, had apparently forgotten that pride goeth before destruction and a haughty spirit before a fall. They had no more chance with these vengeful legislators than Al Capone would have before a gang of Chicago vigilantes. The senators bullied the witnesses, insulted them, shook their fists at them. They brought as witnesses against them drunken former employees and prostitutes. One of the senators, not to be cheated out of a little innocent gaiety, personally conducted a member of the half-world from her home to the capital. Walsh was the exception. He was severe in his examination but fair in his method of questioning. He eventually managed to force Sinclair to refuse to answer on advice of counsel, which at once made him liable to a charge of contempt of the Senate.

And then something happened which must have been a bombshell to the Senator from Montana and his brother. E. L. Doheny took the stand and grudgingly testified that it was he — the friend of the Walshes — who had given Fall the mysterious one hundred thousand dollars!

He told a good story, a plausible story, a story that strengthens one's belief in the essential generosity of human nature. It was that he and Albert B. Fall had been friends in a mining camp forty years ago. They had parted in tears. "Goodbye, Ed, bless you." "Goodbye, Al, may God be with you." Everyone knows that there is no place on earth for the cultivation of friendships like a claim-jumping, faro-playing, gun-toting mining camp. The companionship of these two old prospectors was like unto that of David and Jonathan, except that in forty years they seldom saw each other. In the meantime E. L. Doheny had become a very rich man and Albert B. Fall, now a senator, was in constant financial distress. It was not until Fall became Secretary of the Interior — and there were oil leases to be got — that this friendship, so long in the bud, finally burst into bloom. "What?" said the millionaire, "let my old friend suffer while I live in plenty? Surely not. Here (to his son) is a little black bag with a hundred thousand dollars in currency in it. Take it to my pal What's-his-name, the Secretary of the Interior, and get his note for it. Never shall it be said that E. L. Doheny went back on Alfred J. Fall, if I have the name right."

This touching anecdote failed to draw tears to the eyes of the Montana Savonarola. Perhaps Senator Walsh knew what was coming. Besides, he had lived a long time among mining men in the West. At any rate, it must be said of him that he pursued his old friend, and his brother's, with the same remorseless energy that he had shown against his old enemy.

What was the outcome of all these inquisitions, the torture of witnesses innocent and guilty alike, the epileptic convulsions of the newspapers? To sum it up it was this: Sinclair was adjudged guilty of contempt of the Senate, a sentiment which he shared with not a few of his fellow-citizens. He received three months in the District jail for this and another three months for tailing members of the jury panel in the conspiracy case against him, a practice common enough among Department of Justice lawyers as well as those for the defense. He was acquitted on the really important charge of conspiracy to bribe a public official. In the Doheny case the jury decided that the one hundred thousand dollars in the little black bag was not intended as a bribe, but before another jury Fall was convicted of bribery in accepting it. In other words one jury found that when Doheny gave Fall the money it was a loan and another that when Fall received it it was a bribe! *Fiat justitia!*

This was practically the end of the commotion. Sinclair, a romantic soul, thought Fall would "defend his honor" by shooting Walsh. "He carries a pearl-handled forty-four in a suitcase," said the optimist. But happily this lethal weapon remained in the suitcase and did no harm. Perhaps Fall was in the state of mind of a "bad man" whom John Gaffey of Los Angeles used to tell about. He was a gunfighter and the terror of the community. One day he went into a saloon and delivered his customary rodomontade. A little prospector, who had come back as usual empty-handed from the hills, became so dissatisfied with the speech that he spat tobacco juice in the bad man's eye. The hero clapped his hand to his eye and ran from the place. When he came back the next day, the bartender said scornfully:

"You're some bad man, you are. Lettin' that little rooster spit in your eye. I thought you was goin' to plug him."

"I couldn't," pleaded the bravo. "Y'see he spit in my pistol eye."

[At this point, my father's written narrative ends. The following paragraph is fished from my memory of what he said to me eight years after the event. P.D.]

I came out of the mess with my own reputation somewhat tarnished. You know that I was a character witness for Harry Sinclair at his trial. I was urged by some of my friends — many of whom had been also Sinclair's — not to do it. I confess that I nearly weakened but Harry Whitney persuaded me to appear. As brave as a lion himself, Harry expected the same leonine qualities in his friends. Not that a character witness carries much weight at a trial. Even Bluebeard or Benedict Arnold, if they had ever been haled before the court, could have found someone to swear to the saintliness of their characters. And Sinco was no saint. He was, after all, an oil man. But he generously wrote me later that my appearance was responsible for his acquittal on the important charge. I hope he was right. It would be pleasant to think that friendship, so cruelly slandered and misused throughout the affair, should finally be allowed to score one small point.

And it is perhaps a blessing that poor Harding died when he did. At his death he was still a popular hero and unwarned of the disaster that was to fall on so many of his friends and companions. When you think of it, sudden death is often a historical mercy. Caesar's assassination was less a personal tragedy than Napoleon's defeat and exile. If Booth's bullet had missed Lincoln, perhaps that great man would have faced impeachment as his successor did. At best, the lives of those who live too long dribble out in anticlimax.

The rule would seem to be to enjoy life while you are young, and escape from it when you grow old. The best escape is to enter the world of pure fantasy by writing your memoirs. I am grateful to you for hounding me into it myself. It's a much better world than the other one. The dreary facts you have lived are erased by the pleasant fictions your memory sends in as substitutes. And thus is woven that vast and tangled web of error, prejudice and special pleading we call history.

Commentary

I AM OFTEN asked what it is like to be the son of a famous father. I never know how to answer because actually the question is based on the false premise that celebrities somehow differ from the rest of us. The manufacture of publicity having become a major industry in our time, we are far more celebrity-conscious than we ever were in the past. Because we see a man's name in the newspapers, or stamped in gilt on the back of a book, or his face spread across hundreds of square feet on a motion picture screen, we tend to set him apart as one of a different and superior breed. We find it hard to think of him as enjoying the normal pleasures or suffering the normal griefs of the ordinary human being. But that is all a celebrity is: a human being who is a little brighter or handsomer or richer or luckier or more acquisitive or more persuasive on a platform or who can hit, kick or throw a ball better than the rest of us.

When I was a boy, I never knew that Finley Peter Dunne was famous. He was merely my father, a familiar biped subject, like all fathers, to fits of generosity and temper, to toothaches, constipation and broken shoelaces. No man is a celebrity in his own household. He may be respected, but he is not held in awe.

Later, when I had to earn a living by writing, I realized that being the son of a celebrity in the same field might prove to be a handicap. People are always quick to compare the son with the father, usually to the former's disadvantage. Genius rarely strikes twice in the same family. For every Oliver Wendell Holmes, Jr. and William Pitt the Younger, there are a thousand Absaloms and Richard Cromwells: the failures, fools and scapegraces who have dimmed the luster of many a famous name. I had no intention of becoming one of these, nor did I want any success I might achieve attributed to my parentage alone. So, when I started writing short stories and screenplays, I made it a point not to advertise the relationship. I had no hope of scaling the heights my father had scaled, but I wanted sole credit — or blame — for whatever I might accomplish on a lower level. And I didn't want to embarrass him. In this I wasn't entirely successful. Once a critic called a piece of mine unworthy of the name of Dunne. He was half right. It was unworthy of that Dunne, but not of this one. Since I had made no attempt to trade on the relationship, he might have left my father out of it.

Will Rogers, Jr., if he ever reads this, will know what I mean. He started with even more of a handicap. He was inescapably Junior by name and his father's physical image into the bargain. He couldn't hope to play down the relationship. But Bill made his own success in journalism and politics and has every reason to be proud of himself.

Speaking of celebrities and fame, there is a story my mother used to tell about my father and the artist Charles

Dana Gibson. At the time, early in the century, there was a heavyweight contender called Sailor Tom Sharkey. He was a game boy, as Ring Lardner would say, and his face attested to his courage in the ring. It had been beaten almost out of all human semblance — and Sharkey had been born a homely man. According to my mother's story, she and my father and the Gibsons had stopped in at a soda fountain after the theater. While the four were sipping their sodas, a group of men nearby began to stare and whisper among themselves. They had obviously spotted a celebrity. But which celebrity? My father preened himself. So did Dana Gibson. Each obviously thought himself the target of the stares and whispers. Each resented the other's claim to be the center of this flattering attention. My mother and Mrs. Gibson sneaked round behind the group of rubbernecks, with a view to settling the unspoken argument. They heard one of the men whisper excitedly: "That's him all right! That's Sharkey!"

I am inclined to dismiss this anecdote as a mere wifely libel, or perhaps a fiction of Irene Gibson's always nimble and delightful mind. Dana Gibson was a handsome and distinguished man, and my father, while no beauty, in no way resembled a heavyweight boxer or any other kind of athlete. Unless, that is, you can imagine a pugilist in a pince-nez.

Some early pictures of him, particularly *Spy's* caricature done in London early in the century, make him look like Woodrow Wilson. I think the pince-nez must be responsible, for otherwise I can see little resemblance. Where Wilson was tall, lean and pale, my father was shortish, stocky and florid. Although official documents described his eyes as blue, they were as green as is permissible in a human being.

He was not fat in the sense of grossness, but let us say that his silhouette had substance. Early in the twenties, he had almost died of a gall-bladder ailment and several major operations had left him with an unsightly bulge at his midriff. To contain this embonpoint he was forced to wear a sort of abdominal corset. He used to say that H. G. Wells would approve of him. "I am the man of the future," he said. "The new improved model. I carry my alimentary canal on the outside."

I suppose his floridity can be traced to his heavy drinking. As with General Grant, a great deal has been said about my father's love of the bottle, and perhaps the tales about it need to be put in perspective. He was not an alcoholic in the pathological sense. He was always able to swear off the stuff when he had to. During one of his brief adventures in abstemiousness, a heavy-drinking friend asked him how long it took to get over the craving for alcohol. "I can't tell you exactly," he replied, "but it's longer than four months, six days, seven hours and fifteen minutes." Another time, according to his friend Louis Stoddard, the two met on a New York street corner. "Hello, Peter," said Mr. Stoddard, "drinking anything?" "*Anything*," said my father instantly.

No real alcoholic can jest so readily about his infirmity. But it is true that my father drank very heavily indeed. This is not unknown among good writers. Most of them learn that their genius is half inspiring muse and half devouring succubus. Insomnia is only one of the occupational diseases of the craft. The other is a lifelong dread of failure.

There is no momentum in a writer's career, as there is in a doctor's or a banker's or even an actor's or director's. What the writer has written yesterday may provide him with livelihood and reputation, but what he writes tomorrow may lose him both. Every writer of real merit knows the stark horror of the blank page. If it is ever filled to his satisfaction, it is by a process over which he seems to have no control. E. M. Forster describes it as lowering a bucket into the well of the subconscious. Either an idea comes up or it does not. The writer cannot consciously summon it. To change the metaphor, he can only rub his lamp and hope some djinn of inspiration is loitering unemployed in the neighborhood.

The plight of the humorist is even worse. He is under the obligation of being funny with a deadline staring him in the face. A serious writer can sometimes publish second-rate work and get away with it, if only for a while, but a humorist whose wit fails him is lost immediately. His critics and his public are waiting for the chance not to laugh.

My father found the high standard he had set in the early Dooleys impossible to maintain in middle life. He went through agonies in the attempt, but he knew in his heart that he could no longer consistently match the prodigal achievements of his youth. He might produce a good piece twice in a year, but not twice a week as in his early days. He tried and tried hard. He would lock himself in his room for hours at a time, filling the ashtrays with cigarettes and leaving the floor covered with crumpled sheets of foolscap. "It's no good," he would say in despair. "It's just plain no damn good."

He wrote with humor of his problem in an unfinished

essay: "One bright morning in late May or early June I awoke with a consciousness that I had much important work to do. Accordingly, I took a long time over breakfast, studied the morning papers with the greatest care and having exhausted all other devices for postponing labor, like playing with the dog and winding the clock, settled down to work, when suddenly it occurred to me that I had still a small balance left in the bank. It was not only small, it was puny, but large enough to shut the door on Inspiration. Every great artist knows that without inspiration he can't create; so letters and art are left to the working classes. When the Genius calls for Inspiration he finds she is howling at the door of a slave who has locked himself in and, cursing the fate that made him an artist rather than a bricklayer, settled down before a blank pad of paper to 'make copy.' Anyhow, with the thought of my bank balance all Inspiration fled and there was nothing left for a sensible man to do but practice his mashie shots."

But it was not so funny in actual fact. It was a long nightmare ungoverned by clock or calendar. Only whiskey could suppress its terrors. Whiskey and companionship.

And most of my father's friends drank as heavily as he did, even though few of them in his later years were writers. It was a trait of the self-anointed upper class in the America of the twenties. I have seen many a captain of industry or social leader helped to his Pierce-Arrow by his chauffeur after a perfectly normal afternoon in one of the New York clubs. There was no particular stigma attached to it. These men were not called drunkards, as they might have been if they had not been able to afford chauffeurs or Pierce-Arrows. They merely followed the tradition of their caste, as established by eighteenth-century squires, Regency bucks and the dram-taking worthies of Queen Victoria's day. Yes, the nineteenth century boasted as high an alcoholic content as the eighteenth or twentieth. I have good authority for this statement. In a creative writing course at Harvard I wrote an essay which implied that our strait-laced grandfathers had no use for alcohol. My professor, the late G. H. Maynadier, who was a connoisseur and scholar of everything Victorian, took me gently to task for this egregious error. "It isn't true," he assured me earnestly. "Why as a boy I knew and admired your great-uncle. He was a Victorian of Victorians and," he concluded triumphantly, "he was put to bed by his servants every night."

Hilaire Belloc took note of the aristocracy's affinity for alcohol in a couplet my father loved to quote:

> *Like many of the Upper Class*
> *He liked the Sound of Broken Glass.*

My father was not ashamed of his weakness for the bottle. On the contrary, he made fun of drinkers and drinking, including his own. Once, coming out of the Links Club, a club servant slipped and fell on the icy pavement. "Careful," said my father, helping him up. "You might be mistaken for a member." When he judged me old enough to drink, he used to order at the bar a double martini for himself and "a boy's size for my son." He was concerned with the proper schooling of his sons in the fine art of bending the elbow. He was full of good advice. "When traveling abroad," he counseled me, "always stick to the light wine of the country — Scotch whiskey." When I went off to college, my mother had packed my trunks, putting my shoes in the trays on top, but when I opened the trunk in Cambridge, I found that the shoes had been replaced with a dozen full quarts of aged Allegheny red whiskey. Harry Payne Whitney had had several hundred gallons of this noble beverage laid down in charred wood and had shared the treasure with my father, whose intention was not to encourage me to drink, but to save me from the rotgut favored by Harvard undergraduates in Prohibition days. For a few weeks I was one of the most popular members of the freshman class, though as shoeless as my ancestors in the peat-bogs of Ireland.

No, my father was a drinker — and a prodigious one — but not a drunkard. His fondness for the bottle was open, unashamed, and was accepted and even respected as part of the man. De Lancey Nicoll, a distinguished New York lawyer, summed it up perfectly when he dedicated some verses to him at a dinner given in his honor at Southampton. The last verse ended:

> . . . to Peter Dunne
> Our man of fun
> Who drinks a tun
> Without a bun
> The man beloved by everyone.

In the hands of this able attorney, the defense rests. A tun, by the way, contains two hundred and fifty-two gallons.

My father's relationship with his children was a curious one. He frankly didn't understand us and took little active part in our upbringing. He was always something of a remote figure in our household. He told me later that he was scared of us. I think it would be more accurate to say that we bored him. We spoke no language that he understood. He loved us and spoiled us but he was unable to talk with us. Conversation had to wait until we were old enough to understand him and in turn be understood.

He was apparently bewildered by parenthood. Perhaps one reason was that, as in the case of so many other truly brilliant men, he himself never quite outgrew the emotions of childhood.

He liked to have his own way. When he was thwarted, he could become as imperious as any child. I remember that once when I was twelve or thirteen we missed the Friday afternoon express train from New York to Southampton. We had allowed plenty of time, but no porters were available at the Pennsylvania Station traffic ramp. I had just come down from boarding school and we had more luggage than we could carry ourselves. We finally arrived at the train gate just in time to have it slammed in our faces. My father was furious. He sent for the station master. He put in a call to the president of the railroad. He demanded a special train to carry the pair of us the ninety-odd miles to Southampton. He saw nothing unusual in the request. (He and Payne Whitney and some other friends had done exactly that years before when they had missed a race train to Louisville for the Kentucky Derby. They had a special train put on and arranged for the race train to be sidetracked en route so that they would be first to arrive in Louisville.) The station master, a born diplomat, finally averted the crisis by providing us with a limousine for the trip — at the railroad's expense.

Like Mark Twain and other past and present masters of what are now called the needle and the rib, he was sometimes slow to appreciate a joke on himself. Perhaps it was lack of practice, for few ever got the better of him in a battle of wits.

But still he knew how to laugh at himself. He used to tell a story of finding himself at a dinner party seated next to a handsome lady whose face was perfectly familiar but whose name he couldn't for the life of him remember. (His memory for names could only be described as dreadful.) For half an hour he tried desperately to steer the conversation around to where it might provide some clue. Finally she gave him an apparent opening by remarking: "Oh, I saw my brother last week and he sent you fond regards." He answered hopefully: "Oh yes, your brother. Tell me, what's he doing these days?" She gave him a blank look and said: "He's still President of the United States." The lady was Mrs. Douglas Robinson, Theodore Roosevelt's sister.

His sense of humor where it applied to himself was put to a much sterner test on an occasion when he had had an argument with my mother and decided to leave Southampton and go back to New York. I was reading in a hammock on the veranda and saw him come stamping out, hat jammed down on head, face dark with rage and frosty eyes glaring. He banged his stick down on the veranda steps and called in a voice made magnificent by his wrath: "Oombair!" I couldn't figure it out at first, but then it came to me. My mother favored French servants. Our house was always full of Yvonnes, Helenes, Manons and Madeleines. The chauffeur, however, was an American innocuously named Hubert. My father, in his wrath, could only think that there was some damn character on the payroll, probably French like everyone else, who could drive the damn car and take him to New York where a man could be free of his damn women and find a little peace. "Oombair" was a colorful translation of the pallid "Hubert," and far more satisfactory acoustically for expressing a sense of utter frustration. While I was busy with this deduction, he let out one more stentorian "Oombair!" and then took note of my presence.

"Well," he asked angrily, "what are you staring at?"

"Nothing," I answered innocently, "but if by Oombair you mean Hubert, Mother sent him to the village."

"I do mean Hubert, and if I choose to call him Oombair that's my business. I suppose you think I lost my temper?"

"Oh no, sir," I said hastily.

"Then you're either a damn fool or a liar, because I did." Then he suddenly chuckled. "When *Oombair* comes back," he said, "tell him I don't want him."

And he went back into the house. All his rages were summer storms, and the sun never rivaled in brightness the smile that always broke through the clouds to end them.

I tell this tale without a blush, for he loved to have me repeat it. From then on, a chauffeur was always referred to in our family as an Oombair.

Perhaps I am making too much of my father's failure to communicate with his children. The concept embodied in that nauseating word "togetherness" was alien to his time as well as to his nature. Few of my friends were on really intimate terms with their fathers. The modern first-name relationship was unthinkable. You called your father "sir" to his face and "my old man" behind his back. Both appellations were significant. One's father was still very much the Biblical patriarch or Roman paterfamilias of our republic's earlier days.

I have no sons myself, only daughters, so I don't know if I would have done any better than my father did as a Boy's Companion. It seems to me that such relationships must be based on a compatibility of tastes. Since the boy cannot be expected to nourish a man's tastes, the shared enthusiasms must be immature.

Still, I know fathers who are not conspicuously childish but manage to be good companions to their sons. They are all proficient outdoorsmen. They swim, ride, skate, ski and play tennis. They can put up a tent, tie a clove hitch and bring down a high-flying bird with a pattern of small shot.

My father could do none of these things. As a product of urban, lower-middle-class Chicago, he had never been trained in the arts of the outdoors. He never even learned how to drive a car. I have been told he once played tennis, but the only time I ever saw him with a tennis racket in his hand was on my thirteenth birthday, when someone handed him the implement to give me the traditional thirteen smacks on the behind. ("This is the first time," he observed on that occasion, "that I have ever struck one of my children — save in anger.")

As an outdoorsman he was a complete washout. His tastes ran in other directions. He could see no point in spending a damp night under canvas with the mosquitoes when a warm bedroom and a shelf of good books were available. Outdoors life is a deliberate return to the primitive and my father preferred the hard-won blessings of civilization. To his highly civilized mind, the artificial hardships of the outdoorsman seemed an affectation. He once had Mr. Dooley say of that dedicated apostle of the "strenuous life," Theodore Roosevelt: "I'd like to tell me friend Tiddy that they'se a sthrenuse life an' a sthrenuseless life." My father's days were for work and conversation, his evenings for the supreme joy of reading. He recognized the need for some physical exercise, but he used to quote with relish a remark of the English politician Joseph Chamberlain: "In all my life the only exercise I have taken is to walk upstairs to bed, and I intend to discontinue that as soon as I can have a lift installed."

His sons were brought up differently. Spending the winters in a New England boarding school and the summers on Long Island, we had outdoorsmanship thrust upon us. My brother Peter was a noted oarsman and rifle shot, my brother Leonard a demon on the gridiron, and I dabbled at everything from ping-pong to polo. We were taught that hardship makes the man. Not that the hardships were anything but artificial. But the typical American boarding school is a copy of the English public school, which in turn originally drew its grim inspiration from the educational scheme of ancient Sparta. At Middlesex no foxes gnawed at our vitals, but it was a strict rule that every boy had to take a cold shower every morning, even with the thermometer reading well below zero. We used to comb the ice out of our hair running across the campus to breakfast in the murky New England winter dawn. To this day a hot shower fills me with a delicious sense of guilt.

The natural result of all this emphasis on the physical was that games and sports occupied our attention to the exclusion of almost everything else. We had very little in common with our civilized and sedentary father.

He made some attempts to bridge the gap. I used to send him the usual schoolboy letters from Middlesex, devoted exclusively to the doings of the football, hockey or baseball teams. He answered me once: "I am delighted to hear that your Davids overcame the fearsome Goliaths of Groton. Now I shall be able to sleep at night. The suspense had become unbearable. But have you read anything lately?"

He couldn't have stated more clearly his opinion that a man is distinguished by his mind, not his muscles. When my brothers and I belatedly arrived at an understanding of this, he was ready to welcome us as companions and friends.

The one sport engaged in by this resolutely non-sporting man was the game of golf. He was one of the founders of the famous National Club at Southampton. Its full and grandiose title was "The National Golf Links of America," though it was a private club with a rather small membership. Charles B. Macdonald, who had come over from Scotland to win the first American Amateur tournament, had conceived the idea of a course which would combine copies of the most famous and difficult holes in Britain with some fiendish native inventions. He settled on the treeless downs of Long Island near Southampton as an ideal spot for the course and enlisted a few rich men in New York to put up the money. The club became one of the centers of the social life of Southampton, and it was primarily to be near it that our family took to summering in that pleasant resort.

My mother some years before had won the first ladies' championship of France. She used to say she won because all the French girls apparently misunderstood the nature of the game scheduled for that day and turned up to play in high heels and tight skirts. This may have been true, but my mother still played a fine game. She was short but straight.

My father, on the other hand, was short but crooked. When he drove, the safest place to stand was directly in front of the tee. He spent most of his golfing afternoons in the sand traps and bayberry bushes. He had a physical handicap which prevented him from properly gripping the club; the index finger on his right hand had been crippled in a boyhood accident and he was unable to bend it. But for some strange reason he loved the game. He hacked his way round the course in high good humor, happily jeering at his friends who tortured themselves in giving point to Mr. Dooley's description of golf as Scotland's most cheerful gift to the world "with the exciption maybe iv th' theery iv infant damnation." But then he knew he was no athlete and would get no better, while his friends suffered from the delusion common to most dubs that some day they would "break a hundred" and go on from there to challenge Bobby Jones or Walter Hagen. His own several Dooleys on golf were rare fun, but he readily yielded the palm on this subject to Ring Lardner, whose A *Caddy's Diary* is not only superb comedy but a devastating essay on human nature.

Strangely enough, he was quite an armchair expert on polo. His interest in the sport dated back to the days when Harry Payne Whitney organized and trained the famous Big Four, the American team which went to England and handed the British their first defeat in international competition. My father loved both his friend Harry Whitney, and beating the British at anything.

He was secretly proud of me when I took up polo for a brief period before the market crash of 1929. (I was only one of the many who were unhorsed by that catastrophe.) He was delighted when once I scored twelve goals in a game at Palm Beach. As a matter of fact I should have scored fifty that day, because I had behind me H. C. Phipps and his nephew Mike, past and future internationalists. My orders were to ride to goal and wait for them to hit the ball up to me, which they did all afternoon. They thought it was a wonderful joke. But a young woman who did the society news for the Palm Beach paper wrote a stirring account of the game which identified me as the star. According to her account, nothing so heroic had happened on horseback since Henry V led the charge at Agincourt. My father sent a clipping to a friend of his, an old internationalist whose life had been embittered by a son who was bored with polo and played it both unwillingly and badly. This gentleman had once played a kindly practical joke on my father by putting him on what he claimed was a quiet horse, but which had promptly bucked my father off into a stream. The clipping was my father's belated revenge.

Perhaps his own lack of athletic ability contributed to his somewhat uncharacteristic pride in whatever his sons could achieve on the playing fields. Since I had started very young, I shot a fair game of golf when I was still in my teens. He delighted in matching me against those of his friends who thought well of their own games. As I have since learned from personal experience, there is nothing more humiliating to a grown man than to be beaten at golf by a boy of sixteen. Sometimes my father liked to make small bets on these matches.

But on one match there was no bet. I was waiting on the first tee when he came up with a fragile but distinguished-looking man with a white mustache. My father took me aside and asked if I would mind if the stranger played around with us. "He's a new member from Pittsburgh," he said, "and we should treat him with courtesy. But don't offer to bet him," he went on. "The poor fellow's a little strapped and might be embarrassed." I was so impressed with my obligations to the needy that I paid the stranger's caddy at the end of the round, muttering something about his being our guest and so forth. He looked a little surprised, but thanked me most politely and went off. It was then that my father revealed that our impecunious friend was Andrew Mellon. "But he let me pay for his caddy!" I cried.

"You've just learned the first rule for success in high finance," he said, "which is to despise nothing, however small, as long as it's money."

Money, or the lack of it, was always an important factor in our household. We lived like the rich, spent like the rich, and in fact resembled the rich in every way except in being rich.

I suppose that my father could only blame himself for

our extravagance. He set the example. He had the tastes of a Morgan or a Rockefeller. In the great Dooley days the money had rolled in. He was by far the highest-paid writer of his time. He was courted and cultivated by rich men, joined their society, and quite naturally began to live as they did. My mother did her share. She was new-poor as my father was new-rich, and when given the opportunity readily reverted to the style of living of her grandfathers. She honestly believed that to get along with less than four servants was a form of roughing it. And why not, when her friends had five or seven or even twenty?

So my father, after he had begun to find it hard to write and had virtually retired from the editorial field, was faced with the constant problem of finding an income to fill the insatiable maw of our extravagance. Like everybody else in the innocent but greedy twenties, he began to play the market on margin. He did fairly well for a while — it was almost impossible to do otherwise in that steeply rising market — but then disaster struck.

Years later, he told me the story. As he told it, it was a masterpiece of irony. Payne Whitney and some others had decided to do what other enormously wealthy men had done for their less pecunious friends and organize a little killing for him. They told him to buy a certain stock — I forget which stock, but it was one of those subject to manipulation — to buy it at twenty-five and sell it at fifty.

The instructions were clear and explicit, but my father, having pulled off some minor coups of his own, at this point had begun to consider himself a financial genius. So he shrewdly decided to hold off for a while. The stock, as

strings were pulled behind the scenes, rose to thirty and
then to thirty-five. He still cannily held off. When it
jumped to forty, he decided the time had come to buy. His
friends were right after all and the stock was a good investment. He put every nickel he had into it. It went up to
forty-five and then to fifty, where he had been told to sell.
But did he sell? Oh, no. He began to think: "If it goes to
fifty, why not a hundred? What gives those fellows the impression they know more about the market than I do?" So
he held on. He was still firmly holding on the next week,
when his broker finally sold him out at eighteen.

That is the story he told me. It may seem a little too neat
and too pat. He was after all a professional writer and he
had had several years to perfect the tale.

However it happened, by 1927 he was a thoroughly dis-
enchanted financier. At this point, and it was at the height
of the bull market, he was really broke. Then his dearest
friend, Payne Whitney, died and left to him and two other
close friends legacies of half a million dollars each. He was
crushed by his friend's death and stunned by the legacy.
When he came home that night, I saw him in tears for the
first and only time in my memory. He repeated over and
over again that he didn't want the money — he only
wanted his friend back. I never knew a death to affect
him so, before or afterwards. The touching little tribute
to Payne Whitney in the last essay in this book was written from the heart.

The Whitney legacy saved him. He lost a great deal of it
in the crash of 1929, but there was enough left to maintain
him for the nine years he outlived his friend. Towards the

end, my brothers and I were able to help out and he died free of the financial worries which had dogged him for so long.

In view of his own experience, it is quite natural that he looked with suspicion on literature as a potential career for his sons. He wanted us to be bankers, oil men, brokers, lawyers — anything but writers. He was upset when my brother Peter went to work on a newspaper and when I gave voice to my own literary ambitions. "The saying goes that horse-players die broke," he said. "Well so do writers and journalists. If you want a horrible example, look at me. I made more money than any writer can decently expect to make and now I have nothing to show for it. Any dunderhead can go into a bank or a broker's office in his youth and end up a millionaire. Most of them do. There aren't twenty members of the New York Stock Exchange who can converse intelligently on any subject you could name — including the stock market. But they're all glutted with money. Now if you and your brother showed any signs of genius — or even talent — I wouldn't object. But you haven't. At least not yet. Perhaps you have the capability, but you haven't used it. You haven't written anything. Just what gives you the impression you can make a living as a writer?"

I couldn't really answer the question, so I let him find me a job on Wall Street. I joined the hundreds of graduation-fresh Harvards, Yales and Princetons who had been placed by their fathers in the banks and brokers' offices of downtown New York. We were all paid fifteen or twenty dollars a week and spent more than that every evening at the Racquet Club bar. Each of us was confident that some day he would become president of his firm. That was New York in the Indian summer of the Great Boom.

The crash of 1929 put an end to that dream and to my financial career as well. I went to work as a writer after all, for the very good reason that I could see no other way of making a living.

Eventually I drifted out to Hollywood, where writers were better paid than anywhere else. My father suffered the indignity of having his embryo financier transmuted into a screenwriter. The Great Depression had doomed me to the fate worse than death which he had done everything in his power to avert.

He took the blow philosophically. If he considered me a hack, he never told me so. At least he viewed my work with tolerance, if not admiration. His friends have told me that to them he at least pretended to a pride he might not have felt.

At the time of his death, I hadn't accomplished very much. I had published a few short stories and had contributed to the delinquency of several minor films. I had shared screen credit (with Rowland Lee and Dan Totheroh) on one solid hit, *The Count of Monte Cristo*, which can still be seen on television's late, late shows. He wrote me of this: "I enjoyed your movie. If you want to quote me in the advertisements, I will say that it is magnificent, if not Dumas. But perhaps it will bring you a share of the treasure of Monte Cristo. Seriously, it is sound professional work and I congratulate you and your collaborators." From this rather faint praise, I treasured the one word "professional." It was not an adjective he used lightly.

It was at about this time that I realized the respect I had

always had for him was now in some measure being returned. Perhaps it was only because I had proved I was able to make a living with my pen, but I was now promoted into the select circle of his friends and intimates. There was no longer a trace of condescension in his treatment of me. He accepted me — if not as an equal — at least as a fellow professional and friend. At last I was given a passport to the remarkable kingdom of his mind.

It was a revelation. Given access to the intimacy of his thoughts, I understood for the first time the true nature of his genius. I knew now why the rich and powerful had sought him out, why rulers of nations had maneuvered for his friendship, why intellectuals from Henry Adams to Felix Frankfurter had respected him on their own terms. It was not for his wit nor his charm nor his political acumen, but for the quality of his mind. It was sheer intellect which had carried him to the top of his world.

The chief characteristic of his mind was total clarity. He saw through the flesh to the skeleton of things. This is true of all first-class intellects in all fields of thought. Einstein refused to accept the basic paradox in Newton's theory of gravitation, which for a hundred and fifty years all physicists had accepted, and the result was an entirely new concept of the physical world. Toscanini towered above other conductors because he was able to see through a score to the composer's entire intention. There have been better musicologists than Toscanini and better mathematicians than Einstein, but none have rivaled them in clarity of vision.

Given my paternity, I have been interested in political writing all my life. I read every column and editorial I can lay my hands on. It is precisely this quality of clarity that is so often and so sadly lacking on modern editorial pages. Political writers, like the rest of us, are misled by their own passions and partisanships. With the best will in the world, they allow their enthusiasms to becloud their judgments. Their truths may seem true to themselves, but they are not universal truths. For every unclouded Elmer Davis and James Reston, there are a hundred unwitting pamphleteers for special interests or special points of view.

In preparing this book, I have been rereading Mr. Dooley again. The reason for the phenomenal success of the articles is apparent. In every case, the true nature of the subject is made clear. The articles illuminate as they amuse. The reader at once recognizes that he is being shown the inner truth of a man or an issue, in a line, a phrase or a subtle characterization. The affectionately burlesqued "Tiddy Rosenfelt" is in essence the true Theodore Roosevelt. Governor Taft's "report" on the occupation of the Philippines is a true picture of the hypocrisy which always goes hand in hand with imperialism. The American Ambassador to the Court of St. James who was summoned by the king and came "as fast as his hands an' knees wud carry him" is a true exemplar of the Anglophilia which traditionally overcame our envoys to England during this period. " 'Let us pro-ceed,' says th' impartial an' fair-minded judge, 'to th' thrile iv the haynious monsther Cap Dhry-fuss.' " Could any one sentence more clearly convey the true nature of that judicial farce, the Dreyfus Trial?

And his general, nonpolitical philosophy also shone with the same clarity. A line like "Manny a man that cudden't direct ye to the dhrug store on th' corner whin he was

thirty will get a respectful hearin' whin age has further impaired his mind" is not only a gem of wit but a jewel of
truth. So is "A fanatic is a man that does what th' Lord
wud do if he knew th' facts iv the case."

As with my father's pen, so with his tongue. More than
a quarter of a century has elapsed since the last of the long
nights when we fought his insomnia with "life and letters."
I remember too little of what he said. Most of it is lost in
the pathless swamp of my memory. But I do remember
that every thought he expressed was a recurring miracle of
clarity. Every word bore the stamp of truth. I had been to
expensive schools and colleges, but it was through listening to my father that I received my real education, in history,
literature, politics, religion and above all in the worthiest of
all mankind's studies, which is man himself.

In the essay on Theodore Roosevelt which follows, I have
taken the liberty of interpolating one or two excerpts from
other unpublished writings of my father bearing on the
subject, notably the paragraphs on Herbert Hoover and the
brief discussion of the businessman in politics.

FINLEY PETER DUNNE

On Theodore Roosevelt

I HAVE OFTEN wished that an adequate life of Theodore
Roosevelt could be written. James Bishop's is good and
so is Pringle's. Thayer's *Theodore Roosevelt* is inconceivably
leaden. Roosevelt's *Autobiography* proves again how difficult
it is for a man to sit down coldly and write the story of his
own life. But in no case have we a vivid picture of the most
picturesque and the most powerful man in public life in
his time. Perhaps this failure to produce a real, full-length
portrait of this remarkable individual is due to the fact that
Theodore Roosevelt was more many-sided than any man in
our experience. To a student of government he was a statesman, to a political reporter a crafty politician, to a man of
letters an author. He was an explorer, a hunter of big game,
an ornithologist, a lover of poetry, a soldier, an historian. It
is almost impossible to print on paper a satisfactory picture
of such a man. So John Sargent found when he tried to put
one on canvas. The swift brush of the genius failed him
there. His Roosevelt portrait is heavy and utterly unreal
compared with any other of the Sargents I have ever seen.
It is unlovely, of course, alongside the flitting beauty of
Trotty Widener's picture (but what portrait of a man

would not seem coarse in comparison?), and infinitely dull in the presence of that incomparable piece of ridicule, the Wertheim group.

I suppose it is really too early for any man to appraise Roosevelt correctly. His letters, his works, the anecdotes of his family and friends, do not go very far in building up a simulacrum. Letters that a family dares to publish often conceal more than they reveal. Books for publication are a kind of full-dress uniform for parade purposes. Anecdotes are often malicious when they are not flattering and nearly all of them have been told about every great personage in history from the Neanderthal Man to Secretary Ickes. The saying: "The style is the very man" is among the many foolish aphorisms of new members of the French Academy. T.R. had many styles. When he wrote with his own hand, he produced charming articles and books. When he dictated to a typist his style was rude and awkward. So is the style of any man who is so indifferent to his art as to dictate. I tried my best to dissuade him from this pernicious habit. At one time we had offices with the *Metropolitan Magazine* and it annoyed me to hear him bawling out his articles to his secretary. He would rush in, hurl his hat and overcoat on the table and begin a stump speech that was afterwards to appear as a considered essay in a self-respecting magazine.

I told him how I felt, but he only laughed.

"They read all right to me," he said.

"But you're no judge," I said. "You are damaging your reputation as a writer. Look at those wonderful things you wrote about your experiences in South America."

"Oh well," he laughed, "you must suit your implement

to your subject. A pen is all right for a naturalist, with a poetic strain in him —"

"A what?"

"A poetic strain," he said. "You didn't know I had it but I have and I can use it at times. But when you are dealing with politics you feel that you have your enemy in front of you and you must shake your fist at him and roar the Gospel of Righteousness in his deaf ear."

And he resumed his march up and down the room, striking his palm with a clenched fist and shouting an article that no one but himself ever read.

My first acquaintance with Colonel Roosevelt grew, strangely enough, out of an article that was by no means friendly to him. All my impressions of this man of destiny were derived from the New York papers; and the political editors of these papers at the time were all practically controlled by Roosevelt's Republican enemies, Senator Platt and William Barnes. Roosevelt was easy to caricature, so violent were his mannerisms. The picture I had of him in my mind was that of a dude rancher, noisy, something of a bully, class proud, who pretended to a sentiment of democracy that he by no means felt. So one morning, when I was especially peevish and found on my desk a copy of his *Rough Riders*, I was ready to ridicule it to the limit. I wrote a savage review, and finished by having Mr. Dooley say: "No man that bears a gredge again' himsilf'll iver be governor iv a state. An' if Tiddy done it all he ought to say so an' relieve th' suspense. But if I was him I'd call th' book *Alone in Cubia*."

The review caught on, and for a while the book was better known as "Alone in Cuba" than by its real title. Some

years afterward, coming east on the Century, I found Colonel and Mrs. Roosevelt on the train. They had just been at
some sort of meeting in Buffalo.

"Tell him what happened," said Mrs. Roosevelt with
the angelic smile of a loving wife who has a joke on her
husband.

"Well I oughtn't to," said the Colonel, "but I will. At a
reception I was introduced to a very pretty young lady. She
said, 'Oh, Governor, I've read everything you ever wrote.'
'Really! What book did you like best?' 'Why that one, you
know, "Alone in Cuba." ' "

I never knew a man who could take a joke on himself
with better grace. But I must say — going back to the earlier time when my "review" first appeared — that I was astonished when I received this letter from him:

My dear Mr. Dunne:
    I regret to state that my family and intimate friends are de-
lighted with your review of my book. Now I think you owe me
one; and I shall exact that when you next come east you pay me
a visit. I have long wanted the chance of making your acquaintance.

Sincerely yours,
Theodore Roosevelt

He never forgot the "review," nor let me forget it. Years
later, when he was President, he wrote me: "Do come on
and let me see you again soon. I am by no means as much
alone as in Cubia, because I have an ample surrounding of
senators and congressmen, not to speak of railroad men,
Standard Oil men, beef packers, and vendors of patent
medicine, the depth of whose feelings for me cannot be ex-

pressed in words!" But that was later, after we had become friends.

I never got really acquainted with him until the opening of the Republican Convention at Philadelphia in 1900. I was editor-in-chief of the *Chicago Journal* and I gave myself the assignment of covering the convention. The proceedings were tailored in advance by Mark Hanna and the other bosses. Major McKinley was to be renominated. The platform had already been written. The only thing left undecided was the nomination of a candidate for vice president. McKinley, and therefore Hanna, wanted Long of Massachusetts. But strangely enough Tom Platt demanded Roosevelt. The story was told me that Platt pleaded, "He has a great war record and is popular. McKinley's war record is against him."

"Oh," said Hanna, "talk sense. Why do you really want that fellow?"

"Well," said Platt, "I want to get rid of the ——. I don't want him raising hell in my state any longer. I want to bury him!"

Hanna got McKinley on the telephone. The President was at first indignant. He disliked his former Assistant Secretary of the Navy. The two were almost exact opposites in character, in training, in disposition. But the feeling that their ally Platt needed help overcame his opposition. He consented to "bury" Roosevelt in the vice presidency.

The Colonel appeared by no means over-anxious for the place. Platt worked to cajole him into accepting through appeals to his vanity. I remember seeing him buttonholed by a politician called "Mose" Gunst from San Francisco who was telling him "the guntry demands for you to run,

Gov'ner." Day and night he was besieged by emissaries of Platt and Hanna who urged him to accept for the sake of the Republic. His ambition was appealed to, his duty as a soldier. I don't think he was convinced by the claque. My own theory is that he coolly weighed the political possibilities of the position. He might be able to overcome the majority of the Senate with voice and gavel. If he could hammer them into submission he would be the best-loved man in America. He said afterward that he "accepted the nomination because it offered him a quiet and sequestered place in which he could retire and study politics like a philosopher and write books without interruption" — a remark that if he never said anything else that was funny, would alone place him in the front rank of American humorists. Theodore Roosevelt seeking quiet in his life!

But his intention to accept was not known to anyone in the convention when an old friend of mine, Senator Tom Carter of Montana, came up to the press section and said, "Governor Roosevelt wants to see you. Come on down." I can't say I was particularly keen for the meeting. To a somewhat cynical political reporter, a governor of any state was just a governor, and he was nothing more and wouldn't be that much very long. But it suddenly occurred to me that I might gain from him an answer to the question, "Will Roosevelt accept the vice presidential nomination?" So I went down and found the governor most amiable and complimentary. I disregarded his flattery and asked him point-blank, "Will you accept the nomination for vice president?" His face broke into the broadest of his famous grins and he said, "I don't desire the office but there has

been such an apparently unanimous demand from all parts
of the country for my services, that I feel bound to accept.
Now about that article, I wish to say —" But what he
wished to say I never learned. I had only five minutes to
get to the telegraph office and send a flash to my paper. It
was the second and last scoop of my journalistic career.

After he succeeded to the presidency I saw him from time
to time at the White House or at Oyster Bay. In the White
House, my wife and I found him as cordial a host as Mrs.
Roosevelt was a charming and kindly hostess. I must say
that of all the men and women who have occupied this
place in our day, President and Mrs. Roosevelt were so-
cially the most graceful. They seemed to belong there. The
President's table was abundant. I am sure he never tried to
live on his salary and allowance. This much is certain, that
he was less provident than Mr. Coolidge. But he came of
another breed. He drank no spirits himself. He told me
that when he was a boy at Harvard, he got into a fight with
a friend at the Porcellian Club after both of them had
drunk too much whiskey. From that moment, he never
touched the stronger forms of alcohol, but he liked the
French white wines, especially champagne, and took good
care that his guests had plenty of this excellent, if expensive, stimulant. I liked his dinners, but at his lunches we
had what he would call a "bully" time. Mrs. Roosevelt
named them "Dooley lunches" because I once described a
gathering of baseball players, roller skaters, boxers, con-
tortionists and poets as his chosen company for meals. This
was not quite true, but he did like to have amusing people
around him at informal meals and he was utterly indiffer-

ent as to their political position, their social standing, or their wealth. Everybody who wanted to talked up, about art, or politics or poetry or music or war; the President occasionally sending down a booming pleasantry to a friend at the end of the long table. Once he placed me next to M. Jusserand, the French Ambassador. Jusserand and Cecil Spring–Rice were great ambassadors for their countries with Roosevelt in the White House. T.R. felt a deep affection for the Frenchman and Spring-Rice had acted as best man at his wedding in London. Among his other distinctions, M. Jusserand was one of the best living Shakespearean scholars. He spoke the most perfect English with a French accent that made it hard to understand him unless you knew some French. Roosevelt himself was a sound Shakespearean. The three of us first talked about the Baconian theory and agreed that we never knew a man with a spoonful of brains who had really read Shakespeare and Bacon and believed this silly nonsense. Then we got on Shakespeare's plays and there was a lively discussion. T.R. was disposed to question Shakespeare's authorship of *Romeo and Juliet*, recalling, perhaps, the spuriousness of the First Folio of the play. Jusserand began, "But my friend, who but a gr-reat poet could have written zis:

> *Oh, spik again, br-right angel for zou art*
> *As glorious to zis night being o'er my 'ead*
> *As eez a winged messenger of 'Eaven*
> *Unto zee wite upturned wondering eyes of mortals,*
> *Zat fall back to gaze on heem*
> *When he bestrides zee lazy pacing clouds*
> *And sails upon zee bosom of zee air.*

At this moment a soldierly looking man across the table was heard to say to his neighbor, "The Japs have fine artillery. Their shrapnel is wonderful. I once saw a group of twenty men at Port Arthur actually disemboweled by one shell burst."

"What was that? What was that?" the President cried suddenly. "Disemboweled?"

From that moment he left Juliet speechless in the moon on the balcony while he and the major discussed across the table the nature of gunshot wounds in modern warfare.

The ambassador rallied him lightly after lunch.

"I'm sorry," said the President. "I didn't mean to break up our discussion on Shakespeare, but I was deeply interested in what the major said. He was one of our observers at Port Arthur. Major Pershing brought him here."

"It makes little difference," said the Frenchman. "There is quite as much bloodshed as love in Shakespeare — even in *Romeo and Juliet.*"

M. Jusserand himself has told intimately some of his experiences with T.R. One was his appearance at the White House in a silk hat and morning coat and yellow gloves, how the President met him in breeches and heavy walking boots and led him in a hike across country, in the course of which the party were obliged to take off their clothes and swim a cold stream. With all my respect and admiration for this great ambassador, I feel obliged to caution my readers that M. Jusserand was an author as well as a diplomat, in neither of which callings is a man expected to go further in the direction of perfect truth than satisfactory verisimilitude.

T.R. thought a great deal of Spring-Rice, who was a

scholarly gentleman with a rare sense of fun. He liked him better than any Englishman he knew. But, come to think of it, Spring-Rice was an Irishman.

It is surprising how many of the agreeable Englishmen one meets are Irish or Scotch.

As a general thing, T.R. didn't like the diplomats. He thought few of them knew their own business. They were almost as stupid as our own ambassadors. John Fox used to tell of sitting with him when Miss Alice Roosevelt came in.

"Where are you going, Alice?" he asked.

"To a diplomatic reception," she said.

"I suppose," said her father, "there will be many dagoes there. Do you know, John, I divide the human race into two great classes — white men and dagoes. And I don't mind telling you that under the term 'dagoes,' I include the entire diplomatic corps."

Of course this was in fun. But it is a fact that his strong national feeling did lead him often into fierce expressions of animosity to foreign countries. He had the deepest possible love of country — not particularly of its people, or of the form of government molded for them by the retired lawyers on the Supreme Court — but of a spiritual creation, something abstract and intangible that he called America. He was as jealous of her as a lover could be of his mistress, as distrustful of those who sought her good will, as sad over such faults as his doting eye could see in such a heavenly creature, and fiercely resentful of any attack on her honor. He seemed always to have his sword halfway out of its sheath in her defense.

At this point I should like to insert one of many letters I had from him. Most of them have been published by his various biographers. This one I reprint because it paints a picture of his feeling about our foreign relations that is more illuminating than any I could make. Apparently he wrote it at a white heat and with no premeditation.

WHITE HOUSE
Washington

Dec. 3, 1904.

My dear Dunne:

Your letter pleases me so much that I must send you a line in reply. Did you ever happen to read (for your sins) a little volume of mine called *American Ideals?* If you have not, I won't curse you by presenting it to you, but I shall show you some extracts from it when you come on here. I think you will see that I have exactly your theories. You could not protest any more strongly than I would protest against any "social and political campaign among university professors and associations of wholesale pawnbrokers to create an 'Anglo-Saxon alliance.' " I doubt if this movement is as strong now as it was when I was younger. As I said, I shall show you some of the pieces I have written about it, including one I wrote in support of President Cleveland's Venezuelan message — at which time I had promptly volunteered at the War Department for service against England in the event of war.

As I stated in my Frederick the Great statue speech the other day, and as I have stated many, many times, we are not the same as any Old-World race. We are a new race, composed of many Old-World stocks. As you, perhaps, know, I was attacked in the last campaign by the A.P.A. people because of a speech of mine at a New England Society dinner, where, having listened to what I regarded as altogether too much talk about our being transplanted Englishmen, I explained to the assembled guests that I was not English at all and had little English blood

in me; and added that, though it was true I came of one stock
(the Dutch) which the English had overridden in New York,
yet that I also came from another (the Irish) which had in turn
overridden them! As long as I am President there will be no alliance with anybody unless some conditions, which I cannot now
see, arise; but there will be friendliness with everybody. I am as
friendly to the English Government as to the government of
any other European power, but no more so than to any other
government. For the English people I have a sincere regard; and
there are a very limited number of them, like John Morley,
James Bryce, St. Loe Strachey, and my good friend Cecil Spring-
Rice, of whom I am personally fond and whom I like to have
as my guests. But I am not under the slightest illusion about the
English feeling toward us, and the average Englishman is not a
being whom I find congenial or with whom I care to associate.
I wish him well, but I wish him well at a good distance from
me. England has been friendly with us since we have grown so
strong as to make her friendship a matter of more moment to
her than to us. If we quit building our fleet England's friendship
would immediately cool; but I do not think that in this respect
she differs from most of the powers of Continental Europe. If
we get into trouble we cannot count upon the friendship of any
power, or alliance with any power, or blood relationship with
any power; we can count upon our preparedness for war and
upon the fighting edge of our sailors and soldiers. But I do not
want to see bitterness among us against England or against any
other power. I have been a strong homeruler, as you know, and
of course the descendants of the Irish here will cherish bitter
memories against England just as my beloved friend Jacob Riis
hates Germany because of the fate of Schleswig; just as Senator
Nelson hates Russia because of what she has done to the Swedish and Finnish people of Finland; just as Alsatian friends of
mine have hated Germany; as Italian friends have hated Austria.

It is impossible for the American people, or for me, to go into these hatreds, any more than I could have heeded the protest of the Poles against my accepting the statue from the German Emperor. But always remember that I am with you heart and soul in laughing away such a folly as the 'Anglo-Saxon alliance' business. The first part of your article in question pleased me much, and I have myself had letters from Englishmen which exactly and literally reproduced the attitude you described the British public as taking toward the United States; and Sir Edward Clarke's speech at the banquet to Choate the other day reached a point of unconsciously impertinent silliness which could not be caricatured.

I have had a certain share in making the Kiernans of New York a hereditary Harvard family. Kiernan and Daly were two of our best football captains. Nothing has pleased me so much about Harvard — and some things have pleased me very little about Harvard — as the growth of the young Irish, or perhaps I might speak a little more broadly, of the Catholic element in it.

Have you entered Dunne minimus at Groton yet? Pray enter him at once, or he won't get in. All the boys have to be entered in extreme youth. Do write at once and let me know when you have entered him, and I shall send a letter to Endicott Peabody myself about it.

I have been deeply gratified by the support I have received from the young men, Catholic by faith and of Irish descent, this year; and most of all, I am pleased because I got it through no demagogic bid, but because they were convinced that I was their style of a man, and was trying to give everybody a square deal. For instance, I appointed Wynne First Assistant Postmaster General and afterwards promoted him to be Postmaster General; I appointed Lawrence Murray to be Assistant Secretary of Commerce and Labor. As a matter of fact, I did not know that either of them was a Catholic when I appointed him. I appointed each because I thought he was the right man to have in the place. I was pleased to find that they were Catholics, because in the Republican party, until within a short time, there have been so few Catholics, and especially so few Catholics of Irish parentage, that it has been a difficult matter to get them in high position. But of the nine members of the Supreme Court, two are now Catholics of Irish descent; of the seven Ambassadors, one; of the nine members of the Cabinet, one; of the Republican Senators, two; and so on and so on. This is not a bad showing for the Republican party when, as I say, you consider the small percentage of Catholics, and especially of Irish Catholics, which until very recently it has had within the ranks. If Senator Cockrell does not accept the Isthmian Canal Commissionership, I am going to put Major Byrne in. I am the first President who has ever brought the proportion of Catholic chaplains in the army and navy up to the proper level. Twenty years ago I was an ardent worker for the nomination of Phil Sheridan to the Presidency. In fact, my dear fellow, if there has been one thing more than another to which I have bent my energies, it has been to getting all Americans, of whatever creed, and whether of old native or of Irish or German or Scandinavian stock, fused into one people with the same spirit, and governed by the same principle of recognizing in a man nothing whatever but his individual merit.

Goodbye, friend! It is a good thing to have in the country a man to whom a President can write with the frankness and freedom with which I have written to you.

Give my warm regards to Mrs. Dunne.

> Faithfully yours,
> Theodore Roosevelt

I have read this letter over a great many times with delight to think that this fine American felt exactly as I —

an American of Irish parentage — did on this question.

The English, as he pointed out, have always posed a special problem for us. I never had a better time in my life than the months I spent in England, with occasional dashes to Paris and Dublin. The well-bred Englishman is about as agreeable a fellow as you can find anywhere — especially, as I have noted, if he is an Irishman or a Scotchman. If he knows you and likes you he can be the most hospitable of creatures, who will share his (or your) last shilling with you. If England had a decent climate I would rather live there than in any country I know of, provided it was situated in America. But no one who has ever spent much time in England can have failed to observe a slight tinge of contempt mingled with a humorous tolerance, in the attitude of the ruling classes of England towards America and Americans. Of course it is nothing like the aversion, amounting almost to disgust, with which these same Englishmen treat and talk about Canadians, Australians and other "Colonials." Also a great gentleman like Arthur Balfour will conceal it. Perhaps Balfour didn't feel it. He was a real man of the world in the most laudable meaning of the phrase. But a pompous snob like Clarke would show it at once. This rooted animosity to us is something most of our ambassadors to the Court of St. James have overlooked. Indeed, it isn't hard to think that an Englishman in private and an Englishman in public life are two entirely different human animals. In his London club or at his place in the country he may be a man of spotless honesty, open nature, friendliness of spirit and jealous of his honor. But put him in public office where he is called upon to defend his job, his country or what amounts to the same thing, his caste, and he will prove his skill at any diplomatic game from chuck-a-luck to murder.

I have said before that there should be an adequate life of Theodore Roosevelt. Probably in time some wholly detailed mind will apply itself to this work, but it must do so with affection and with honesty and with application of that principle of selection that is the very core of art. The writer will have many documents to study, but one of his main sources of information for the history of this genius and his times must be the reports of his contemporaries, some of them intimate friends and others in a position to observe his acts intimately. His character is not to be caught in the delicate web of a cold and careful contemporary observer. The Roosevelt spirit has threshed itself free of such laces a score of times. And the biographer must be sure of the good faith of his witnesses. Of all sins Roosevelt hated lying most. Yet he was more often accused of double-dealing than any man of his generation. His hatred of falsehood was well known to those who were brought in daily relation to his life, but the slander on his veracity persisted. Of all John Hay's stories of Lincoln, the one that Roosevelt liked best reflected both his abhorrence of untruth and his fondness for physical force as a corrective of sin. In Lincoln's day, people came and gawked in the White House with as much freedom as they do in the Empire State Building today. In fact, Charles A. Dana said that when Secretary Stanton sent him over to the White House to ask what should be done with the Confederate agents to Canada who had been arrested in Maine, he walked straight into the President's office without challenge from anyone. The staff had all gone home. Lincoln came out of the washroom in his shirtsleeves, wiping the soap and water from his hairy arms. Dana told him the nature of his errand. "Dana," said the great President, "what would you do if you had an elephant by the hind leg?" "I'd let him go," said Dana. "Well," said Lincoln, "you go back to Stanton and tell him that."

But it was another Lincoln story that I started to tell when my pen ambled away from it. A cabinet meeting was in session and a man appeared at the door and nodded to the President, who apparently knew him. The visitor spoke with great vehemence. Lincoln smilingly tried to quiet him. But the man grew more violent and was heard to say in a high voice, "Mr. President, I don't believe you are telling the truth." The President said no word in reply. But he seized the visitor by the coat collar and *actually kicked him out of the White House.* With the certain authority of his great physical strength, he held his victim at arm's length and slowly and deliberately booted the man through the anteroom and down the hall to the door and then, releasing him, gave him one magnificent kick down a short flight of stairs to the lawn. Then he returned to the business of the day, only slightly ruffled.

In dealing with stories reflecting on Roosevelt's truthfulness, my biographer must consider the character of the men he was fighting. Of what use would it be to him or his aims to be outspoken to such politicians as Tom Platt, Bill Barnes or Matt Quay or such capitalists as Jim Hill or E. H. Harriman? They were his enemies and the enemies of his faith. Why should he lay his cards on the table before them? No, Theodore Roosevelt was a truth-telling man. He may have practiced what is known in theology as

the "Economics of St. Francis Liguori" — an admirable
saint, but Italian. He was sometimes sparing of facts in
talking with his enemies. Let them draw their own inferences from what he said. The inferences were often vicious.
They were invariably incorrect. But why should he worry
about that? You must never forget that Roosevelt had a
soldier's mind, and that he looked upon his political career
as war against the "forces of evil." "We stand at Armaged-
don and we battle for the Lord," he cried. Dissembling is
an essential part of strategy in war. To accuse Roosevelt of
falsehood because Harriman went away from a visit to the
White House with the impression that Roosevelt had the
same standards of personal integrity that were Harriman's
would be a good deal like calling Robert E. Lee a rascal because he let his soldiers bluff the prudent McClellan by
placing logs fashioned like cannon on their entrenchments.
People are too liable to remember only one part of T.R.'s
famous saying: "Carry a big stick." The other part of the
adage was "speak softly." I think he meant "walk warily,"
for he was not soft of speech.

I must revert again to my belief in the importance of the
individual in the making of history when I repeat that the
financiers and politicians encountered in Theodore Roosevelt a political genius of the first order. Carlyle afforded a
perfect anodyne for the soreness of stupidity when he borrowed from Buffon the saying that genius is the infinite capacity for taking pains. But the frustrate of Cheyne Walk
probably didn't mean that any more than he meant the
other silly things he said. When a genius comes along, the
masses see him and marvel at him as they do at a comet.
The middle class of businessmen find nothing in him to

excite wonder and, if they ever admitted the possibility of
such a thing, would be more liable to ascribe genius to
the Michigan tinker, Henry Ford, than to the Bedford
tinker, John Bunyan. But the highly intelligent classes see
the prodigy clearly. The elder J. P. Morgan, being something of a genius himself, was first to understand Theodore
Roosevelt. He gave way to him over the Reading strike, si-
lenced the fool Baer who had proclaimed that he was or-
dained by God to keep down wages, and saw to it that the
leaders of the union were secretly bribed. He was repaid a
hundredfold when Roosevelt, with utter disregard for the
statutes, let the United States Steel Company grab the
Tennessee Coal Company away from the crippled or bankrupt Grant Schley.

Hill — the railroad Hill — had more of the stigmata attributed to genius by the pathologists. When he was angry
his great hairy face became distorted, his eyeballs turned
in, he stuttered and gasped broken invective and altogether
gave the appearance of a man in an epileptic convulsion. I
have always thought that in 1900 and thereafter, Hill was a
good deal more than half mad. His egomania was terrifying.
His plans for power had been thwarted by Roosevelt, and
when Teddy's name was mentioned, he frothed at the
mouth. I don't mean this as a figure of speech. It is actually
a true description of a physical phenomenon. And what
else but madness could it be in a man to advocate repealing
the immigration laws and flooding this country with
"cheap labor"? He visited this belief on Henry Cannon and
myself one day, when he joined us at lunch at the Savarin
restaurant. I thought he was joking when he cried, "Why
should I have to pay a fireman six dollars a day for work

that a Chinaman would do for fifty cents?" But Cannon, who was his banker and friend, told me he meant what he said, and I was convinced of it when he stopped me later in the day in front of the Sub-Treasury building and, holding me with a paw like a grizzly bear's, pounded my chest with a roll of blueprints while he shouted: "This country is ruined by the wages paid the working men. Let down the bars!" His wildness made him look like a Blake picture of the Prophet Elijah in one of his least playful moods. But he never ascended to Heaven in a spectacular, or any other, way. Roosevelt threw a sprag into a wheel of that chariot and the old fellow died cursing the man who had spoiled his exit.

Yes, Theodore the Great was confronted by the ablest and the most remorseless financiers of all time. They held the politicians in their hands completely. But Roosevelt's intuitions were a thousand times as certain as Hanna's wisdom or the slyness and cunning of Matt Quay and Tom Platt. His political clairvoyance was strengthened by his resentment of the control of government by the "Money Power." Up to his time the direction of legislation at Washington by the rich men of the country was almost taken for granted. Even under Cleveland the public was treated to the spectacle of the Secretary of the Treasury, Carlisle, trying to sneak through the back door of a New York restaurant and get his orders on the Treasury's policy from a small group of Wall Street financiers. But Roosevelt, unlike the average Washington politician, was used to money. It had no sacredness in his eyes. He was brought up among people who had it and he was moderately well off himself. His father had left each of the children between fifteen and twenty thousand a year and you may be sure that this did not diminish when nursed on the ample financial bosom of Edith Roosevelt. To this he added several thousand dollars a year from his writings. It must be remembered also, that he often held highly remunerative public offices. Not as many as Calvin Coolidge who, as the Irish say, "never did a tap of work" from the time he left Amherst College, but lived always on the salaries of the offices he managed to pick up. But at one time or another, Roosevelt was a member of the New York State Legislature, Commissioner of Police in New York City, Civil Service Commissioner, Assistant Secretary of the Navy, Vice President and President. But even if his income had not been supplemented by these windfalls, even if it had been less than his father left him, he would still have felt instinctively the resentment of every man who felt proud of his country and was jealous of its honor against the uncouth usurpation of the government's functions by "malefactors of great wealth."

These "Titans," as the newspapers of the day loved to call them, fought among themselves for control of the northwestern railways with utter disregard of the effect of the brawl on the public interest and the stockholders. Suddenly the President stepped in and smote them hip and thigh. They fought back for a time, but they were beaten the minute the Big Stick whirled.

The three marked capitalists in the battle of 1901 and the years following were Morgan, Harriman and Hill. We thought at the time it was a war of the worlds, but the present generation knows little of it and probably cares less. But in our day it was big stuff and we watched the conduct of the principal actors with profound interest.

Morgan chuckled and conceded defeat with the urbanity of a monarch who has been outmaneuvered in diplomacy by a rival emperor. Hill raved. Harriman was a born gambler and he took his losses with all the aplomb of Jack Hamlin. Roosevelt had destroyed his racket, which was to acquire such political control of New York and other states as would enable him to destroy Morgan's financial ascendancy. He playfully regretted that he and the President didn't see eye to eye on public matters. Each thought he was right. But it was a difference in opinion that made markets and horse races, and so forth. Meanwhile, he coolly bided his time, which came when his adversary turned over the Government at Washington to William Howard Taft.

Taft, with his brother Charlie to nudge his elbow, dealt cards that were entirely satisfactory to the gentlemen who placidly accepted the brevet of "Captain of Industry" or "Empire Builder" and probably really did think they were heroes of that "Romance of Business" of which we subsequently have read a good deal of slop. But the comedy nearly came to an end in 1907, even with its all-star cast. After the great actors had departed this life or retired, it bogged down pretty badly in 1921. It was revived by the speculative fury of the Stock Exchange and by the press agent work of newspaper and magazine writers who spread the delusion that these "financial wizards" of the twenties were all supermen and not — as most of them were — empty-headed and cold-hearted gamblers. Finally, its sham jewels and its tawdry scenery were flooded out by the freshet which the members of the Stock Exchange agreed in pronouncing the "debbicle" of 1929. Toward the end, with all its false splendor, it was fairly shabby to the experienced eye. No one in his senses would think of comparing the clownish troupers of the 1920s, the vendors of poisonous synthetic foods, to the pirates of an older age. Hill and Harriman and Morgan were more of the Drake and Frobisher school; these later were imitations of the kind of pirate that lurks in the backwaters of the Chinese rivers. Who would think of comparing Insull to Rockefeller, "Young Jack" Morgan to "J.P.," Cravath to Whiting, the Van Sweringens to Harriman and Hill?

Yet there are those who still clamor for what they call a "business administration" in Washington. "What we need," says the customer's man in the broker's office, "is a good businessman in the White House." This sounds good to the infatuated oafs (and I to my regret have been one of them) who gamble in stocks on the advice of these gentry. But they delude both their clients and themselves. The belief that a businessman is somehow better qualified than his fellow-citizens to run the country is one of the curious political myths of our time.

It is a fact that up to the time of Herbert Hoover's election no President had ever been a businessman in the strict meaning of the word, and most of them could be described, without detraction, as professional politicians. This includes Jefferson, the Adamses, Lincoln and both Roosevelts.

There is a good reason for this. No two human activities could be more widely separate than the conduct of a business and the government of a nation. Business is a matter of barter and trade for gain. Its essence is to sell something for more than you paid for it and to manufacture, purchase, organize and advertise towards this end. The government has nothing to sell except its own securities and these are readily disposed of at the highest prices to investors who think them safer — even if they are issued by scurvy politicians — than the stocks and bonds of their own companies.

The government, theoretically at least, is intended for the promotion of the general welfare. It has to deal from day to day with the mutable conditions of human kind — its needs, desires, wishes, whims, anxieties, opinions and prejudices — all as changeable as the channels of the Ganges River. The National Administration is supposed to act for the good of the country rather than the private gain of individuals. One of the most successful British Chancellors of the Exchequer, Birkenhead, told me that when he quitted office he was "stony broke." The same was true of the younger Pitt. It was true in some degree also of the two greatest Secretaries of the Treasury in our history: Alexander Hamilton and Hugh McCulloch. And the most prominent "businessman" in government in recent years, if you except Andrew Mellon, was a failure. The good Secretary Alger could compute to a decimal point the cost and selling price of a hundred thousand running feet of pine, but when the logistics of the Spanish-American War were left to him: the transportation of arms, supplies and troops to Cuba, he so boggled the job that if it hadn't been for the vast superiority of our ships, and the greater alertness of the commanders, we should have had a fairly bad time of it during the summer of 1898.

Only a fool would blame poor Mr. Hoover for the market crash of 1929. He was no more responsible for that disas-

ter than he was for the delirium of speculation that pre-
ceded it. But in the following three years of his presidency this capable man of business could do nothing to
halt the decline which followed. He was betrayed by his
background. His experience as a mining stock promoter
was of no use to him in what was essentially a political
crisis. His ideas were laudable, but he failed to act on
them with any sense of conviction. He seemed afraid of
power. It took an unashamed politician in the person of
Franklin Roosevelt to use the government as it was meant
to be used — as a political instrument for the common welfare, the stockbrokers included but not voting.

And so, human nature being what it is, the winds of
abuse blow at gale force from Wall Street towards the
White House. The political fury of the stockbroking caste
against their rescuer is a most peculiar phenomenon. History offers no parallel insanity, except perhaps in the
warped mind of John Wilkes Booth, whose bullet laid
low the one man who might have spared the South the
horrors of Reconstruction.

But then, no American President can wish for greater
fortune than to be cordially hated by his greedier fellow-
citizens. The history books will have little to say of the
nonentities in the White House who only succeeded in bor-
ing the people to death. But Jefferson, Jackson, Lincoln,
Wilson, the two Roosevelts will be remembered for as long
as this republic survives.

Almost the same epithets are being applied to Franklin
as were applied to Theodore. If I ever see F.D.R. again I
must remind him that he is singularly blessed in his enemies — but then, he doesn't need me to tell him about

that. In deliberately inviting the sputtering fire of the arm-chair pirates, he is proving himself as adroit in politics as his great cousin was.

It may be a sign of old age, but it seems to me that to-day's political invective is sharper, fouler, less tolerant than it was in the days of my youth. The patriots of my time spoke freely of the horsewhip and the punch in the nose as legitimate methods of political persuasion, but there was none of today's snarling hatred of an opponent, nor did individuals who blandly accept the designation of "gentleman" invent scatological stories about a political enemy's wife.

An ancient acquaintance of mine, a banker of interna-tional reputation, would cheerfully enter a plot to assassi-nate our President — if he could find someone else to do the deed, put up the money and take the blame! His emo-tions, as in his fiscal dealings, are tempered by his love of betting on a sure thing. Only a few years ago, when his bank nearly went under in the crash, this same fellow came to me in panic and asked what I thought the market would do, asked *me*, as innocent of finance as he is of courage! Fearing the worst, he took Draconian measures. He had his wife fire the servants, the first recourse of all withered plutocrats, and chartered his yacht to a rum-runner. Now, with the greater part of his millions restored, he is ready once more to assert himself in the affairs of state.

He detects a plot to sovietize America, masterminded by none other than my friend Felix Frankfurter, and abet-ted by the columnists Walter Lippmann and David Law-rence. All three, as he points out, are Jews, and therefore a constant threat to pure Aryan financiers. But why waste my time writing of such a mushhead?

I have been asked why I don't do some Dooleys on Adolf Hitler. The answer is that I cannot. Insanity and racial murder are not fit topics for one who would be considered a humorist. I fear that I am like my friend the banker: if I had a gun in my hand and Hitler in front of me I would use it — provided that I had waiting for me a fast getaway car with one of Al Capone's drivers at the wheel. And that is the real tragedy of our age, that those who live by hate contaminate us all and drag us down to their level.

But perhaps the worst thing that has happened to us is that we are losing our political humor. George Ade, who is two years older than I am, tells me that his failing eyes detect the same signs mine do. A candidate for high office these days must ape in dreariness the pronouncements of a Calvin Coolidge or a Herbert Hoover. There is no place for the sly jests of a Lincoln or the Homeric laughter of a Roosevelt. I'm glad that I'm not a young man, for I fear that today, Mr. Dooley's irreverence would be considered treasonable.

But not in Theodore Roosevelt's time. He valued humor on a par with the other qualities which mark the civilized man: intelligence, charity and courage. He even pretended to take as much interest in my work as I took in his. He was good enough to write me in 1907: "Let me repeat that Dooley, especially when he writes about Teddy Rosenfelt, has no more interested and amused reader than said Rosenfelt himself." Since he was my most cherished source of copy, this could be taken to mean that he missed little that

I wrote. Certainly I missed none of his actions. They were my bread and butter. I once listed my assets as a political commentator for him. I put him at ninety per cent. He was always good for a story and the humor wrote itself.

He didn't mind what I said about him because he was a large man. He was even large enough to laugh at himself. Once, at a White House luncheon, he was talking of making a dive in one of the navy's submarines and was extracting much pleasure from the horrified protests of some members of his entourage. He asked me for my opinion and I said that it was perfectly all right for him to go "as long as you take Fairbanks with you." Fairbanks was the fatuous politician who was currently vice president. I will always remember the shocked silence at the table, broken by the President's great booming laugh. He ended the argument by saying that he'd go if I'd go. Since he knew I wouldn't enter a Central Park rowboat on the biggest kind of a bet, he was perfectly safe in making the suggestion.

An era ended with his death. Whichever of the Elysiums his spirit has chosen to roam — and he will have had his choice of them — it will not be a dull place. The saints will have to go disguised as boxers, scholars, jockeys, prestidigitators and — I may hope — minor journalists who see nothing sacrilegious in laughter. And, even in a halo, Theodore Roosevelt will be good copy and a good friend.

Commentary

THE LAST of the essays my father left to me is a tribute to Mark Twain, but, in the pattern of this book, it touches on other subjects as well. It could be subtitled an essay on friendship. I think it is fitting that man's humanity to man should be the theme of the last professional words he ever wrote.

To Peter Dunne, friendship was a large word and a large emotion. When it came to his friends, this caustic wit and deflater of sentimentality was himself a man of deep sentiment. I don't mean this as a paradox; there is the distinction between sentiment and sentimentality.

When he spoke of his friends, he glowed. There is no other word for it. The ties which bound him to them were almost tangible, almost visible.

He spoke often of Mark Twain and always with this same inner illumination. But there was more to their relationship than friendship. There was the tie of mutual professional respect. As my father makes clear in the essay itself, he considered Mark Twain the greatest of American writers: "Emerson and Clemens our greatest writers; Emerson and Clemens, Hawthorne, Poe, Whitman, Abraham

Lincoln." I think this opinion is worth repeating as the final, mature judgment of a professional writer and literary scholar of the first rank.

Mark Twain, for his part, was an admirer of Mr. Dooley and most cordial to his creator. He accepted the younger writer as a compatible professional soul, one of his own breed and stamp. This acceptance was instant and instinctive. They belonged to the same rare species: the American humorist whose work transcended mere humor and became an important social force.

The relationship between the older humorist and the younger was echoed in my father's later friendship with Ring Lardner. Again there was a bridging of generations and again there was mutual professional respect. Again the older man, in this case my father, accepted the younger without question as one of his own select breed.

These three men, Mark Twain born in 1835, Peter Dunne in 1867, Ring Lardner in 1885, embodied a direct line of succession in American letters. Through the channel of their work ran the mainstream of American humorous social criticism. There have been other humorists, and good ones, but no others captured the mood of the country, satirized its foibles, mirrored its soul as effectively as the Mississippi River pilot, the Irish-American reporter and the Michigan sports writer. They were not jokesmiths or gagmen. They were social historians. To read them today is to gain an understanding of the American spirit of past decades few novelists or factual historians can provide.

Their precise and delicate tool was humor. We Americans have always prided ourselves on our humor. We have long boasted of our ability to laugh at ourselves. But I

wonder if our boast hasn't become to some extent an
empty one. My father thought so, as his rueful paragraph
on the subject in the last essay makes clear. We often talked
about it, particularly when the topic of reviving Mr. Dooley came up, as it frequently did.

"Humor," he told me, "especially political humor, is a
privilege of the innocent and the secure. As a nation we
have lost both our innocence and our security. As a matter
of fact, this is true of the entire world. There is little humor
to be found in revolution, and today revolution of one
kind or another is the principal business of mankind. No
one can be permitted to laugh at a cause he must be carefully prepared to die for. The fanatic is the most humorless
creature on earth, but he is the one the people will turn to
more and more as fears and tensions grow less and less tolerable. Humor is only effective as a political weapon when
the victim has enough humor in himself to perceive that
he has been wounded. It couldn't even scratch the hide of a
Hitler or a Stalin, because they are entirely lacking in this
saving grace. A government which is inept or venal or
arrogant can be reformed with humor, but not a government which has become a prison.

"It doesn't matter if the prison state is leftist or rightist,
revolutionary or counter-revolutionary. They're all alike. A
jail is a jail and neither prisoners nor jailers have reason for
laughter. Humor goes hand-in-hand with the independent
spirit. If one declines, so does the other. Only free people
can laugh, and those who forget how to laugh may soon
forget how to be free."

This statement is fished from my memory of many con-
versations. I cannot guarantee its total verbal accuracy ex-

cept for the last sentence, which I wrote down at the time
he spoke it, intending to have him include it in one of the
essays.

If he was right, if a decline in political humor is a symp-
tom of the erosion of liberty, then America has even more
cause for concern today than she did at the time of his
death. The mainstream seems to have dried up. The
mighty torrent has been replaced by aimless rivulets. Most
modern American humor is peripheral, nonvital, safe.
When it comes close to politics, close to the gut interests
of our society, it trickles away. Satire seems as out-of-date
as the whalebone corset and the ambrotype. Of its recent
major practitioners, James Thurber is dead and only E. B.
White, with his delicate and pungent wit, is left to carry on
a great tradition; and even White is not as widely read as
he deserves to be. Perhaps future generations will recog-
nize the brilliance of this unassuming genius. But the present one seems to prefer its politics unsauced with wit.
Politically, we have become as passionate and solemn as
children at play. We have denied ourselves the adult grace
of humor.

In today's uneasy world, caution seems to be the watch-
word among political satirists, where their great predecessors were reckless, irreverent and even raucous. We invite
the smile, the polite titter, but not the great uninhibited
belly-laugh of our grandfathers. We seem to fear that loud
laughter, like Joshua's ungentle trumpets, might blow
down the gossamer walls we have erected in the name of
security. If this is a necessary precaution, the necessity itself should alarm us. I think people would like to laugh.
Motion picture producers can tell you that even inferior

comedies will make money. The infinitely dull comedy shows on television apparently hold vast audiences spellbound. A sports columnist who relieves the dreary solemnity of today's sporting page with a few dim rays of wit is hailed as a major humorist. Yes, people would like to laugh and I suspect they would like to laugh at some of the persons and institutions now, by common usage, taboo. But I wonder if they — if we — still dare.

Perhaps this is the crux of it, as my father sensed. We no longer dare. As he feared, we have begun to equate irreverence with disloyalty. It seems to me that public officials, appointed or elected, need humorous critics as deer need wolves, to kill off the misfits and improve the health and stamina of the survivors. If the wolves are forbidden to perform their natural function, everyone is loser: the humorists, the officials and the public. But as things stand today, few humorists are willing to pay the price of being thought at best cranks and at worst disloyal. Perhaps this explains why the most widely read modern American writers are virtually humorless. Our major novelists and playwrights are concerned with tragedy, disillusionment and decadence. We still search our national conscience, long a native characteristic of ours, but we do it without wit. We have become sophisticated, and therefore sad. We have lost our innocence. Even that once sublimely innocent art, the American motion picture, has succumbed to the same trend.

Certainly to go back and reread Mark Twain and Artemus Ward, Peter Dunne and George Ade, is to recapture a vision of innocence. The Victorian mirage of a constantly improving world still held firm on their horizon.

Their eyes were clear, but clear with optimism. They may have had their doubts about human nature, but there was none of the innate pessimism of a Kafka or an Orwell or a Tennessee Williams. When they struck out at injustice, it was in the faith that justice would ultimately prevail. The same faith glowed more naïvely in the romantic tales of O. Henry and Richard Harding Davis. The shopgirl starving to death in an attic is rescued by a handsome millionaire, the young aristocrat in the Bowery flophouse by the same millionaire's beautiful sister. My father himself said of his friend Davis that his world was one in which "the women are beautiful, the young men gallant and the busdrivers humorous." In this one sentence, he re-created an era now gone beyond recall. But it seemed permanent then.

Finley Peter Dunne was no Pangloss. His optimism was streaked with cynicism and fatalism, as became a son of Ireland. He was far from naïve. But he could not have been a child of his century and not shared the common belief in the permanence and the essential rightness of human progress.

Even the revolutionaries of the nineteenth century were disciples of Victorian permanence. Marx's perfect Communist society was conceived as a permanent cure for the economic ills of man, as Utopian in its way as the fantasies of Wells and as immutable as the perfect laissez-faire state of Ricardo or Bentham.

This sense of permanence, this lovely illusion of security, reached into the social as well as the political life of the time. The family, the home, the land, the business were there to stay, to be received from the father and handed down to the son.

Friendship, too, was permanent. You were bound to your friend by an intangible sacrament, as binding as the tangible sacrament of marriage, stronger even than Polonius's "hoops of steel." When my father called a man his friend he was not referring to a casual acquaintance or a golfing partner but to someone as firmly and as lastingly related to him as the members of his own family.

His friends were an extraordinary group of men and women. They had to be to capture his affection. I knew only a few of them well. Most of them were vague Olympian figures who used to stroll grandly into our house with a puppy for Christmas or to take me for a wildly exciting ride in a Stutz Bearcat.

Theodore Roosevelt I remember mostly as an expanse of serge waistcoat crossed by a heavy gold watch chain. Whenever he came to the house, I was invited to punch this ample target. I would whale away with both hands while the Colonel cried encouragement in the voice which had so often stirred the multitudes. Once, at Oyster Bay, I barked my knuckles on the watch chain and burst into unmanly tears. To my surprise and gratitude, I was not cast into outer darkness but given a piggy-back ride to the bathroom, where the former President of the United States bathed my knuckles in iodine.

I remember the warm, faintly accented voice of Walter Damrosch, when, at a children's concert in Carnegie Hall, he announced that the orchestra would now play Schubert's "Unfinished Symphony at the request of Master

Philip Dunne." I almost suffocated with pride and embarrassment. I needn't have been proud, or at least not for myself. He was paying a compliment to his friend my father, not to me.

The divinity who took me for a ride in his Bearcat was Robert Collier, the publisher, who was my godfather and for many years my father's closest friend.

He was to have been the subject of an entire chapter in these memoirs, but my father died before the chapter could be written. I wish I could fill the gap myself, but beyond the car ride, I have very little personal memory of Bob Collier. He died prematurely in 1918, when I was ten years old. From all my father and others who knew him told me of him, his memory deserves to be kept green. He was a gay, reckless, laughing Irishman. He was the Beau Sabreur of journalism in his time, conducting in his *Collier's Weekly* a hard-hitting but literate crusade for the truth. After his death, *Collier's* fell into the hands of pygmies, was turned into a gutless slick magazine and finally expired of its own inanity, a dissolution by that time long overdue.

Perhaps Bob Collier was fated to die young. He worked hard, drank hard and played hard. The only sports he enjoyed were those which involved the imminent risk of breaking his neck, such as polo, fox-hunting and driving a racing car.

He was one of the very early flyers in this country. I believe that his instructor was the famous English pilot, Tom Sopwith. Flying was a very different affair in 1910 from the safe and managed business it had become in 1940 when my wife and I obtained our licenses. One thing you didn't do in 1910 was fly at night, but Bob Collier did. According to my father, he once flew at midnight from the polo field at Meadowbrook on Long Island to his country place in New Jersey with two friends strapped to the wings of his rickety biplane.

I emphasize the reckless side of his nature mostly to correct a great injustice done him by my own industry a few years back. A motion picture laid in his period presented him as a leading supporting character. It made him, of all things, into a languid society flâneur, a weedy fashion plate with a finely arched eyebrow and a mouth full of hot potatoes. I shall not identify the film because its writer, producer and director are all friends of mine and acted through ignorance rather than malice. The great shame is that they would have had a much better picture if they had done a little research and presented Bob Collier as he really was. The moral of this is: always do your homework. I hope this paragraph will help to soothe my godfather's offended spirit.

He loved elaborate jokes, such as his threat to send Mark Twain a baby elephant for Christmas. The story is told in Albert Paine's readable biography of Mark Twain: the mounting suspense at the Clemens house in the country, the arrival of bales of hay and bushels of carrots, the appearance of a supposed elephant trainer from Barnum and Bailey's circus to prepare the way.

According to my father, the joke originated at lunch one day when Mark Twain remarked that he thought a baby elephant was "the playfullest and most amusing little cuss in the world. I wish I owned one."

"Why don't you buy one?" asked Collier.

"I can't afford it."

"Nonsense. I'll buy you one for Christmas."

"You will? You'll buy me a baby elephant? This is more than anyone could expect. I didn't know there could be such a friendship in this miserable world. Send it along. I'll hang up a stocking for it."

Paine ends his version of the story in something of an anticlimax: merely that the elephant finally arrived, "two feet long and made of cloth and cotton — one of the finest toy elephants ever seen anywhere."

My father quarreled with this understatement. "I wonder if Paine isn't wrong in his conclusion to this tale," he wrote. "The way he tells it is tame and not what I remember, although I had had to go to Europe and didn't come back until after the hoax had been perpetrated. But we had worked on it pretty hard before I left — Collier, Payne Whitney, Frank Garvan and I. We spared no pains in preparing this joke on one of the most painstaking jokers of our period. It was arranged that a special train was to be hired, with a band in the passenger coach and a flat-car in front with an enormous packing case guarded by six Indian mahouts in turbans with ankuses in their hands. The train was to stop at Redfield, the mahouts would salaam, Mark would open the box and pull out hundreds of pounds of excelsior until he came upon a tiny toy elephant from Schwartz's! It was months afterward when I got back to America and I supposed the denouement had taken place as planned. Against even Paine's testimony I prefer to think it did. It was so much more in agreement with the stature of a proper joke on the most gigantic joker of the age. Also it was much more Collieresque." That word "Collieresque" is evocative indeed.

My father's association with Collier was professional as well as personal. In 1915, with Mark Sullivan as editor, he contributed a regular page of editorials and comment to *Collier's Weekly*. One of the principal functions of this page was to present the point of view of Preparedness. In 1917, when Sullivan retired, he took over as editor.

When Collier died in 1918, he bequeathed the property by will to my father, Payne Whitney and Frank Garvan. The three men promptly refused the bequest and turned the magazine over to Mrs. Collier. It appeared that there was not enough in the estate for Mrs. Collier unless the magazine were included. The gesture represented an enormous sacrifice for my father, but he didn't hesitate to make it. It was the final act of a friend, such an act as describes his dedication to friendship far more clearly than any words I can muster.

His friends entered his life at different periods, but all remained his friends to the end. From his Chicago newspaper days there were George Ade, Brand Whitlock and Charles Dillingham, who later became a successful theatrical producer in New York.

Broadway was not my father's true element, but he had many close friends among the theater people, notably Dillingham, Charles Frohman and Ethel Barrymore.

Miss Barrymore had the dubious honor of being my godmother, and my father in turn was godfather to her son Sammy Colt. Miss Barrymore had a sense of humor I can only describe as elegant. When I met her in Hollywood after a lapse of years, I was a little diffident about approaching her, wondering if she would remember me. She noticed my indecision and apparently understood it, for she came straight up to me, held out her hand and said, with the Barrymore smile, "Perhaps you don't remember me, but I'm your godmother." Our professional paths crossed only once, on the motion picture *Pinky*. Her performance won her an Academy Award nomination, in her case a supererogatory honor, but it meant a great deal to me to have contributed to the part in which she won it.

She was one of the few women who could match wit and intellect with my father. She was direct, outspoken and devoid of false pride. He loved to tell the story of a dinner party he and my mother gave at which she was the guest of honor. The guests were assembled in tailcoats and fashionable décolletage, champagne and badinage were flowing, Miss Barrymore as usual was the center of attention, when suddenly the doorbell rang and there on the doorstep stood a gaunt, melancholy young man, hatless and coatless, unshaven, his shoulders hunched against a biting December wind. It was Miss Barrymore's younger brother John. She swept to the door and surveyed him calmly, but with the knowledge that something appropriately dramatic was expected of her. She rose as always to the occasion. "Jack Barrymore," she asked in that unforgettable voice: "have you hocked your overcoat again?"

I wish that my father had lived to write his memories of her. It would have been a chapter informed with love. He loved her for many reasons, but most of all because she could make him laugh. The combination of beauty, brains and talent is not uncommon, but it is rare indeed to find humor as an added ingredient. I believe that her name will be one of the few from the theater to survive our era, and join those of Mrs. Siddons, Bernhardt and Duse in the pantheon of the unforgettable.

Speaking of names, I suspect that these notes may seem to some like an exercise in the popular sport of name-dropping. If so, there is no way I can avoid it. Celebrities have a way of attracting each other. An actor meets all the important politicians, peers and pugilists, a painter or a composer cannot avoid publishers and ladies of fashion. Even an atomic scientist will occasionally be found feeding at Sardi's or Chasen's. An "Establishment," to use the modern phrase, does exist, and within it a celebrity finds his friends among other celebrities. The same thing was true in my father's day. When he moved from Chicago to New York, the writers, politicians and other leaders of opinion were waiting for him. The same sort of reception committee was on deck when he went to Washington and to London. His own fame doomed him to the company of the famous.

It is a pleasure then, to come to one friend whose only claim to public renown was that he had a racehorse named after him. Scholars of racing will remember John P. Grier, Harry Whitney's superb three-year-old whose misfortune was that he came up in the same year as Man O' War and spent his career chasing the chestnut tail of Riddle's nonpareil.

John P. Grier, the horse, will go down in sporting history along with Sir Thomas Lipton and tennis's Bill Johnston as one of the great Second Bests. But John P. Grier, the man, was a first-class human being. My father had known him well in Chicago and had picked him to be best man at his wedding. Before that, they had traveled together in Europe. He was a successful financier and a generous but tough-minded man. After my father's funeral in 1936, he invited me to lunch at the Links Club and lured me into a defense of F.D.R. in that sanctuary of Roosevelt hatred. He told me that for four years he and my father and Wayne Johnson had carried the standard of the Democracy virtually all by themselves. I can't say that I enjoyed the experience. The conversation hadn't lasted ten minutes before a gentleman of seventy, the head of a famous corporation, offered to punch me in the nose for daring to suggest that my friend, that doughty old Bull Mooser Harold Ickes, was not a paid functionary of Moscow. He really believed it. To his amiable mind, any supporter of the New Deal was in fact a traitor. It was no funnier then than now in the telling. It only seemed unreal, and more than a little insane.

Wayne Johnson, another close friend of my father's later years, was a successful corporation lawyer and a most attractive man. In 1934, there was some talk of running him as a Democratic candidate for the Senate from Montana, where he had originated. He asked my father for advice and received a characteristic reply: "My own opinion is that you ought to go out for it. In my time I have talked with many public men and without exception they have maintained that Big Politics (which includes and consolidates all kinds) is incomparably the most satisfactory of human pursuits. The control and leadership of men. That is the thing to exercise the mind to the very end. It seems to be a preservative of health and life too. Statesmen live a long time, unfortunately, in some cases, for their country. In this respect, it is almost as antiseptic as avarice."

The last line is pure Dooley. The rest of the letter echoes the philosophy of William C. Whitney, a man who more than any other single individual influenced the direction of my father's life.

Whitney is one of the great unknowns in American political history. Yet he wrote some of its most important chapters and for many years wielded behind the scenes a power equaled only by that of the much better-known Mark Hanna. As political manager of both Cleveland campaigns, he broke the post–Civil War hegemony of the Republican Party. As Cleveland's Secretary of the Navy, he was a pioneer in developing modern American sea power. He was as successful in private life as in public and made himself a millionaire among millionaires. He was a patron of the arts and a sportsman who first developed the great racing stables now carried on by his grandchildren. But politics remained the passion of his life.

In the young Finley Peter Dunne he found one who shared his enthusiasm for this greatest of all indoor and outdoor sports. An intellectual and witty man himself, he relished my father's intellect and wit.

He has been called my father's Maecenas, but the description doesn't hold, for he offered him no gift but hospitality. There was no need to. My father at the time of their friendship was at the height of his creative powers and was earning what was for a writer a fabulous amount of money. Their relationship was based not on money but on mutual liking and respect. It has been suggested that

Whitney persuaded him to become editor of the New York *Morning Telegraph,* which they hoped to make into a sort of American *Figaro,* primarily as a means of insuring that the daily lunches Whitney delighted in would be continued. Whatever his motives, his sudden death in 1904 put an end to their plans.

My father's friendship with Whitney had two major effects on his life. It taught him the habit of extravagance. Arriving in New York fresh from Chicago, caught up at once in the Whitney circle, he learned no other way to live than the Whitney way. It was not ostentation. You simply felt entitled to the best, demanded it — and paid for it.

It also provided him with two lifelong friends in Whitney's sons, Harry Payne, and Payne. The latter was, with Bob Collier and Frank Garvan, the closest friend he had. Not long after my father's death, a friend of his made the bitter statement that the Whitneys had "ruined Peter as a writer and made him half a millionaire." The reference, of course, was to Payne Whitney's legacy. There was enough of the epigram about this statement to give it some currency around New York at the time.

Not all epigrams are true and in my own opinion this one is false. My father's literary output dwindled for reasons other than his friendships, even those with men of Lucullan tastes. As he himself admitted, when he didn't need the money he found it hard to write, and before the legacy every penny he possessed he had earned himself. And there were other reasons besides his comparative affluence. He had suffered recurring illnesses. To some extent, the prodigal outpourings of his youth had exhausted him. He had run out of appropriate subjects. Finally, in his later

years, the world itself moved out of the purview of the
humorist. As he said in one of these essays, insanity and
racial murder are not fit subjects for humor. And yet a revived Mr. Dooley could not have pretended that such
things didn't exist.

A Mr. Dooley who avoided controversial subjects would
have been unthinkable. Humorists like Will Rogers and
Irvin Cobb could stay cautiously out on the periphery, but
Finley Peter Dunne had won his fame by going straight
to the heart of every issue. He had dared the giants in their
own castles. He made the choice himself: if he could not
laugh, he would remain silent.

As for the two younger Whitneys, they were his friends.
This is an uncomplicated view of the relationship and will
serve as the basis for no epigrams, but it was his own. I see
no reason to improve on it.

He kept many of his old friends in Chicago, notably
Robert Hammill, Michael Monahan and Michael Straus.
His letters to them are a delight, as well as providing vivid
impressions of life in New York at the time. Like many
professional writers, he didn't like to spend his talent on
letters. His stern critical sense required that each letter be
as polished as a professional piece. Those that he finally
brought himself to write are therefore very much worth the
reading. As a curiosity, I should like to quote here a rare
example, a little poem in prose he sent in 1902 to Irene
Langhorne Gibson in response to a verse she had written
to him:

> I never knew, Irene my dear, that you could versify. Although
> it really should be clear to me, at least, you needn't fear to fail
> at anything you try. The Sapphic fragment from your pen is

worthy of a loftier theme. To ask Apollo's helping when you write inflammable men, does not a generous heart beseem. I'm really crushed enough, God knows, at thinking I must stay in town. I hardly could resist your prose and now you try to rhyme me down. . . . I wish I were of noble birth; I wish I wore a coronet. I'd travel all around the earth, I'd fill the world with endless mirth, I'd surely whoop it up, you bet. But now I think of it, I'd not. I never would to Shivaz go or Timbuctoo or Tommyrot. For me there's but one garden spot. It's Greenwood on the C & O. And there I'd thrive, mild and serene, consume the Colonel's mountain grog, play sqush and drive with dear Irene, hold hands with Nanny, fair if lean; and kick the moist and faithful dog. But here I sit to toil condemned, beside the many-voic-ed sea; in sheets of Irish dialect hemmed, my temper sadly sawed and phlegmed (new word), my brow with perspiration gemmed, my chin unshaved, my hair unkemmed, my hatred of the world unstemmed; by doubt distraught, by fear o'erwhe'med. Oh, this demnition grind be demn'd! Come back, Irene, come back to me. From Algy Gordon-Lennox flee; from Fleming and from Fitzhugh Lee. Come back, Irene, to

F.P.D.

"The Colonel" in this foolery is Mrs. Gibson's father, that Colonel Langhorne whom my father used to call "the Chauncey Depew of the South," and "Nanny, fair if lean" is her sister, the about-to-be Lady Astor. The coronet belonged to Gordon-Lennox.

Mrs. Gibson, as a young girl, and in her maturity when I knew her, was the most attractive member of an extremely attractive family. Among the famously beautiful Langhorne sisters, she was prima inter pares.

She was one of those women who gain in charm as they grow older. She had tremendous natural dignity and a wicked wit. In her youth she had been the embodiment of the lovely cool goddesses who did service as the heroines of Richard Harding Davis's literary gallantries, as well as of her husband's famous "Gibson Girl" cartoons. In later years, she retained her shining qualities undimmed.

In my father's soul there lurked more than a little of the condescension towards women which marked the Victorian era. He betrays it in these essays. Women are referred to with conscious gallantry or not at all. They are always the pure and fluffily dressed darlings of the Victorian ideal. But he never condescended to Irene Gibson. He wouldn't have dared.

He loved to tell the story of the one time when he thought he had caught her at a disadvantage, but underestimated the resources of her wit. Before she had married Dana Gibson, she had had many beaux, as boy-friends were called in that more gracious time. Suitors from all over the world had made the pilgrimage to the Langhorne estate in Greenwood, Virginia. Among them had been a titled Englishman of great social and diplomatic prominence. Many years later, this same gentleman came to Washington on a mission for the British Foreign Office. The Gibsons gave a dinner party for him in New York. My father told me the story:

For days before Lord ——'s arrival, Irene tortured Dana with praise of him. His charm, his good looks, his intelligence, his style. She had very nearly accepted his suit and married him. Perhaps she should have. Perhaps she had missed the great opportunity of her life, and so forth. It was all fun, of course, a lady exercising her inalienable right of teasing her husband about a former rival. Dana took it all with his usual good nature and aplomb. After all, they had been married for more than thirty years. Then the paragon arrived. He was bald and fat. He was a crashing bore. His voice resembled the neighing of a horse, and when he laughed — always at his own jokes — a drop appeared and quivered on the end of his nose. His soup gurgled down his gullet with the sound of a bathroom drain in need of a plumber. He drank too much and made remarks about America which did credit neither to his profession nor his breeding. Dana, your mother, and I were exchanging glances across the table, trying to suppress our mirth. Irene appeared unruffled. She presided over the debacle with her usual cool dignity and charm. When her disastrous guest of honor finally left, Dana and I took him to the front door. Then we returned, eager for our moment of triumph. Dana was rubbing his hands in glee and his eyes glowed as Scipio's must have glowed at Zama. Here was a total victory after a lifetime of defeat — here was total revenge. But his Hannibal had disappeared. Irene was nowhere to be found. We searched the downstairs and your mother went upstairs to look for her, without success. Then we heard a small sound — perhaps it was a giggle — and found her. She had crawled under the dining-room table.

The friends of my father's I knew best were those he used to meet at the National Club in Southampton in his later years. There was Judge O'Brien, mentioned earlier in these notes, the patriarch of a vast and attractive clan. There was Patrick Francis Murphy, the erudite leather merchant who was the only nonsoporific after-dinner speaker I have ever heard. I was too young to have heard Chauncey Depew, whom my father had known from his Chicago days and to whom he had once addressed a letter in a famous double pun: "Chauncey M. Depot, care of the Grand Central Depew." But even the celebrated Depew couldn't have been much more entertaining than the elegant and satirical Murphy.

There was Charles B. Macdonald, the founder of the National, a vast, imperious Scotsman who was the target for some of my father's most quoted private jests. When Macdonald, who had introduced the game to America, published a book titled: *Scotland's Gift — Golf,* my father urged him to retitle it: *Scotland's* ONLY *Gift — Golf.* As President of the Links Club, Macdonald endowed his fellow members with an enormous portrait of himself, painted, I believe, by Gari Melchers. It was truly heroic, both in size and conception. It showed Macdonald standing on a wind-swept links in a pose reminiscent of Napoleon at Austerlitz, attended by a diminutive but worshipping caddy. When a new member asked my father whose portrait it was, he answered readily, "Nobody's. It's an allegorical painting representing Modesty."

Macdonald's son-in-law, H. J. Whigham, was also one of my father's lifelong friends. An Englishman by birth, he had been a war correspondent in Cuba in 1898 and then had settled down in New York to make his mark in American journalism. He edited the liberal *Metropolitan Magazine,* to which both my father and Theodore Roosevelt made frequent contributions. Jim Whigham, who became my own friend after my father's death, was famous as a brilliant conversationalist. But once you turned the record on, there was no way to turn it off. Jim would roll on and on, a relentless Mississippi of bon mots and beautifully turned phrases. My father used to employ him as what he called a "Bore Repellent." Once he and some friends were cornered by a particularly obnoxious club bore. The evening had become nearly intolerable; the bore's thick hide had turned away all my father's increasingly pointed shafts, when, as he told it, "Jim Whigham stuck his head into the room. I signaled to him frantically to join us. No ship-wrecked mariner seeing a rescuing craft change course at his signal could know greater joy than I did when Jim cruised over and anchored his stern at our table. I asked him one question to start things off, and that blessed Englishman understood at once what was required of him, leaned forward, fixed his monocle in his eye and began to fire a cannonade of words which in fifteen minutes blasted his victim away from the table and clear out into the street. I even began to feel a little sorry for the poor fellow. He had so clearly met his master."

Bores have always been a natural hazard of club life. Once my father was playing cards with some men at the Racquet Club when a famous specimen of the breed hove into view, obviously looking for a game. One of the men at the table said quickly, "For God's sake don't let him come over here. He's the biggest bore in New York."

"I'll bet you five hundred dollars I know a bigger one," said my father.

"It's a bet. Who's your candidate?"

"Your brother George," said my father, calmly.

The other man glared at him, then pulled out his wallet, counted out five hundred-dollar bills and shoved them across the table. "Take the money," he said. "I didn't know you knew him."

As this anecdote shows, my father's wit was often rough, and sometimes malicious. The story has often been told of how when he was playing golf with the notoriously parsimonious Marshall Field (the first of that name) in Chicago, he advised the merchant to put a dollar bill on his ball, on the grounds that he "could make a dollar go farther than anyone in the world." Of the financier Russell Sage, also a celebrated miser, he wrote a friend: "Russell Sage says he would give thirty cents to see you and he would kill a man for twenty-five." (But my mother had the best Russell Sage story. She had gone with another woman to Sage's office to ask for a contribution to the Red Cross. The millionaire asked to see a list of people who had already contributed. He found the item: "Mrs. Russell Sage, $100." He took his pen, wrote "Mr. and" before his wife's name and handed the list back to my mother. "And what's more," she reported, "he was hurt because I didn't thank him.")

My father had no mercy on Nicholas Murray Butler when that President of Columbia University refused to abandon the Republican Party on the issue of Prohibition. He used him with unreasonable savagery, as once when Butler, in the locker room at the National, accused him of letting himself become portly. He answered, with a great deal more malice than kindliness: "Yes, my fat goes under my belt, but yours goes under your hat."

Sometimes his shot sailed far over the head of its target. This is the price one sometimes pays for too much erudition. He once referred to a somewhat unappetizing New York publisher as a "upas tree," after the fabulous and lethal shrub which is reputed to destroy all life around it. His victim ran into my brother at a party and asked him querulously, "What does your father mean, going around calling me a eucalyptus tree?"

The humorous insult has always been a trademark of American social intercourse. In its lowest form, it is the lingua franca on all levels of male society. "You old son of a bitch" is a common salutation of esteem. Al Smith's emotional grunt of "you old potato" when he was reconciled with F.D.R. is an example.

The dialogue of George F. Babbitt and his friends, as satirically reported by Sinclair Lewis, teems with vapid raillery of this type. On a somewhat higher level, Groucho Marx, Jack Benny and Bob Hope have refined the insult into an entire comedy technique. On a higher level still was Mark Twain's use of affectionate invective, examples of which are quoted in the following essay. My father used it in the same way, not promiscuously, but only when it applied, and always with wit.

His much-beloved friend Frank Garvan used it on all occasions — if he liked you. I could always calculate my current rating with "Uncle Frank" by the degree of virulence in his greeting. If he merely said "Hello Phil," I knew I was in disfavor. If I stood well with him, he was totally unprintable. This rambuctious and opinionated little Irishman was a leader of the New York bar and had held several important posts in government.

Frank Garvan was in many ways the most intimate of my father's friends. It was an easy relationship: the long years of familiarity had eliminated any possibility of unwelcome surprises. Garvan had the gift of total loyalty. In his later years, my father could always count on him for undemanding companionship.

I cannot begin to make a list which would include all of my father's friends. There were too many I didn't know,

or knew only by hearsay. There were the editors and po-
litical writers John Phillips, Ida M. Tarbell, Richard Har-
ding Davis, Ray Stannard Baker, Arthur Brisbane, William
Allen White, Franklin P. Adams, Brand Whitlock, Nor-
man Hapgood, Mark Sullivan and Frederick U. Adams.
There were the novelists, playwrights, philosophers and
essayists William Dean Howells, John Fox, Jr., Thomas
Bailey Aldrich, Rudyard Kipling, Anthony Hope, Hilaire
Belloc, James M. Barrie, William James and Jack London.
In the theater, there were Charles Dillingham, John Drew,
Charles Frohman, Ethel Barrymore, Henry Irving and
Mrs. Patrick Campbell. There were men of politics and
large affairs like the Roosevelts, Al Smith, Felix Frank-
furter, William C. Whitney, Bernard Baruch, Joseph H.
Choate, Charles W. Eliot and Elihu Root.

His friends included men and women, the famous and
the obscure, the radical and the conservative, Americans
and foreigners, drunkards and teetotallers, priests and athe-
ists, near-scoundrels and near-saints. But all were alike in
being large human beings. All were gifted with humor, including the ability to laugh at themselves. My father used
to enjoy exchanging scurrilous stories about Jews with the
great soprano Alma Gluck and equally scurrilous stories
about Catholics with Father Duffy of the "Fighting 69th."
He would damn the Democrats with Al Smith and the
Republicans with Elihu Root.

His tolerance was almost without limit. The latchstring
of the door to his friendship always hung out. He only
barred the pompous, the predatory — and perhaps the pro-
hibitionist. I might add to this alliterative group the people who called him "Pete." This diminutive infuriated him

and no friend of his would have thought of using it. After his death, I could always spot the pretenders among the many who claimed to have been his intimates; they were the ones who referred to him as "Pete," or "Old Pete" or even "good Old Pete." No real friend of his would have thus risked the punch in the nose he so often threatened for impertinence but never, to my knowledge, delivered. (The closest he ever came to actual mayhem was when a Beverly Hills doctor called him "sweetheart" after the fashion of the healers popular among the movie aristocracy. I barely restrained him from whacking the incautious medico over the head with his own stethoscope.)

He accepted the obligations of friendship as well as the benefits. He could and did speak out for Harry Sinclair, the indicted oil millionaire, and Art Young, the radical cartoonist who had been jailed for his political activities during World War I. If he could not approve of what they had done, they were not thereby diminished in his eyes as human beings. He never expected angelic behavior of a species which had not been conceived as angels.

Most of his friends are gone now. A few will survive in the glare of history, a few more in the half-light of specialized scholarship; many have already joined the countless billions of human beings whose fate is the total darkness of oblivion. But to him they were all equal, equally illumined by the light of friendship.

Not all of his friends were contemporaries. Some he never met, except in the spirit. They were those he found in books. In many ways, they were his closest companions, especially in his last years.

All his life he had been an omnivorous reader. He never

went to college, but I will state without hesitation that he was the best-read man I ever knew. Our house was full of books, crowding the bookcases, piled in the hallways, on tables and in the corners of rooms. Each week, a fresh consignment would arrive from his booksellers and every year a truck load was sent off to various charities.

He used to read at night, sometimes all night long. No matter at what time I awoke, I could see the light shining under his door. If I went into his room, I always found him cheerful. I was never quite sure whether he read to relieve his insomnia or welcomed insomnia as giving him further opportunity to read.

Perhaps that is how I remember him best: the faded blue dressing gown round his shoulders, a cigarette pinched between his middle finger and that permanently straight index finger, the bed table and the bed itself piled high with books. The still sharp green eyes would look up through their pince-nez and the wide mouth would spread even wider in a radiant grin. "Come in," he would say. "Come in and we will discuss life and letters." He would shove some books out of the way to make room and we would settle down to a conversation which often lasted until dawn.

In his last year, he began to reread perennial favorites of his, as if to revive and reinforce old friendships as his days drew in. He kept them always at his bedside: Boswell's *Life of Samuel Johnson*, Burton's *Anatomy of Melancholy* and the *Essays* of Montaigne. He spoke of Johnson and Montaigne, each so much like him in so many ways, almost as if they were alive and in communication with him. It was no morbid fancy; it was simply that across the centuries he had made them his friends.

Finally, he added one more volume to this select group: General Grant's *Memoirs*. Grant had written this great work of history while he was dying of cancer of the throat — my father's ailment — in order to pay off his debts and provide for his family. My father could not help but feel a sense of kinship with the old warrior fighting his last lonely battle against a foe far more terrible than the armies he had vanquished.

I have never regretted urging him into his own last battle. I think it helped him to have work to do.

Certainly in all his life he was never afraid of battle. To him it was part of the human condition. To this extent he was a moralist. He felt that each man's passport to society must be earned by contributing his skill or talent to the utmost of his powers. The writer's contribution, as he saw it, was to entertain, to shed light, to cultivate the truth. Throughout his life, his own contribution had been a large one. If these essays succeed in augmenting it, even in the slightest degree, then all the effort that went into their writing was not undertaken in vain.

On Mark Twain

W E ARE NOW, December 1935, celebrating the centenary of Mark Twain's birth and it is almost as funny as anything that great humorist ever wrote.

I'm glad it's being done if it quickens the sale of Mark Twain's books. All through his married life his one dominating thought was the care of his family. When his beloved wife and his beautiful daughter Jean died his affection centered on his surviving child, who returned it by giving all her slender strength toward the softening of his declining years. And even Mark Twain's works needed a certain amount of pushing. At the time H. H. Rogers took hold of his affairs and compelled *Harper's* (through George Harvey) to waken the public to the value of his books, his income from royalties was considerably less than five thousand a year.

Still the centenary is funny. Mark himself would have enjoyed it. He always maintained that although his own success had been due to his appeal to intelligence he would have made much more money if he could have got all the stupid people of the country to buy his books.

His centenary has inflamed to a Mark Twain frenzy all

the hebetude of our fair land. Hundreds upon hundreds of preachers have delivered eulogies on this unbending athe- ist.

A regiment of Boy Scouts stormed the Mayor's office in New York and demanded that he buy the Fifth Avenue house where our genius lived for a few years before his death.

I don't know how many essays have been written about him: "The Real Mark Twain," "The Mark Twain I Knew," "The Mark Twain I Didn't Know," "The Mark Twain Who Kicked Me Downstairs," and so forth. Mark would have enjoyed it. He always had a boyish delight in the circus. Publicity never scared him. If he didn't suffer fools gladly he suffered them patiently. He knew what a vast propor- tion of the population of the world they comprise and how mischievous they can be when their dull prejudices or in- ferior susceptibilities are wounded. But how he would have laughed at their antics in 1935!

Still if any centennial anniversary should be celebrated it is that of our unequaled humorist. Emerson and Clemens our greatest writers; Emerson and Clemens, Hawthorne, Poe, Whitman, Abraham Lincoln. No "centenary" can be too vivacious, no monument too high for him and his fame.

One of the strangest fables that has grown up about Mark Twain is that he was secretly a writer of filthy sexual tales. Indeed, one book reviewer in New York came out the other day in a furious demand on the heir to the Clem- ens estate to produce these mysterious obscenities. He wrote in effect, "You have no right to withhold from the great libidinous American public, which I represent, even the most ignoble utterances of this superb but wicked genius. Give us the dirt!" I'm afraid this apostle of lewdness must remain unsatisfied. One of the reasons why "Mark Twain's Dirty Stories" has never been published is that Mark Twain didn't write dirty stories!

It is sad, but it is true. It was the habit of the good old man to sit up in bed in the morning and write notes or articles on matters that interested him. Most of them were fierce letters to editors of newspapers on things he didn't like. Being a sensible humorist and one unaccustomed to writing for fun, he destroyed these letters after he had spilled all the bile and ill-nature that troubled him in the early mornings and was once again able to take a more cheerful view of life. "I write these things just to keep my hand in," he told me. "A writer must never stop practicing. He can't know when he will be called on to go back to his desk and write for his living. If his hand is out he'll have a hard time. Besides, if I write I can let my breakfast get cold. I was always used to a cold breakfast when I was a young man in the West and I detest piping hot rolls, sizzling bacon and eggs and steaming coffee. When my breakfast is properly chilled I eat it and then resume my writing, like Paderewski who does the five finger exercise for hours every morning . . ."

I didn't know Mark Twain as well as H. H. Rogers did, or William Dean Howells or Thomas Bailey Aldrich or that glorious Irishman Robert Collier, whom he fairly adored. But I saw a good deal of him at one time and my experience agreed with that of his more intimate friends. He never told me a lubricous story. That may have been due to the fact that I never told him one. I find that the wag who has one of these jests to tell can only be sure of an audience in another fellow who has one ready to fire back at him. Not that I have any particular objection to filth as such. I've read a good deal of it, from the *Satyricon* to *Europa*. But I am no good at telling stories, chaste or otherwise. I always forget the point. The only "bad" tale he ever wrote was the *Conversation at the Court of Queen Elizabeth*. But that was in no sense pornographic. It dealt with the same form of amusement that was the subject of Maxfield Parrish's great picture which used to hang behind the bar of the Knickerbocker Hotel, later went to the Racquet Club and now is I know not where.

I must make one exception to my general statement that Mark never told a rowdy story. One day at lunch in London with Edwin Abbey, the painter, he repeated a pleasant talk he had given to a company of art students in Paris. It was not particularly bad. In these days it might be told at a cocktail party of men and women. I have heard worse. But Abbey liked it so much that, at one of those wonderful suppers Henry Irving used to give at the Lyceum on Saturday nights, he called on Mark to repeat the tale. As I say, it was not particularly bad. It would pass without comment in a small crowd. But to attempt to tell it to three score British cabinet ministers, financiers, M.P.'s, barristers and diplomats whom Irving loved to intersperse with his painters, musicians, writers, playwrights and actors was to invite disaster. Mark had not spoken a minute before he knew he had blundered. He told us so after the supper. But he seemed utterly unconcerned amid the general embarrassment. He went on with his tale in that same steady, even drawl that he called his "infirmity of speech," and sat down with a serene smile upon his face amid the furious applause of the four or five Americans present. The only other person at the table who showed amusement at the recital was the host, Henry Irving. He beamed appreciation of the wit of his old crony, whom he had introduced as "My old friend, my deah friend, that great writer whose name is familiar at every English fireside — er — ah — Samuel Mark Clemens." And when Mark sat down the actor shook him warmly by the hand and murmured, "Splendid, old boy. Magnificent!"

But however cleanly his writings were his language at times was enough to raise the hair. Like everybody in the West in his time or even in mine, profanity was part of the currency of ordinary conversation among men. We swore so much that our oaths lost their only true value, that is, as emphasis for a really heartfelt utterance, like the single "damn" in the life history of the old parson at the bridge at Lexington. Mr. Clemens was aware of this failing and warned me against it. He was always warning me against sins that he was equally guilty of or more so. "You should not swear. You should not swear, especially in the presence of the young. I never realized more how powerful the force of example is than I did yesterday. You know I'm a little careless in my language. I'm not as bad as you are, or Collier. I have some respect for the proprieties. But I'll admit I do sometimes forget myself in spite of my attempts to reform. Well, a few weeks ago we hired a waitress, a pleasant, innocent young Irish girl. The second day she quit. She went to my daughter and said, 'I'd like to stay here but I just can't stand Mr. Clemens's language.' My daughter is good at managing people. She made some trifling excuse for me. She said I was insane or had been brought up in Troy or something. Anyhow the girl stayed on. Yesterday I was sitting at the table when I heard her call out to the cook, 'For God's sake Lizzie what in hell's the matter with you? Don't you know that Goddamned old tiger is out there hollering for his chops?' Such, my boy, is the force of example that this innocent child in two weeks had learned to talk as I do, only better. If you give an example, make it a good one. Mine always is, if I stop to think — and have the time."

His power of objurgation was prodigious, appalling, unrestrained. As a rule he felt kindly toward individuals in private or public life. He could put up with most people. But there were three men of whom he never spoke except with rage. One was a bad poet of the same name as his, who traded, or so he thought, on a wholly fictitious relationship. He described this poetaster to George Harvey in language that George, who was himself a free-spoken man, could only repeat in a whisper. Another one of his hatreds was Bret Harte. Once Henry James, the flawless, the sedate, the impeccable Henry asked him, "Do you know Bret Harte?" "Yes," Mark replied readily, "I know the son of a bitch." But it was against William Randolph Hearst that his wildest rage was directed, the same William Randolph Hearst who has appointed himself journalistic master of ceremonies for the centenary. Mark's outbursts against Bret Harte were formidable but his scorn and hatred of Hearst were beyond description. He had never had any business or social relations with the editor and publisher that I know of. It could not have been that Hearst had excited his rage because of attacks on H. H. Rogers, for everybody was attacking his friend at the time and the Hearst newspapers were comparatively lenient. Yet at the mention of the laird of San Simeon the old humorist and philosopher would rake his memory for the invective of the Mississippi steamboat, the western mining camp and the print shop, and pour forth such language as Ernest Hemingway would hesitate to put in the mouth of one of his matadors. And when Hearst ran for mayor or governor, I forget which it was, Mark wrote a lot of scurrilous unprintable doggerel about him which was circulated among his friends. And this may be where the rumor of his pornography began. There must have been some deep reason for this abhorrence. If I ever see Hearst again I must ask him.

With these exceptions the great writer was a mild, kindly, clean-spoken, clean-living gentleman, always most courteous and polite with women, and they adored him. I remember his coming to my house for supper one night. There were other distinguished people there but the ladies had eyes only for him in his white flannels and the crimson gown and mortarboard of a D.C.L. of Oxford. He was immensely popular in England. I am told that when his doctorate was conferred on him the undergraduates at the Sheldonian Theatre outdid themselves in friendly riotousness.

He knew everybody. Princes and potentates everywhere sought him out but he remained unaffected and simple. In his own private circle he was worshipped. I have no other word for it. His friends adored him not only as a great writer but for his own fearlessness, his loyalty, his rightmindedness. He was modest when he was rich, modest and generous; he was undaunted by poverty. In this connection I must tell a story about him while it is in my mind. He was an inveterate cigar smoker. The first thing he did in the morning when he awoke was to light a cigar; the last thing he did at night was to put one out. While money was pouring into his purse from the publishing business in which he had ventured his small fortune, he smoked the best and most expensive cigars. They were quite as good as J. P. Morgan's, who had his made especially for him. But when the crash came, when the publishing business failed, and Mark Twain's fortune disappeared, he went to work as resolutely as Walter Scott or General Grant ever did, to earn and save money to pay his creditors. It was lucky for him that he had a sagacious friend in Rogers so that his term of privation was shorter than that of the great Scotsman. But there was a time when he felt that in honor he could afford no luxury, no indulgence, no waste. His creditors must be paid. And one of the first comforts he put aside was his beloved cigar. But he couldn't renounce it entirely; he had to smoke. In his earliest boyhood in Hannibal he had learned the habit and he had continued it until it was no longer a habit or a luxury. It was a necessity, an essential part of his physical and mental well-being. He made up his mind that if he must smoke or die he would buy only the cheapest cigars. After all, most of our physical pleasures are attributable to a teasing of one or the other of the mucous membranes of the body. For this purpose why wouldn't a bad cigar be as useful as a good one? Why not, indeed? He first interviewed a manufacturer in Philadelphia who turned out a product that was generally known as the Stinkadora Manuro. Mark found these cigars quite bad enough to satisfy his desire for martyrdom but the dealer wanted too much for them. He asked four cents apiece even in bulk and this Mark thought was extravagant. He eventually settled on the popular disinfectant known as the Pittsburgh stogie. These stogies are long, wan tubes, wrapped in the noble tobacco leaves of Connecticut or Wisconsin. I don't know what they are filled with. The aroma suggests at various times excelsior, rubber and leather findings. Mark used to buy them by the bale at an average cost of three cents per cigar. When he went out in the morning he loaded his pockets with them, sometimes carrying as much as fifty or sixty cents worth of them. He was most generous, almost profuse in offering them to his friends. I think he would have been even more so with his enemies. He would have given a whole box to Hearst. If you offered him a Corona Corona or a Romeo and Juliet perfecto, he would wave it aside. "Why do you smoke those things? Such useless extravagance! Sixty cents for a cigar? Good God, man alive, don't you realize that you could feed a whole family in Flatbush for a day on sixty cents if you wanted to? Try one of these of mine. They cost me three cents apiece and *they — are —worth — every — penny of it.* I never think of smoking any other."

So great was his cunning, so engaging his smile when he proffered the poisonous rope, that only a man of iron will could refuse. And the joy on his face as he puffed on his stogie and watched his victim's contortions and choking was positively ecstatic. It seemed at one time as if all his friends would drop away from him. But his fortunes changed suddenly for the better. Through the financial wizardry of Rogers and the intelligent diligence of his publishers, his fears for the security of his family were dissolved and he was again in receipt of a very large income.

At this time he turned up in London. William Gillette,

the playwright and actor, who had known him in Hartford
when Mark's fame was at its zenith, promptly got up a dinner
for him. That was easy enough. No man in London even
at the height of the season would decline an invitation to
meet Mark Twain. The chef of the Savoy was famous and
could be depended on to provide the best of food and
drink. The only thing to trouble the host was how to get
cigars that the guest of honor could smoke. It was clear that
he wouldn't touch a good cigar and there was nothing that
approached a Pittsburgh stogie to be found in London. It
was too late to send to America for a supply. So Gillette,
who was a man of infinite resource, dispatched a messenger
to Italy where he had heard the government tobacco monopoly catered to the most depraved tastes in tobacco. The
agent had some difficulty in finding anything like a substitute for Pittsburgh's greatest gift to the nation. The most
venomous specimens of the government's artistry had
straws in them and to get them going you had to build a
fire under them.

This wouldn't do at all. But eventually in Naples, where
you were sure to find the worst of everything, he discovered
a cigar that bore an adequate resemblance to the stogie. It
was a long, lean cigar, somewhat more swarthy in com-
plexion than the pale chloritic yellowish-green of our American product, but having an aroma that would penetrate the
ordinary gas mask.

Gillette was delighted. After a perfect dinner, a waiter
passed the cigars around. In one hand he carried a box of
Oppenheim's best; in the other a box of the Italian substitute for the stogie, which he placed before the guest of
honor. Mark picked up one of these perilous things, shud-

dered, turned pale and replaced it in the box. Then he cried: "Waiter! Come back here with those actual cigars." And he took a handful and laid them beside his plate.

Gillette was amazed. "Why, Mr. Clemens," he said, "don't you like those others? They are exactly like your stogies."

"That," said Mark, "is one of many reasons why I abhor them."

"But," Gillette said, "you used to like them. You gave them to your friends. You even made me smoke one."

"So I did, William. So I did," Mark responded. "But those were my sad days. I couldn't afford anything better than those disreputable inventions. I suffered but I'm not built to suffer alone. I like to share my distress with my friends. You were one of them. It gave me much pleasure to watch the manly pain you bore for my sake. But there is no longer any need for such playfulness. Please have those dangerous weapons removed. They might catch fire. And remember this, my friend, there is no poorer or more unsatisfactory or more unprofitable form of economy than trying to save money on cigars. Always buy the best, William. Always buy the best."

It was through Robert Collier that I knew Mark Twain — Robert Collier, his much loved friend and mine. Of that journalistic genius I shall speak again in these notes.

In New York after the death of that lovely creature Jean, Mark Twain tried to brighten his life a little by going to theaters, having friends come to his house and making new friends with the younger generation. I was lucky enough to be among this group. He always treated Collier and me as if we were still in our adolescence although when

I first met him in 1899, I had been a hard-boiled newspaper-man for fifteen years, had written four or five books and edited or published about that many newspapers and magazines. He would say, "I like you young fellows. I like to have you around me. But you mustn't expect me to listen to your opinions. They are too immature. Wait till you and Collier have made a reputation. Then you can talk to me and I will stay awake." I think that one day I squared accounts with him for this and similar admonitions. In his last years, he, who had once been rather shy, took hungrily to the publicity that was poured on him. He liked attention; he even demanded it. In the streets of New York he was a more marked figure than Theodore Roosevelt or J. P. Morgan. His noble countenance, his splendid head would distinguish him in any crowd, however great, but when he took to wearing white clothes — a sensible thing to do but a conspicuous one — no one who had ever seen a picture of him in the papers could miss him.

One bright spring afternoon I met him at the crowded corner of Fifth Avenue and 42nd Street. As usual we stopped to exchange our customary banter about the ignorance of youth and the impotence of age. Thousands and thousands of men, women and children passed us and every mother's son and daughter turned his head to look at the picturesque figure. Some of them stopped and listened. At one time there must have been fifteen or twenty typical New York rufuses gawking at him. Mark loved it. His face was aflame. His eyes shone. He talked better and louder than I had ever heard him. Finally I said, "Let's get out of here and go over to the Century and have a drink."

"I'm not a member of the Century. What's the matter with staying here?"

"But aren't you embarrassed standing here in these crowds talking to a celebrity?" I said.

He answered like a man coming out of a trance. His eyes were wide open and staring. He stammered, "Wh-wh-why, do *you* think these people are looking at *you*? Why, you conceited fellow, they're looking at *me!*"

Then the fact dawned on him that youth had at last rebelled. His face broke into a great grin. "Oh, come on over to the Century and have a drink."

"But you just said you weren't a member."

"I'm not. That makes my hospitality all the more remarkable. What could be finer than to entertain a friend at a club where you're not a member?"

"But I'm a member."

"I knew that or I wouldn't have invited you to have a drink."

The most openhanded of men, he loved to pretend that he was stingy. One day I was lunching with him and he said, "This is very pleasant. Why can't we keep it up? Suppose we get some fellows who write for a living and lunch together every Tuesday. Let's see who we'll have. Collier is all right. He is not strictly speaking a man of culture. He is only a publisher. But he has literary associations. So far as a man in his ignorant trade can be, he's a man of letters. How about Howells?"

"He's a great friend of mine. Howells by all means."

"Well, that's settled. We won't have George Harvey. He's a good fellow but he lacks beauty. He is almost homely enough to be good-looking but not quite. How about H. H. Rogers?"

"I thought you said this was to be a literary lunch."

"So it is."

"Then why ask Rogers?"

"Why ask Rogers?" Mark cried. "Why ask Rogers? To pay for the lunch, you idiot."

When I knew him best most of his old friends had died. Only a little while after he had rented the house at 21 Fifth Avenue, Thomas Bailey Aldrich, a great wit and a charming poet and storyteller, ceased to come to New York. He was very ill. Strange how literary reputations flare up and die down. Only a few days ago I had the greatest difficulty in getting copies of those two exquisite drolleries by Aldrich: *Prudence Palfrey* and *Marjorie Daw*. The book salesman had never heard of them.

Aldrich was one of Mark's best friends, so good a one in fact, that when he sent him an autographed copy of one of his books, he inscribed it, "To Thomas Bailey Aldrich from his only friend, S. L. Clemens." But Tom Aldrich was a dying man and only William Dean Howells remained of Mark's earliest friends. He always had a deep affection for the round, rosy-cheeked little novelist, who was among the most delightful writers of his day until he took to using the typewriter, that assassin of style. Howells had a delicate wit, although he could express himself at times with sufficient emphasis about men and things he didn't like. He was by way of being a Socialist, but he never acted on his theories. He disliked and disparaged most of our modern writers. He lost all his smiling good nature when he talked about Stevenson, George Meredith, Rudyard

Kipling, and told me he "couldn't stand them." He was forever digging up unknown writers, chiefly Spanish, and urging American readers to buy their works, although his own Spanish was of the slightest and the authors were even less widely known in Barcelona than in Kansas City. Who can know an author by translation? He thought no episode was possible that he couldn't imagine happening in the little Ohio town where he was born, or in Cambridge, Massachusetts, where he lived as editor of the *Atlantic Monthly*. In spite of his inveterate parochialism, he wrote more than one fine novel. *The Lady of the Aroostook* was one, and *The Rise of Silas Lapham* another; while his little essays composed when he was consul at Venice and called *Venetian Life* are still marvels of delicate fun and graceful English. It seemed strange that intimacy should develop between this mild storyteller, whose vision was limited to the civilities of American life, and Mark Twain, who had actually shot buffalo on the plains, mined for gold, drunk coffee with the desperado and twenty-three-times murderer Slade, and seen men shot and hanged. But if you knew Howells you could understand. For he was always genial even when most dogmatic in his unfavorable opinion of everybody except Flaubert and Mark Twain, from Shakespeare to Stevenson. He was full of drolleries and he did appreciate, if not quite adequately, the genius of Mark Twain. And he put his appreciation in words. So they got on together famously.

Mark was a good deal of a radical in politics — foreign politics. At home he was more conservative. In the Cleveland – Blaine campaign he was a "mugwump." He was conservative but he hated tyranny. He went cheerfully with

Howells and Collier on the committee to receive Maxim Gorki, when the Russian Nihilist came over here, was overwhelmed by a greeting that he knew was far beyond his due as a man of letters, and went home in tears. The New York *World* discovered that Gorki was living at a Fifth Avenue hotel with a lady not his wife, and with the delicacy characteristic of that great journal published the fact and got the hotelkeepers, who had never been known before to ask their guests to show marriage licenses, to kick the poor bewildered Russian into the street. But Mark was never a Socialist or a Communist. He thought too poorly of the human race to believe they could ever be got to live together in amity. "They'll go on murdering each other and robbing each other, cheating each other and lying about each other to the end of time no matter what form of government they choose," he said. Nor was Howells by any means a Marx or a Liebknecht. His candidate for president was Brand Whitlock, whose mild opinions on free trade, civil service reform, government supervision of railways, etc., represented to the kind and gentle novelist the very last word in Revolution.

By the way, Whitlock once came within an ace of being nominated and elected vice president. Brand was a most likeable fellow, an old friend of mine in Chicago where we worked together on the newspapers. He afterwards went to Toledo, studied law with Frank Hurd, and became mayor of the town. In 1916 President Wilson looked about for a Democrat to run with him for vice president and *in petto*, as they say at the Vatican, decided on Whitlock. Brand was indeed well qualified. He was a kind man, a popular public official, an excellent writer. His record as our Minister in Brussels before we got into the war was good. In appearance he was attractive. He had the pleasantest manners in the world and if he had to he could fight and fight hard. But, unfortunately for his future as a statesman, while abroad he fell a victim to the English pronunciation of our uncommon language. The letter "a" destroyed him. Not having gone to Oxford or Harvard, his Boeotian ear betrayed him. So when he went to see the President he told him that the Germans were not the "bond of ruffians" pictured by the papers but "when they left their own lond they lost their gentleness ond condidly adopted harsh measures." He would have been all right if he had stuck to the short a's of Chicago and Toledo. The President knew that perfectly correct language. But Wilson was a schoolmaster and a precisian in English. He quickly erased his old friend's name from his list of potential running-mates. It was a good thing for Whitlock. It enabled him to go on with his writing. This gentle fellow would have hated presiding over the Senate and listening to the billingsgate of such creatures as Heflin and Bilbo. (Was Bilbo in the Senate then? It doesn't matter; there were others of the same stamp.)

Whitlock used to laugh ruefully over this misadventure. "It is all due to my habit of imitation," he said. "I take my color from my surroundings and talk like the people I live with. So does everyone, but I'm the worst. But you've got to admit this much in my favor. If I am an imitator I'm a bad one."

But to get back to Mark Twain. I could talk about him forever, if anyone would listen to me — he was so much the greatest figure in American letters, so much the most picturesque figure in the life of New York; and he had such a capacity for friendship as no other man approached. I don't know when or why it was that he began to dress in white, but he did look fine in those snowy flannels. He hated dyed clothes of any kind but he loathed black clothes as a symbol of death and decay. Once he had a chance to pour out his feelings on this subject. As I have said, Thomas Bailey Aldrich was one of his dearest friends. Aldrich, in fact, was a friendly man. Everybody liked him who knew him. The very thing he said to Oliver Wendell Holmes might be said about him. The doctor was discoursing on his capacity for making friends. "Why," he said, "if I were stranded on a cannibal island and met the king of the cannibals —"

"Yes," said Aldrich, "you would pick an acquaintance with him."

After his death, Mrs. Aldrich decided that some permanent memorial to her husband should be created, so she filled the old frame house at Portsmouth, New Hampshire, with pictures, books, manuscripts and other memorabilia of her husband and made a charming place of it. I was appointed one of the committee to help dedicate this memorial. The committee included also Mark Twain, W. D. Howells, Thomas Nelson Page, R. W. Gilder and Colonel Higginson. One bright, warm June day in 1908 the hundreds of Aldrich's friends who were asked gathered in a hall in Portsmouth. Most of us came from neighboring summer places, and were dressed in our summer clothes, the men in flannels, the ladies in light, fluffy dresses. The hall presented a cheerful appearance, perfectly suited to the character of the good fellow whose memory we were there to honor. That is, it was until there entered upon this gay scene of seasonably dressed, cheerful men and women, young and old, a lank figure, clothed from head to foot in black — black frock coat, black shoes, black tie — and carrying in its hand a black silk hat. It was the evangel of white clothes! It was Mark Twain! He sat down alongside Howells, who immediately began to tease him. "What did you think this was — a funeral in winter?" he said. "You should have worn galoshes and had a crape band on your hat." "I don't give a damn what you say," Mark shouted. "You can't make me feel any worse, any more idiotically foolish than I did when I came in and saw you fellows in flannels and all those darling girls in muslin. It was Paine, my secretary, who I thought was also my friend, who made me dress up like an undertaker. He said these were the commemoration exercises for a dead friend and I must dress in black. I will see him after the meeting. I will do nothing to disgrace myself or my friends. I will not act without thought. But as soon after these exercises are over that I can do so without appearing irreverent I am going to kill him."

Fortunately Mark was not able to carry out his design on his secretary. When called upon he began his speech with a heartrending appeal for sympathy, because he had appeared draped in black. It was genuine, too. But his audience didn't respond in kind to his anger and grief. They started to laugh. Mark Twain looked them over and laughed with them. Then he commenced one of the most rollicking speeches I ever heard. And he and Paine went home arm-in-arm. There was no blood shed.

Once the New York *Evening Post* treated me severely

for something I wrote to the effect that Clemens's writings were not mere drollery, that he could be at times severe, and even harsh. Anyone who will read *Innocents Abroad, Roughing It* and *A Tramp Abroad* will see what I mean. In fact his treatment of his dull, half-educated fellow passengers on the *Quaker City* was deeply resented. Mark Twain was in truth an extremely serious-minded man, subject to long fits of melancholy and disposed to violent opinions on political and religious questions. His *What is Man?* is fully as characteristic of his genius as his *Jumping Frog.* I laughed a great deal more over Artemus Ward when I first read him than I ever did over Mark Twain, and a great deal more over George Ade than over Artemus Ward. But I liked Ade's somewhat sad, quiet tale of Doc Horn better even than I liked the *Fables.* Ade is now a very old man. Why, he's two years older than I am. Think of it! Yet my ancient friend goes on writing with all his old skill. It is remarkable. But it shows that a virtuous simple life invariably is rewarded with a vigorous and happy old age — maybe. I hope I will be able to write as freshly and attractively when and if I get to his age as he does.

But, of course, Mark Twain's greatest friend at the end was Henry Huddlestone Rogers, the active head of the Standard Oil Company of New Jersey. In a vague way I knew that Rogers had helped Clemens out of his financial difficulties, but I had no conception of the magnitude of his assistance. Clemens knew the publishing business thoroughly, especially the "subscription" business, i.e., the sale of books by canvassers, and I believe he never sold his own to "the trade," holding that publishers and booksellers got too much and authors too little out of the existing practices of the business. His niece married Charles Webster, an active figure in the publishing business, and in the eighties Mark went into a partnership with this young fellow, Mark supplying the money and, as it turned out, the large business vision that made the firm of Webster and Company so successful for a while. Their first coup was General Grant's *Memoirs*. Grant, in spite of all his dreary mistakes in business, where he became the prey of Ferdinand Ward, one of the most flagrant swindlers of his time, was still the greatest figure in American life. He and Mark were close friends and the latter had once tried to persuade him to publish his recollections. Now, just as Webster and Company started going Mark heard that The Century Company was dickering with the General for his book. Dickering is the word. The Century people were a nice, gentlemanly, honorable group. But they were timid. They couldn't see their way quite to making an advance payment of twenty-five thousand dollars, although they would spend twice that much printing tiny poems by tiny poets. Mark heard of this and went to see Grant. "Why, General," he said. "I'll give you my check for twenty-five thousand dollars this minute if you promise me the book." Eventually Webster and Company got the *Memoirs*. It was a wonderful book and the sales were unprecedented. Up to 1912 the sum of $450,000 in royalties had been paid to General Grant or his estate. Grant worked and worked and in less than two years had turned in more than three hundred thousand words of copy. All this time he was suffering from cancer of the throat. When his work was finished and he knew his family was safe, he died. He wrote the last page of his *Memoirs* on July 1, 1885. He died July 28, 1885. I think he was glad to die.

Why Webster and Company failed after this start, I don't know. But one day the humorist found that his publishing company was bankrupt and that he himself was faced with the necessity of spending the rest of his life writing to pay off an enormous debt. It was then that Rogers came upon the scene and it was about Rogers that Mark wanted to talk when he called me up one morning and asked me to drop in at "21" on my way downtown.

At that time *Everybody's Magazine,* now extinct, was printing a series of articles by Tom Lawson, whose roguery was almost as much envied in Wall Street, New York, as in State Street, Boston, where he usually operated. In these articles Lawson pretended to expose the wickedness of Rogers and others. He could write pretty well and the publishers of the magazines were so infatuated with the success of his articles that one of them in a public address actually compared him to Jesus Christ!

Mark at once told me why he had sent for me. "Can't you," he asked me, "write a Dooley about —— Lawson and the —— publisher of that —— magazine?" (You can fill in the blanks to suit your taste; go as far as you like and your words will seem shy and delicate in comparison with the original.) "I have tried to flatten out these ——. I have written thousands of words but I am always just cussing. If I could keep my faculty for humor uppermost I'd laugh the dogs out of the country. But I can't. I get too mad."

I told him that although I liked Rogers from what little I knew about him, I couldn't go to the defense of any of the

Standard Oil people. I was brought up in the West to hate
the Rockefellers. Also I felt that Lawson and his gang were
pretty cheap game. "I suppose so," he said. "But never
mind. I don't imagine Rogers would want you to, anyway.
He doesn't mind these attacks much."

I was glad afterwards that I didn't write the article. When
I got to know Rogers better we talked about Lawson. "I
never saw the fellow for more than five minutes in my life.
You don't suppose I'd have that kind of vermin around my
office, do you?"

"Then why don't you denounce his lies?"

"That's the trouble," said Rogers benignly. "Lawson is a
liar when he says I talked to him at any length on any subject. The most I ever did was to give him a broker's order
and that through my secretary. But Lawson is getting his
stuff from Burrage, an old partner of mine who has since
turned on me. Burrage and I worked together and as we
were fighting thieves we had to use the weapons and methods most convenient for that kind of a scrap. Burrage tells
Lawson of talks he and I had together, Lawson magnifies
them a hundred diameters, paints them in terrible colors,
dresses them up fantastically and puts them out as parleys
between himself and me. They are really lies as he tells
them but there is enough truth in them to make it awkward
to contradict them."

But to return to 21 Fifth Avenue and Mark Twain.

"I wonder," he said, "if you ever heard what Rogers did
for me? No? Well, when Webster and Company failed I
was all but destroyed. I had assumed that I was to be a man
of leisure for the rest of my life, with an income more than
enough to pay for all the necessities and luxuries of life and

to provide amply for my family. Of course I would write occasionally, but only to amuse myself and my friends. The
dream was too beautiful to last. One day I found that I
must grind out copy for the rest of my days to pay my
creditors. I was hopeless. And some of the creditors were angry, impatient and mean. Then Rogers came to my rescue.
I had never done a single thing for him in my life. He was
a much pleasanter companion for me than I was for him.
He was blessed with the greatest gift of humor I have ever
known in any man. I never had to cheer him up but often
he pulled me out of one of those infernos of melancholy
that I am liable to fall into at any time. When he heard of
my troubles he came straight to me and offered to handle
my financial affairs. Besides the Webster concern I was
heavily interested in a company that owned patents for a
typesetting machine. Rogers said, 'Let me handle these people. You stop walking the floor.' Unfortunately the machine was a failure and is now in some museum. Then he
turned his attention to the publishing company and decided that it must be placed in bankruptcy at once. This
was done and Rogers, who was himself a considerable cred-
itor, called a creditors' meeting. He didn't like the way
some of the creditors were acting. He thought they were
heartless. Most of them had made plenty of money out of
us, much, much more than we owed them, but these fellows were the most exacting of the lot. That hardened Rogers and when he was hard, he was hard. He settled down to
a nice quiet talk with these men. 'Gentlemen,' he said, 'you
all know how deeply I feel toward Mr. Clemens. He is my
best friend. But business is business and we must not let
our sentiments interfere with our interests. I therefore pro-

pose that we turn over the copyrights on Mr. Clemens's books to Mrs. Clemens, to whom the company owes sixty thousand dollars, and keep for ourselves the tangible assets, such as presses, type, furniture, etc. This may seem hard on Mrs. Clemens but — well, business is business, you know, and I think she will realize considerable out of these copyrights — in time.'

"And," Mark went on, "it turned out that the copyrights were by far the most valuable assets of the company. The presses and furniture and other things went for not more than a quarter of the debt but from the copyrights I was able to pay the creditors to the last cent."

What Rogers had seen in Mark Twain's books was what Mark himself had seen in Grant's *Memoirs* — that is, their enormous possibilities. But these possibilities must be developed. So this true friend went to work and applied all his genius in finance to re-establishing the Clemens fortune. I don't know what were his financial relations with George Harvey, then the head of Harper Brothers, but they were of a nature to cause Harvey to sign a contract with Clemens whereby for a long term he was to receive a minimum of (I have been told) thirty-two thousand a year and as much more as the books could earn in royalties. The whole came to a large sum, for under energetic management, the books sold in great numbers and our good Mark was not only able to pay his creditors in full but to live at ease and to leave a substantial estate. And it all came out of Rogers's quick decision to appeal to the venality of these rapacious small-time financiers and give them the comfortable feeling that they were robbing an unprotected woman.

But Rogers did not stop here. He continued to direct the Clemens fortunes. He invested Mark's money for him and always, strangely enough, in stocks that rose in value. "He is a wizard," Mark said. "He never makes a bad investment. Every single thing he has done for me has been profitable."

Now that he was handling Mark's affairs Rogers was in his element. He put all his skill in finance, all his adroitness, all his reputation at the service of his friend. Charles Frohman, a great theatrical producer and a great man, thought he would like to present a play made out of *Huckleberry Finn.* He consulted his partners and they agreed to finance the enterprise. He saw Mark Twain, and Mark turned him over to Rogers. Mark always had an extraordinarily high opinion of the Jews as a group. He liked them. He thought they were far, far more intelligent than any other people. He was to learn how badly matched the smartest of them was against a New Englander who had been trained in finance by John D. Rockefeller. The first thing Rogers did was to invite the group to 26 Broadway.

Charlie Dillingham told me the story.

"They were dumbfounded by the invitation," said Charles. "All except Charles Frohman and myself. I was the only goy in the group and Rogers knew me. And Frohman, as you know, cared little about money, was quite as bold as Rogers and would have bankrupted himself to produce what he thought was an artistic success. But to the others twenty-six Broadway was a Holy Place — the more Holy because Forbidden. In Rogers's office they were anesthetized by an atmosphere not of millions or hundreds of millions but of billions. Even Abe Erlanger was silent and a little pale. As for Al Hayman, whose favorite saying at a meeting when some famous writer's or artist's name was brought up, was: 'What's the use of talking about that guy? He ain't got a cent,' Al would have taken off his shoes at the door if anyone had suggested it. Rogers was all courtesy, all soothing politeness. He talked seriously about the theater, frivolously about finance. Finally, he said, 'Well, gentlemen, we are all busy men' — at the word 'we,' old man Harris gulped — 'so let's get to work on this contract with Mark Twain. I think you will find it satisfactory.' And he produced the contract. They pretended to read it but I don't think they did. Finally Erlanger, who in the course of any business meeting always swore he was being gypped and threatened to punch somebody in the nose, remarked, 'Gentlemen, I think we can agree on anything our friend Mr. Rogers proposes.' At the words 'our friend' Rogers beamed. They all signed and were escorted to the door. We went uptown to Hayman's office and spent that afternoon in a discussion over the division of the profits and made so much noise that the neighbors sent for the police."

"Would there have been a great profit if the play had not failed?" I asked.

"Listen," Charles replied. "Do you know what forty thousand dollars a week gross represents? You don't, of course. Well, I'll tell you. It represents capacity at the New Amsterdam. And if we had played to capacity at the New Amsterdam, after paying Mark Twain's royalties and the playwright's and the high-priced company which was the only kind that Charles Frohman would ever manage, and the other expenses, we might have come out even. I don't say we would. But we might. After that experience Al Hayman never liked to hear us talk about Rogers. He never spoke ill of him but he seemed to think the mere mention of Rogers's name was a reflection on his own aptitude for business."

No wonder Mark Twain could write about Henry Rogers in *A Tribute* which Rogers would not let Paine publish: "His character is full of fine graces but the finest is this: that he can load you down with crushing obligations and then so conduct himself that you never feel their weight. If he would only require something in return. But that is not his nature; it would not occur to him. He was born serene, patient, all-enduring where a friend is concerned. He is not only the best friend I have ever had, but is the best man I have known."

Mark emphasized the delicacy of Rogers's generous offices. The irritable genus of authors has a greater hatred of patronage than most people. They rebel against what Patrick Francis Murphy used to call "the unconscious arrogance of conscious wealth" — an arrogance that has caused more revolutions than the most savage misrule. A notable instance of this was Richard Henry Stoddard's reply to Andrew Carnegie's invitation to dinner. Andrew didn't know Stoddard but that didn't prevent him from asking anyone to dinner. He thought he was conferring a favor. The furious poet replied, "For his ignorance and his impudence Mr. Andrew Carnegie one day will find himself in bed with his arse done up in arnica."

We talked about Rogers by the hour. I had no thought that twenty years later a similar generosity would be extended to a minor humorist when the great heart of Payne

Whitney rescued him from the abyss of debt into which he had been plunged by reckless gambling. I think that if Payne had lived he would not have left me a fortune by will. He would have "worked my affairs" out. He was Rogers's equal in business acumen when he found it was necessary to exercise a quality on which he placed no great value. He was as cool as Rogers, as indefatigable, and his financial resources were much larger. I could say with equal truth of him what Mark Twain said of his friend: "I have not known his equal among men for lovable qualities." I am sure that if he had lived he would have worked with characteristic patience to get me out of my difficulties and would have done it in such a manner as to relieve me as much as possible from a sense of obligation. But he didn't have time. The summons of Death was too urgent. He knew that his life might end at any moment. He must hurry to save his friends. So in great haste he changed his will and left me a bequest that enabled me to pay all my debts and walk again with my head erect. For this I will bless him — and his — forever.

Mark once said he and I would collaborate on an essay "De Amicitia" that would be better than Cicero's. He once said of me, "he is blessed beyond reason with friends." Beyond reason is right. But reason has no more to do with friendship than money, or propinquity, or kindred pursuits or anything else that you can mention and say, "This is why they are friends." It consists of imponderables infinitely remote from the comprehension of those meager souls who think of the sources of friendship as something tangible.

I have indeed been singularly blessed with friends, and

I never lost one except by death. I have also been blessed
with my enemies. They comprise some of the worst writers
in the world. Sometimes I am scared by the thought that
they hate me because I am really one of them and have escaped from their dingy company by miraculous good luck.
Perhaps so. But I am indifferent to what they say or think.
They are the scum of the earth.

The saddest feature of old age is not one's own progressive enfeeblement, but the loss of one's friends. Many of
mine are dead. In a short time — or so I am advised — I
may meet them in Paradise, that is, if they are satisfied
with their surroundings and they have not thought the
regulations too irksome. Otherwise I shall probably find
them camping out somewhere in ultra-stellar space, for
they were all independent fellows, and if things didn't go
well with them wouldn't hesitate to go forth and rough it
for all eternity. But I think they will be in Heaven, for
their sins were such as a loving Father could only smile
upon, and they harmed no one except in battle.

Postscript

IT IS OFTEN said that the reason Mr. Dooley is read today only by scholars and political experts is that the Irish dialect presents an insurmountable hurdle to the modern lay reader. The brogue, what my father called "the mild and aisy Elizabethan English of the southern Irishman," is no longer a familiar sound in our land.

I am often asked why the articles were written in dialect in the first place. Finley Peter Dunne was a master of lucid and graceful English, as he proved in the nondialect essays he wrote for *Collier's Weekly* and the *American Magazine*. Why then did he deliberately take the risk of obscuring his message by writing in a dialect which might not outlive — and which indeed has failed to outlive — the era in which it flourished?

Franklin P. Adams has given what I believe to be the correct answer: "The expression of that social consciousness as articulated in the Dooley sketches would never have been printed unless they were written in dialect. For editors, fearful of calling names, feel that the advertisers and the politicians and the social leaders — money, politics and social ambition being the Achilles heels of editors and publishers — are journalism's sacred cows. But if pretense and hypocrisy are attacked by the office clown, especially in dialect, the crooks and the shammers think that it is All in Fun. And when the Dunnes and the Lardners die, the papers print editorials saying that there was no malice in their writing and no bitterness in their humor. Few popular writers ever wrote more maliciously and bitterly than Lardner and Dunne. They resented injustice, they loathed sham, and they hated the selfish stupidity that went with them."

This fits in perfectly with my father's own version of how he happened to begin writing in dialect: "While I was writing editorials for the [Chicago] *Post*, we became engaged in a bitter fight with the crooks in the city council. McAuliff [the editor] and I were both municipal reformers but our publisher wasn't so eager. He was nervous about libel suits and loans at banks that were interested in the franchises for sale in the council. It occurred to me that while it might be dangerous to call an alderman a thief in English no one could sue if a comic Irishman denounced the statesman as a thief . . . I think the articles were effective. The crooks were ridiculed by their friends who delighted in reading these articles aloud in public places, and, as they were nearly all natural Irish comedians, doing it well. If I had written the same thing in English I would have inevitably been pistoled or slugged, as other critics were. But my victims did not dare to complain. They felt bound to smile and treat these highly libelous articles as mere humorous skits."

In his later years, my father felt keenly his obvious losses in general readership. Granted that some of the articles which dealt with specific political events and personalities of their time were already dated, there were many others which were timeless and deserved to survive as literature. Only the dialect apparently stood in their way.

For this reason, he acceded to the urging of his friends and "translated" a few of the articles into plain English, with the intention of publishing them. I include them here in a final section with some of my own favorites I have taken the liberty of "translating" in the same way. I have chosen widely different topics in order to provide the broadest possible sample of my father's work. In some cases I have followed his precedent in editing the text.

I have also "translated" a few choice Dooleyisms which can stand by themselves out of their context. They are samples of the lines that were read aloud at a million American breakfast tables when they appeared in the newspapers, and made Mr. Dooley the wit, sage and national folk-hero of his time.

"Archey Road" was what the Irish of my father's youth called Chicago's Archer Avenue, stretching from the heart of the city to the quiet suburbs. Here — "forninst th' gas-house and beyant Healey's slough and not far from the polis station" — lived Martin Dooley, saloonkeeper and Doctor of Philosophy.

In F.P.D.'s words: "He reads the newspapers with solemn care, heartily hates them, and accepts all they print for the sake of drowning Hennessy's rising protests against his logic. From the cool heights of life in the Archey Road . . . he observes the passing show, and meditates thereon. His impressions are transferred to the desensitized plate of Mr. Hennessy's mind, where they can do no harm."

Father Kelly is the parish priest. Hogan is a friend whose erudition enables Mr. Dooley to make an occasional classical or literary allusion.

A Book Review

This is one of the best-known and most frequently quoted of the articles. It led directly to the friendship between F.P.D. and Theodore Roosevelt.

"Well, sir," said Mr. Dooley, "I just got hold of a book, Hennessy, that suits me up to the handle, a grand book, the grandest ever seen. You know I'm not much troubled by literature, having many worries of my own, but I'm not prejudiced against books. I am not. When a real good book comes along I'm as quick as anyone to say it isn't so bad, and this here book is fine. I tell you 'tis fine."

"What is it?" Mr. Hennessy asked languidly.

" 'Tis 'The Biography of a Hero by One who Knows.' 'Tis 'The Daring Exploits of a Brave Man by an Actual Eye Witness.' 'Tis 'The Account of the Destruction of Spanish Power in the Antilles,' as it fell from the lips of Teddy Roosevelt and was taken down by his own hands.

"You see it was this way, Hennessy, as I read the book. When Teddy was blown up in the harbor of Havana, he concluded there must be war. He debated the question long and earnestly and finally passed a joint resolution declaring war. So far so good. But there was no one to carry it on. What should he do? I'll let the genial author tell the story in his own words:

" 'The Secretary of War had offered me,' he says, 'the command of a regiment,' he says, 'but I couldn't consent to remain in Tampa while perhaps less audacious heroes were at the front,' he says. 'Besides,' he says, 'I felt I was incompetent to command a regiment raised by another,' he says. 'I determined to raise one of my own,' he says. 'I selected from among my acquaintances in the West,' he says, 'men that had traveled with me across the desert and storm-wreathed mountain,' he says, 'sharing my burdens and at times confronting perils almost as great as any that beset my path,' he says. 'Together we had faced the terrors of the large but violent West,' he says, 'and these brave men had seen me with my trusty rifle shooting down the buffalo, the elk, the moose, the grizzly bear, the mountain goat,' he says, 'the silver man, and other ferocious beasts of those parts,' he says. 'And they never flinched,' he says. 'In a few days I had them perfectly tamed,' he says, 'and ready to go anywhere I led,' he says. 'On the transport going to Cuba,' he says, 'I would stand beside one of these rough men treating him as an equal, which he was in everything but birth, education, rank and courage, and together we would look up at the admirable stars in that tolerable southern sky and quote the Bible from Walt Whitman,' he says. 'Honest, loyal, true-hearted lads, how kind I was to them,' he says.

" 'We had no sooner landed in Cuba than it became necessary for me to take command of the army, which I did at once. A number of days were spent by me reconnoitering, attended only by my brave and fluent bodyguard, Richard Harding Davis. I discovered that the enemy was entrenched on the top of San Juan hill immediately in front of me. At this time it became apparent that I was handicapped by the presence of the army,' he says. 'One day when I was about to charge a blockhouse sturdily defended by an army corps under General Tamale, the brave Castilian that I afterwards killed with a small ink eraser that I always carry, I ran into the entire military force of the United States lying on its stomach. 'If you won't fight,' says I, 'let me go through,' I says. 'Who are you?' says they. 'Colonel Roosevelt,' says I. 'Oh, excuse me,' says the general in command (if my memory serves me true it was Miles) rising to his knees and saluting. This showed me it would be impossible to carry the war to a successful conclusion unless I was free, so I sent the army home and attacked San Juan hill. Armed only with a small thirty-two which I used in the West to shoot the fleet prairie dog, I climbed that precipitous ascent in the face of the most galling fire I ever knew or heard of. But I had a few rounds of gall myself and what cared I? I dashed madly on, cheering as I went. The Spanish troops were drawn up in a long line in the formation known among military men as a long line. I fired at the man nearest to me and I knew by the expression of his face that the trusty bullet went home. It passed through his frame, he fell, and one little home in far-off Catalonia was made happy by the thought that its representative had been killed by the future Governor of New York. The bullet sped on in its mad flight and passed through the entire line, finally embedding itself in the abdomen of the Archbishop of Santiago eight miles away. This ended the war.'

" 'There has been some discussion as to who was the first man to reach the summit of San Juan hill. I will not attempt to dispute the merits of the many gallant soldiers, statesmen, correspondents and Kinetoscope men who claim the distinction. They are all brave men and if they wish to wear my laurels they may. I have so many anyhow that it keeps me broke having them blocked and ironed. But I will say for the benefit of Posterity that I was the only man I saw. And I had a telescope.'

"I have tried, Hennessy," Mr. Dooley continued, "to give you a fair idea of the contents of this remarkable book, but what I've told you is only what Hogan calls an outline of the principal points. You'll have to read the book yourself to get a true conception. I haven't time to tell you the work Teddy did in arming and equipping himself, how he fed himself, how he steadied himself in battle and encouraged himself with a few well-chosen words when the sky was darkest. You'll have to take a squint into the book yourself to learn those things."

"I won't do it," said Mr. Hennessy. "I think Teddy Roosevelt is all right, and if he wants to blow his own horn leave him do it."

"True for you," said Mr. Dooley, "and if his valiant deeds didn't get into this book, it would be a long time before they appeared in General Shafter's history of the war. No man that bears a grudge against himself will ever be governor of a state. And if Teddy did it all he ought to say so and relieve the suspense. But if I was him I'd call the book *Alone in Cuba.*"

Shaughnessy

F.P.D. sometimes sang in a minor key, particularly in the earlier sketches. John McKenna was Mr. Dooley's first "straight man." Later he was replaced by Mr. Hennessy.

"John," said Mr. Dooley, "when you come to think of it, the heroes of the world — and by them I mean the lads that have buckled on the gloves and gone out to do the best they could — they're not in it with the quiet people you never hear of from one end of the year to another."

"I believe it," said Mr. McKenna, "for my mother told me so."

"Sure," said Mr. Dooley, "I know it's an old story. The world's been full of it from the beginning; and will be full of it till, as Father Kelly says, the payroll's closed. But I was thinking more of it the other night than ever before, when I went to see Shaughnessy marry off his only daughter. You know Shaughnessy — a quiet man that came into the Road before the fire. He worked for Larkin, the contractor, for near twenty years without skip or break, and saw the family grow up by candlelight. The oldest boy was intended for a priest. It's a poor family that hasn't someone that's being educated for the priesthood while all the rest wear themselves to skeletons for him, and call him Father John or Father Mike when he comes home once a year, lighthearted and free, to eat with them.

"Shaughnessy's lad went wrong in his lungs, and they fought death for him for five years, sending him out to the West and having masses said for him; and poor devil, he kept coming back cross and cruel, with the fire in his cheeks, till one day he lay down and says he: 'Pa,' he says, 'I'm going to give up,' he says. 'And I only ask that you'll have the mass sung over me by some man besides Father Kelly,' he says. And he went, and Shaughnessy came clumping down the aisle like a man in a trance.

"Well, the next one was a girl, and she didn't die, but the less said the sooner mended. Then there was Terrence, a big, bold, curly-headed lad that cocked his hat at any man — or woman for the matter of that — and that broke the back of a policeman and swam to the crib, and was champion of the South Side at handball. And he went. Then the good woman passed away. And the twins they grew to be the prettiest pair that ever went to first communion; and one night there was a light in the window of Shaughnessy's house till three in the morning. I remember it, for I had quite a crowd of William Joyce's men in, and we wondered at it, and went home when the lamp in Shaughnessy's window was blown out.

"There was the one girl left — Theresa, a big, clean-looking child that I saw grow up from hello to good evening. She thought only of the old man, and he leaned on her like a crutch. She was out to meet him in the evening; and in the morning he, the simple old man, would stop to blow a kiss at her and wave his dinner-pail, looking up and down the road to see that no one was watching him.

"I don't know what possessed the young Donahue, from the Nineteenth. I never thought much of him, a stuck-up, easy-come lad that never had anything but a civil word, and is president of the sodality. But he came in, and married Theresa Shaughnessy last Thursday night. The old man took on twenty years, but he was as brave as a general of the army. He cracked jokes and he made speeches; and he took the pipes from under the elbow of Hogan, the blind man, and played 'The Wind that Shakes the Barley' till you'd have worn your leg to a smoke for wanting to dance. Then he went to the door with the two of them; and says he, 'Well,' he says, 'Jim, be good to her,' he says, and shook hands with her through the carriage window.

"Him and me sat a long time smoking across the stove. Finally, says I, 'Well,' I says, 'I must be moving.' 'What's the hurry?' says he. 'I've got to go,' says I. 'Wait a moment,' says he. 'Theresa will' — he stopped right there for a minute, holding to the back of the chair. 'Well,' he says, 'if you've got to go, you must,' he says. 'I'll show you out,' he says. And he came with me to the door, holding the lamp over his head. I looked back at him as I went by; and he was sitting by the stove, with his elbows on his knees and the empty pipe between his teeth."

Christian Science and Doctors

"What's Christian Science?" asked Mr. Hennessy.

"It's one way of getting the money," said Mr. Dooley.

"But what's it like?" asked Mr. Hennessy.

"Well," said Mr. Dooley, "you have something the matter with you. You have a leg cut off."

"The Lord save us!"

"That is, you think you have," Mr. Dooley went on. "You think you have a leg cut off. You say to yourself, 'More expense. A wooden leg.' You think you have lost it but you're wrong. You're as well as ever, only you don't know it. You call up a Christian Scientist, or your wife does. Not many men are Christian Scientists, but nearly all women are, in one way or another. Your wife calls up a Christian Scientist, and says she, 'My husband thinks he's lost a leg,' she says. 'Nonsense,' says the Christian Scientist, she says, for she's a woman too. 'Nonsense,' says she. 'No one ever lost a leg,' she says. 'Well it's strange,' says the wife. 'He's mislaid it, then,' she says, 'for he hasn't got it.' 'He only thinks he's lost it,' says the Christian Scientist. 'Let him think it on again. Let him put his mind to it,' she says, 'and I'll put mine, and we'll put our minds to it, and it will be all right,' she says."

"Sure, it's foolishness," said Mr. Hennessy.

"Well, sir, who can tell?" said Mr. Dooley. "If it wasn't for medical progress, I'd be sure the Christian Scientists was wrong. But the doctor who attended me when I was young would be thought as lunatical if he was alive today as the most Christian Scientist that ever reduced a swelling over a long distance telephone. He introduced near the whole parish into this life of sin and sorrow; he gave us calomel with a shovel, bled us like a police captain; and never thought any medicine was good if it didn't choke you going down. I can see him now as he came up driving an old gray and yellow horse in a buggy. He had whiskers that he could tie in a knot around his waist, and him and the priest was the only two men in the neighborhood that carried a gold watch. Everybody thought he was a great man, but they wouldn't let him treat a spavin in these days. He'd tackle anything from pneumonia to premature baldness. He never heard of microbes and neither did I till a few years ago when I was told they was a kind of animal or bug that crawled around in you like spiders. I saw pictures of them in the papers with eyes like poached eggs till I dreamed one night I was a hayloft full of bats. Then the young Doc down the street set me right. He says the microbes is a vegetable and every man is like a conservatory full of millions of these potted plants. Some are good for you, and some are bad. When the tuberoses and geraniums is flourishing and lifting their dainty petals to the sun, you're healthy, but when the other flowers get the best of these nosegays 'tis time to call in a doctor. The doctor is a kind of gardener for you. It's his business to encourage the good microbes, making two pansies grow where one grew before, and to hoe out the Canadian thistles and the milkweed.

"Between the Christian Scientist and the Doc it's a question of whether you want to be treated like a lunatic or like a can of preserved vegetables.

"Father Kelly says the styles of medicine change like the

styles of hats. When he was a boy they gave you quinine for whatever ailed you and now they give you strychnine and next year they'll be giving you prussic acid. He says they're finding new things the matter with you every day and old things that have to be taken out until the time is coming when not more than half of us will be real and the rest will be rubber. He says they ought to enforce the law of assault with a deadly weapon against the doctors. He says that if they knew less about poison and more about gruel, and opened fewer patients and more windows, there'd not be so many Christian Scientists. He says the difference between Christian Scientists and doctors is that the Christian Scientists think there's no such thing as disease, and doctors think there isn't anything else. And there you are."

"What do you think about it?" asked Mr. Hennessy.

"I think," said Mr. Dooley, "that if the Christian Scientists had some science and the doctors more Christianity, it wouldn't make any difference which you called in — if you had a good nurse."

The Pursuit of Riches

"Dear me, I wish I had money," said Mr. Hennessy.

"A man," said Mr. Dooley, "has more fun wishing for the things he hasn't got than enjoying the things he has got. Life, Hennessy, is like a Pullman dining car: a fine bill of fare but nothing to eat. You go in fresh and hungry, tuck your napkin in your collar, and square away at the list of groceries that the colored man hands you. What'll you have first? You think you'd like to be famous, and you order a dish of fame and bid the waiter make it good and hot. He's gone an age, and when he comes back your appetite has departed. You taste the order, and says you: 'Why it's cold and full of broken glass!' 'That's the way we always serve fame on this car,' says the waiter. 'Don't you think you'd like money for the second course? Mister Rockefeller over there has had forty-two helpings,' says he. 'It don't seem to agree with him,' says you, 'but you may bring me some,' you say. Away he goes, and stays till you're bald and your teeth fall out and you sit drumming on the table and looking out at the scenery. By-and-by he comes back with your order, but just as he's going to hand it to you Rockefeller grabs the plate. 'What kind of a car is this?' says you. 'Don't I get anything to eat? Can't you give me a little happiness?' 'I don't recommend the happiness,' says the waiter. 'It's canned, and it killed the last man that tried it.' 'Well, gracious,' says you, 'I've got to have something. Give me a little good health, and I'll try to make a meal out of that.' 'Sorry, sir,' says the colored man, 'but we're all out of good health. Besides,' he says, taking you gently by the arm, 'we're coming into the depot and you'll have to get out,' he says.

"And there you are. You'll never get money unless you fix the waiter and grab the dishes away from the other passengers. And you won't do that. So you'll never be rich. No poor man ever will be. One of the strangest things about life is that the poor, who need the money most, are the very ones that never have it. A poor man is a poor man, and a rich man is a rich man. You're either born poor or rich. It doesn't make any difference whether you have money to begin with. If you're born to be rich you'll be rich, and if you're born to be poor you'll be poor.

"A poor man, Hennessy, is a man that refuses to cash in. You don't get anything for nothing, and to gather in a million of those beautiful green promises you have to go down every day with something under your arm to the great pawnshop. When you want four dollars, you hock the clock. When Rockefeller wants ten million, he puts up his peace of mind or his health or something equally valuable. If you'd hock your priceless habit of sleeping late in the morning, you'd be able to tell the time of day when you get up without going to the corner drugstore.

"I have a lot of things around here I could cash in if I cared for money. I have the priceless gift of laziness. It's made me what I am. I have my good health. You can always raise money on that. And I have my friends. I don't know that I could get much on them, but if I wanted to be a millionaire, I'd tuck you and Hogan and Donahue under my arm and carry you down to the pawnshop.

"No, Hennessy, you and I, my friend, weren't cut out to be millionaires. If you had nothing but money, you'd have nothing but money."

"Life is full of disappointments," said Mr. Hennessy.

"It is," said Mr. Dooley, "if you feel that way. It's true that a good many have tried it, and none have come back for a post-graduate course. But still it ain't so bad a career for a young man. You never get what you order, but it's pretty good if your appetite ain't keen and you care for the scenery."

The Power of Love

On St. Patrick's Day, 1897, Bob Fitzsimmons knocked
out Jim Corbett in the fourteenth round with his famous
"solar plexus punch" to win the heavyweight championship of the world.

This short piece was Ring Lardner's favorite Dooley.
Lardner used a similar obliquely humorous approach
twenty-five years later in his famous coverage of a World
Series. But *The Power of Love* is a great deal more than a
humorous report of a prize fight.

"It was this way," said Mr. Hennessy, sparring at Mr. Dooley.
"Fitz led his right light on the head, then he stuck his thumb in
Corbett's heart, and that was the end of the fight and of Pompa-
dour Jim. I told you how it would come out. The punch over
the heart did the business."

"Not at all," said Mr. Dooley. "Not at all. It was Mrs.
Fitzsimmons did the business. Did you see the picture of that
lady? Did you? Well, it would have gone hard with the lad if
he'd lost the fight in the ring. He'd have to lose another at
home. I'll bet five dollars that the first lady of the land licks
the champ without the aid of a stove lid. I know it.

"As my good friend John L. Sullivan says, it's a great comfort to have little reminders of home near by when you're

fighting. John had none, poor lad; and that accounts for the way he went down at last.

"The home influence is felt in every walk of life. When Corbett was pounding the first gentleman of the land like a man shingling a roof, the first lady of the land stood in the corner, cheering on the bruised and bleeding hero. 'Darling,' she says, 'think of your home, my love. Think,' she says, 'of our little child learning his catechism in Rahway, New Jersey,' she says, 'and paste him,' she says, 'in the slats. Don't hit him on the jaw,' she says. 'He's well-trained there. But tuck your loving hooks into his diseased and aching ribs,' she says. 'Ah, love!' she says, 'recall the happy golden days of our courtship, when we walked the country lane in the light of the moon,' she says, 'and hurl your maulies into his hoops,' she says. 'Hit him in the slats!'

"And Fitz looked over his shoulder and saw her face, and strange feelings of tenderness came over him; and he thought to himself: 'What is so good as the love of a pure woman? If I don't nail this large man, she'll probably kick in my head.' And with this sacred sentiment in his heart he went over and jolted Corbett one over the laths that retired him to the home for decayed actors.

"It was a woman's love that did it, Hennessy. I'll make a bet with you that, if the first lady of the land had been in the ring instead of the first gentleman, Corbett wouldn't have lasted one round. I'd like to have such a wife as that. I'd do the cooking, and leave the fighting to her. There ought to be more like her. The trouble with the race we're bringing up is that the fair sect, as Shakespeare calls them, lacks interest in their duty to their husbands. It's the business of men to fight, and the business of their wives to make them fight. You may talk of the immorality of nailing a man on the jaw, but it's in this way only that the world increases in happiness and the race in strength.

Did you see anyone the other day that wasn't asking to know how the fight came out? They might say that they regarded the exhibition as brutal and disgusting, but divvle a one of them but was waiting around the corner for the returns.

"Father Kelly mentioned the scrap in his sermon last Sunday. He said it was a disgraceful and corrupting affair, and he was ashamed to see the young men of the parish taking such an interest in it in Lent. But late Wednesday afternoon he came bustling down the street. 'Nice day,' he says. It was pouring rain. 'Fine,' says I. 'There was no parade today,' he says. 'No,' says I. 'Too bad,' says he and started to go. Then he turned, and says he, 'By the way, how did that foul and outrageous affair in Carson City come out?' 'Fitz,' says I, 'in the fourteenth.' 'You don't say,' he says, dancing around. 'Good,' he says. 'I told Father Doyle this morning at breakfast that if that red-headed man ever got one punch at the other lad, I'd bet him a new cassock — Oh, dear!' he says, 'what am I saying?' 'You're saying,' says I, 'what nine-tenths of the people, laymen and clergy, are saying,' says I. 'Well,' he says, 'I guess you're right,' he says. 'After all,' he says, 'and under all, we're mere brutes; and it only takes two lads more brutal than the rest to expose the streak in the best of us. Force rules the world, and the churches are empty when the blood begins to flow,' he says. 'It's too bad,' he says. 'Tell me, was Corbett badly hurt?' he says."

The Crusade Against Vice

"Vice," said Mr. Dooley, "is a creature of such hideous mien, as Hogan says, that the more you see it the better you like it. I'd be afraid to enter upon a crusade against vice for fear I might prefer it to the virtuous life of a respectable liquor dealer. But anyhow the crusade has started, and before many months I'll be looking under the table when I sit down to a peaceful game of solitaire to see if a policeman in citizens' clothes ain't concealed there.

"The city of New York, Hennessy, sets the fashion of vice and starts the crusade against it. Then everybody else takes it up. There's crusades and crusaders in every hamlet in the land and places that are cursed with nothing worse than pitching horseshoes send to the neighboring big city for a case of vice to suppress. We're in the midst of a crusade now, and there isn't a policeman in town who isn't trembling for his job.

"As a people, Hennessy, we're the greatest crusaders that ever were — for a short distance. But the trouble is the crusade doesn't last after the first sprint. The crusaders drop out of the procession to take a drink or put a little money on the ace and by the time the end of the line of march is reached the boss crusader is alone in the job and his former followers are hurling bricks at him from the windows of policy shops. The boss crusader always gets the double cross. If I wanted to send my good name down to the generations with Cap Kidd and Jesse James I'd lead a movement for the suppression of vice.

"You see, Hennessy, it's this way: the lads elected to office and put on the police force are in need of a little loose change, and the only way they can get it is by negotiating with vice. Tammany can't raise any money on the churches; it won't do for them to raid a gents' furnishing store for keeping disorderly neckties in the window. They've got to get the money where it's coming to them and it's only coming to them where the law and vile human nature have a strangle hold on each other. A policeman goes after vice as an officer of the law and comes away as a philosopher.

"Well, the lads go on using the revised statutes as a sandbag, and by and by the captain of the police station gets to a point where his steam yacht bumps into a canoe of the president of the Standard Oil Company and then there's the divvle to pay. It's been a dull summer anyhow and people are looking for a change and a little diversion, and somebody who doesn't remember what happened to the last man that led a crusade against vice, gets up and, says he: 'This here city is a veritable Sodom and it must be cleaned out,' and everybody takes a broom at it. The churches appoint committees and so does the Stock Exchange and the Brewers' Society and after a while other organizations jump into the fray, as Hogan says. The man that objects to canary birds in windows, street-music, vivisection, profanity, expensive funerals, open streetcars and other vices, takes a hand. It is resolved by the Insomnia Club that now's the time to make a flying wedge against the divvlish hurdy-gurdy and meetings are called to burn the police in oil for not arresting the criminals who sell vegetables at the top of their lungs. Someone invents an anti-vice cocktail. Lectures are delivered to small bodies of preachers on how to detect vice so that no one can palm off counterfeit vice on them and make them think it is good. The police become active and when the police are active it is a good time for decent men to wear marriage certificates outside of their coats. Heinous monsters are nailed in the act of hoisting in a shell of beer in a German Garden; husbands wait in the police station to be ready to bail out their wives when they're arrested for shopping after four o'clock; and there's more joy over one sinner returned to the station than for ninety and nine that have reformed.

"The boss crusader is having the time of his life all the while. His picture is in the papers every morning and his sermons are a directory of places of amusement. He says to himself 'I am improving the world and my name will go down to the generations as the greatest vice buster of the century. When I get through there won't be enough crime left in this city to amuse a stranger from Hannibal, Missouri for twenty minutes,' he says.

"That's where he's wrong. After a while people get tired of the pastime. They want somewhere to go nights. Most people ain't vicious, Hennessy, and it takes vice to hunt vice.

"That accounts for policemen.

"Besides, the horse show or the football game or something else exciting diverts their attention and one day the boss crusader finds that he's alone in Sodom.

" 'Vice ain't so bad after all. I notice business was better when it was rampant,' says one lad. 'Sure you're right,' says another. 'I haven't sold a single pink shirt since they closed the faro games,' says he. 'The theater business ain't what it was when there was more vice,' says another. 'This ain't no Connecticut village,' he says. 'And it's no use trying to introduce sumptuary legislation in this imperial American city,' he says, 'where people come pursued by the sheriff from every corner of the world,' he says. 'You can't make laws for this community that would suit a New England village,' he says, 'where,' he says, 'the people are too uncivilized to be immoral,' he says. 'Vice,' he says, 'goes a long way toward making life bearable,' he says. 'A little vice now and then is relished by the best of men,' he says. 'Who's this reformer lad anyhow, interfering with the liberty of the individual and,' he says, 'making it hard to rent houses on the side streets?' he says. 'I bet you if you investigate you'll find that he's no better than he should be himself,' he says. And the best the boss crusader gets out of it is to be able to escape from town in a wig and false whiskers. Then the captain of police that's been spending his vacation in the district where a man has to be a Rocky Mountain sheep to be a policeman, returns to his old place, puts up his hat on the rack and says, 'Garrity, if anybody calls you can tell him to put it in an envelope and leave it in my box. And if you got a good man handy I wish you'd send him over and have him punch the bishop's head. His Grace is getting too gay.'

"And there you are, Hennessy. The crusade is over and vice is rampant again. I'm afraid, my lad, that the friends of vice are too strong in this world of sin for the friends of virtue. The good man, the crusader, only works at the crusade once in five years, and only when he has time to spare from his other duties. It's a pastime for him. But the defense of vice is a business with the other lad and he nails away at it, weekdays and Sundays, holy days and fish days, morning, noon and night."

"They ought to hang some of them politicians," said Mr. Hennessy angrily.

"Well," said Dooley, "I don't know. I don't expect to gather calla lilies in Hogan's turnip patch. Why should I expect to pick bunches of spotless statesmen from the graduating class of the house of correction?"

The Philippine Peace

This bitter and courageous article had a direct effect on the course of American policy. It was one of several powerful blows struck by F.P.D. against the cruelty and hypocrisy of colonialism as our once innocent nation had begun to practice it in the Philippines. In another article he satirized a popular American view of the islanders: "It is not for those wretched and degraded creatures, without a mind or a shirt of their own, to give lessons in politeness and liberty to a nation that manufactures more dressed beef than any other imperial nation in the world."

"It's strange we don't hear much talk about the Philippines," said Mr. Hennessy.

"The reason is," said Mr. Dooley, "that everything is perfectly quiet there. We don't talk about Ohio or Iowa or any of our other possessions because there's nothing doing in those parts. The people are going ahead, garnering the products of the soil, sending their children to school, worshipping on Sunday in the churches and thanking Heaven for the blessings of free government and the protection of the flag above them.

"So it is in the Philippines. I know, for my friend Governor Taft says so, and there's a man that understands contentment when he sees it. The Filipinos, he says, are satisfied with our rule. And I believe him. A man that isn't satisfied when he's had enough is a glutton. They're satisfied and happy and slowly but surely they're acquiring that love for the government that floats over them that will make them good citizens without a vote or a right to trial by jury. I know it. Governor Taft says so.

"Says he, 'The Philippines is one or more of the beautiful jewels in the diadem of our fair nation. Formerly our fair nation didn't care for jewels, but did up her hair with side combs, but she's been abroad some since and she came back with beautiful golden hair that is better for having a tiara. She is not as young as she was. The simple home-loving maiden that our fathers knew has disappeared and in her place we find a Columbia, gentlemen, with maturer charms, a knowledge of European customs and not averse to a cigarette.

" 'The Philippines raise unknown quantities of produce, none of which fortunately can come into this country. My business kept me in Manila or I would tell you what they are. Besides, some of our loyal subjects are getting to be good shots.

" 'Passing to the political situation, I will say it is good. Not perhaps as good as yours or mine, but good. Every once in a while when I think of it, an election is held. Unfortunately it usually happens that those elected have not yet surrendered. In the Philippines, the office seeks the man, but as he is also pursued by the soldiery, it is not always easy to catch him and fit it on him. The country may be divided into two parts, politically — where the insurrection continues and where it will soon be. The brave but I fear not altogether cheery army controls the insurrected parts by martial law, but the civil authorities are supreme in their own house. The difference between civil law and martial law in the Philippines is what kind of coat the judge wears. The result is much the same. The two branches work in perfect harmony. We bag them in the city and they round them up in the country.

" 'It is not always necessary to kill a Filipino American right away. My desire is to educate them slowly in the ways and customs of the country. We are giving hundreds of these poor benighted heathen the well-known, old-fashioned American water cure. Of course you know how it is done. A Filipino, we'll say, never heard of the history of this country. He is met by one of our sturdy lads in black and blue who asks him to cheer for Abraham Lincoln. He refuses. He is then placed on the grass and given a drink, a bayonet being fixed in his mouth so he cannot reject the hospitality. Under the influence of the hose that cheers but does not inebriate, he soon warms or perhaps I might say swells up to a realization of the grandeur of his adoptive country. One gallon makes him give three groans for the Constitution. At four gallons, he will ask to be wrapped in the flag. At the dew point he sings "Yankee Doodle." Occasionally we run across a stubborn and rebellious man who would strain at my idea of human rights and swallow the Pacific Ocean, but I must say most of these little fellows are less hollow in their pretensions.

" 'Naturally we have had to take a good many customs from the Spaniards, but we have improved on them. Among the most useful Spanish custom is reconcentration. Our reconcentration camps are among the most thickly populated in the world. I was talking with a Spanish gentleman the other day who had been away for a long time and he said he wouldn't know the country. Even the faces of the people on the streets have changed. They seemed glad to see him.

" 'I have not considered it advisable to introduce any fads like trial by jury of your peers into my administration. Plain straightforward dealing is my motto. A Filipino at his best has only learned half his duty to mankind. He can be tried but he can't try his fellow man. It takes him too long. But in time I hope to have them trained to a point where they can be good men and true at the inquest.

" 'I hope I have told you enough to show you that the stories of disorder are greatly exaggerated. The country is progressing splendidly, the ocean still laps the shore, the mountains are there and apparently quite happy; the flag floats free and well-guarded over the government offices, and the cheery people go and come on their errands — go out alone and come back with the troops. Everywhere happiness, content and love of the step-mother country, except in places where there are people. Gentlemen, I thank you.'

"And there you are, Hennessy. I hope this lucid story will quiet the wagging tongues of scandal and that people will let the Philippines stew in their own happiness."

"But sure they might do something for them," said Mr. Hennessy.

"They will," said Mr. Dooley. "They'll give them a measure of freedom."

"But when?"

"When they'll stand still long enough to be measured," said Mr. Dooley.

Youth and Age

"I see that Teddy — " Mr. Dooley began.

"Don't be disrespectful," said Mr. Hennessy.

"I'm not disrespectful," said Mr. Dooley. "I'm affectionate. I'm familiar. But I'm not disrespectful. I may be burned at the stake for it. Whenever anything happens in this country, a committee of prominent businessmen, clergymen and college professors meets and resolves to go out and lynch a few familiar Democrats.

"I wonder why it is the clergy is so much more excitable than any other people. You take a man with small side whiskers, a long coat and a white choker, a man that wouldn't harm a spider and that floats like an Angel of Peace, as Hogan says, over a mixed quartette choir, and let anything stirring happen and he'll send up the premiums on fire insurance. Let a bad man do a bad deed and the preachers are all for quartering everybody that can't recite the thirty-nine articles on his head. If somebody starts a fire, they grab up a can of kerosene and begin to burn down the block. It is a good thing preachers don't go to Congress. When they're calm they'd wipe out all the laws and when they're excited, they'd wipe out all the population. They're never two jumps from the thumbscrew. It is queer that the best of men at times should feel like the worst toward those between.

"But anyhow, I see that Teddy is the youngest President we've ever had, and some of the papers are wondering whether he's old enough for the responsibilities of the office. He isn't afraid, but a good many are, that a man of only forty-two or three, who hasn't lost a tooth, and maybe has gained a few, a mere child, who ought to be playing 'Run, sheep, run,' at Oyster Bay, will not be able to conduct the business of Government with the proper amount of infirmity.

"I wonder sometimes, Hennessy, when is a man old enough. I've seen the age limit rising ever since I went into public life. When I was a young lad, a fellow would come out of college or the reform school or whatever was his alma mater, knock down the first old man in his way and leap to the front. Every time school let out, some aged statesman went back like Cincinnati to his farm and was glad to get there safely. You could mark the progress of youth by the wreck of spectacles, gold-headed walking sticks, unreal teeth, and pretended hair.

"In the old days, a man was a man when he voted — at twenty-one in Boston, at eighteen in the sixth ward. A man of thirty was counted mature, a man of forty was looked on as a patriarch and when a man got to be fifty, the family put his chair in the corner and gave him the back bedroom.

"But nowadays, by heavens, a man doesn't get started till he's too old to run. The race of life has settled down to something between a limp and hobble. It is the old man's time. An orator is a boy orator as long as he can speak without the aid of a dental surgeon; an actor is a boy actor until he's so old he can't play King Lear without putting a little of the bloom of youth on his cheeks out of the youth-jar. There's no such thing as age. If Methuselah were alive, he'd be captain of a football team. When a man gets to ninety, he's just beginning to feel strong enough for work. Anybody that tries to do anything before he's an uncomfortable risk for the life insurance company is snubbed for youthful impertinence.

"They say respect for old age is gone out. That may be true, but if it is so, it is because us old lads are still doing things on the trapeze. I don't want any man's respect. It means I don't count. So when I come to think it over, I agree with the papers. President Teddy is too young for the office. What is needed is a man of — well, a man of my age. And I don't know as I'm quite ripe enough. I'm going out now to roll my hoop."

"Go on with you," said Mr. Hennessy. "When do you think a man is old enough?"

"Well," said Mr. Dooley, "a man is old enough to vote when he can vote, he's old enough to work when he can work. And he's old enough to be President when he becomes President. If he ain't, it will age him."

On Titans of Finance

This is a combination made by F.P.D. of two articles written on the same subject. The misbehavior of what Theodore Roosevelt called the "malefactors of great wealth"
was an obvious and favorite target of Mr. Dooley.

"Well, sir," said Mr. Dooley, "I see the Titans of Finance
have clutched each other by the throat and engaged in a death
struggle. Glory be, when business gets above selling tenpenny
nails in a brown-paper cornucopia, it's hard to tell it from murder."

"What's a Titan of Finance?" asked Mr. Hennessy.

"A Titan of Finance," said Mr. Dooley, "is a man that's got
more money than he can carry without being disorderly. There's
no intoxicant in the world, Hennessy, like money. It goes to the
head quicker than the whiskey the druggist makes in his back
room. A little money taken from friends in a social way or for
the stomach's sake is not so bad. A man can make money slowly
and go on increasing his capacity till he can carry his load without staggering and do nothing violent with a million or two
aboard. But some of these lads have been trying to consume the
entire output, and it looks to me as though it was about time to
call in the police."

"Didn't they slap a fine on John D. Rockefeller?" asked Mr. Hennessy.

"They did. They did so," said Mr. Dooley. "Twenty-nine million dollars. The charges was that John D. was going around loaded up to the guards with Standard Oil, exceeding the speed limit in acquiring money, and singing 'A charge to keep I have,' till the neighbors could stand it no longer. Judge Kenesaw Mt. Landis says: 'You're an old offender and I'll have to make an example of you. Twenty-nine million dollars or fifty-eight million days. Call the next case, Mister Clerk!'

"Well, sir, glory be but times have changed when they land my great and good friend John D. with a fine that's equal to three million drunk and disorderly cases. It would have been cheaper if he'd taken to drink early in life.

"Did he pay the fine? He did not. Of course he could if he wanted to. He wouldn't have to pawn anything to get the money, you can bet on that. All he'd have to do would be to put his hand down in his pocket, skin twenty-nine million dollar bills off his roll and hurl them at the clerk.

"But he refused to pay as a matter of principle. It's not that he needs the money. He doesn't care for money in the passionate way you and I do, Hennessy. The likes of us are as crazy about a dollar as a man is about his child when he has only one. But my friend John D., having a large and growing family of dollars, takes only a kind of general interest in them. He's issued a statement saying that he's a custodian of money appointed by himself. He looks after his own money and the money of other people. He takes it and puts it where it won't hurt them and they won't spoil it. He's a kind of a society for the prevention of cruelty to money. If he finds a man misusing his money he takes it away from him and adopts it. Every Saturday night he lets the man see it for a few hours. So he's surprised to find out that when, with the purest intentions in the world, he's caught trying to coax our little money to his home where it'll find congenial surroundings and have other money to play with, the people try to lynch him and the police arrest him for abduction.

"So as a matter of principle he appealed the case. An appeal, Hennessy, is where you ask one court to show its contempt for another court. You'd think John D. would bow his head reverently in the awful presence of Kenesaw Mt. Landis and sob out, 'Thanks, your honor. This here noble fine fills me with joy!' But he doesn't. He's like myself. Him and me bow to the decisions of the courts only if they bow first.

"I have great respect for the judiciary, as fine a lot of cross and indignant men as you'll find anywhere. I have the same respect for them as they have for each other. But you can't be too careful about what decisions you bow to. A decision that seems agreeable may turn out like an acquaintance you scrape up at a picnic. You may be ashamed of it tomorrow. Many's the time I've bowed to a decree of a court, only to see it go up gaily to the Supreme Court, knock at the door and be kicked downstairs by an angry old gentleman in a black silk petticoat. A decree of the court has got to be pretty venerable before I do more than greet it with a pleasant smile. And my friend John D. sees it the same way I do."

"Well," said Mr. Hennessy. "It's time he got what was coming to him."

"I'll not say you're wrong," said Mr. Dooley. "But put yourself in the poor lad's place. He thinks he's doing a great service to the world collecting all the money in sight. It might remain in incompetent hands if he didn't get it. It would be a shame to leave it where it would be mistreated. The only trouble with John D. is that he doesn't put himself in my place. As the father of about thirty dollars I want to bring them up myself in my own foolish way. I may not do what's right by them. I may be too indulgent with them. Their home life may not be happy.

Perhaps it's clear that if they went to the Rockefeller institution for the care of money they'd be in better surroundings, but when my philanthropic friend tries to carry them off I raise a cry of 'Police' and a mob of people that never had a dollar of their own, and never will have one, pounce on the poor misguided man, the police pinch him, and the government condemns the institution and lets out the inmates and a good many of them go to the bad."

"Do you think he'll ever serve out his fine?" asked Mr. Hennessy.

"I don't know," said Mr. Dooley. "But if he does, when he comes out at the end of fifty-eight million years, he'll find a great many changes in men's hats and the means of transportation, but not much in anything else. He may find flying machines, and even excursions to the moon, but he'll see a good many people still walking to their work."

Some Observations by Mr. Dooley

No matter whether the Constitution follows the flag or not, the Supreme Court follows the election returns.

I care not who makes the laws of the nation if I can get out an injunction.

It is as hard for a rich man to enter the Kingdom of Heaven as it is for a poor man to get out of Purgatory.

Trust everybody — but cut the cards.

A woman's sense of humor is usually in her husband's name.

A man that would expect to train lobsters to fly in a year is called a lunatic; but a man that thinks men can be turned into angels by an election is called a reformer and remains at large.

The trouble with most of us is that we swallow political ideas before they're ripe and they don't agree with us.

People tell me to be frank, but how can I when I don't dare to know myself?

It's a good thing that funeral sermons are not composed in the confessional.

Miracles are laughed at by a nation that reads thirty million newspapers a day and supports Wall Street.

The presidency is the highest office in the gift of the people. The vice presidency is the next highest and the lowest. It isn't a crime exactly. You can't be sent to jail for it, but it's a kind of disgrace.

Would I send a boy to college? Well, at the age when a boy is fit to be in college I wouldn't have him around the house.

I never knew a politician to go wrong until he'd been contaminated by contact with a businessman. Whenever I see an alderman and a banker walking down the street together, I know the Recording Angel will have to order another bottle of ink.

I know a lot about children. Not being an author, I'm a great critic.

I'm strong for any revolution that isn't going to happen in my day.

Being an editor is a hard job, but a fascinating one. There's nothing so hard as minding your own business and an editor never has to do that.

The Democratic Party is never so good as when it's broke, when respectable people speak of it in whispers, and when it has no leaders and only one principle, to go in and take it away from the other fellows.

A reformer tries to get into office on a flying machine. He succeeds now and then, but the odds are a hundred to one on the lad that tunnels through.

I can see in my mind the day when explosives will be so explosive and guns will shoot so far that only the folks that stay at home will be killed, and life insurance agents will be advising people to go into the army.

The enthusiasm of this country always makes me think of a

bonfire on an ice floe. It burns bright as long as you feed it, and it looks good, but it doesn't take hold, somehow, on the ice.

Though I'd make a map from memory and gossip of any other man, for myself I'm still uncharted.

A man with a face that looks as if someone had thrown it at him in anger nearly always marries before he is old enough to vote.

The past always looks better than it was. It's only pleasant because it isn't here.

We haul little strips of iron to pile up in little buildings which are called skyscrapers, but not by the sky. I've been up to the top of the very highest building in town, and I wasn't any nearer Heaven than when I was in the street.

We're a great people. We are that. And the best of it is, we know we are.

The war is over — the part you see in the picture papers. But the tax collector will continue his part with relentless fury. Cavalry charges are not the only ones in a real war.

That's the beauty of election statistics: they're not burdened with anything like the facts.

The hand that rocks the scales in the grocery store is the hand that rules the world.

There are no friends at cards or world politics.

The world is full of crooks, but let us thank Heaven they put in part of their time cheating each other.

To be enjoyable, a will must be at one and the same time a practical joke on the heirs and an advertisement of the man that made it.

The reason you have no money is because you don't love it for itself alone. Money won't ever surrender to such a flirt.

The truth is a tough boss in literature. He don't even pay board wages, and if you go to work for him you want to have a job on the side.

If greatness and goodness went hand in hand, it's small chance any of us would have of seeing our picture in the papers.

History is a post-mortem examination. It tells you what a country died of. But I'd like to know what it lived of.

Women haven't the right to vote, but they have the privilege of controlling the man you elect. If I could fly do you think I'd want to walk?

No man is a hero to his undertaker.

Many a man that couldn't direct you to the drugstore on the corner when he was thirty will get a respectful hearing when age has further impaired his mind.

In my heart I think if people marry it ought to be for life. The laws are altogether too lenient with them.

In England a man is presumed to be innocent till he's proved guilty and they take it for granted he's guilty. In this country a man is presumed to be guilty until he's proved guilty and after that he's presumed to be innocent.

If you'd turn on the gas in the darkest heart, you'd find it had a good reason for the worst thing it has done, a good virtuous reason, like needing the money, or punishing the wicked, or teaching people a lesson to be more careful, or protecting the liberties of mankind, or needing the money.

A Mormon is a man that has the bad taste and the religion to do what a good many other men are restrained from doing by conscientious scruples and the police.

When we Americans are through with the English language, it will look as if it had been run over by a musical comedy.

Do I think republics are ungrateful? I do. That's why they continue to be republics.

Among men, wet eye means a dry heart.

Uneasy, as Hogan says, is the head that wears a crown. Other heads are uneasy too, but you don't hear of them.

The trouble with this house is that it's occupied entirely by human beings. If it was a vacant house, it could easily be kept clean.

The further you get away from any period the better you can write about it. You aren't subject to interruptions by people that were there.

All you've got to do is believe what you hear, and if you do that enough, after a while you'll hear what you believe.